The
Merrimack Valley Works
Volume I

———

Charles J. Pouliot

The Merrimack Valley Works - Volume I

Copyright © 2021 by Charles J. Pouliot

A statement on my copyright use:

Under the "fair use" defense, I may make limited use of an original author's work without asking permission. Pursuant to 17 U.S. Code § 107, certain uses of copyrighted material "for purposes such as criticism, comment, news reporting, teaching, scholarship, or research, is not an infringement of copyright."

As a matter of policy, fair use is based on the belief that the public is entitled to freely use portions of copyrighted materials for purposes of commentary and criticism. The fair use privilege is perhaps the most significant limitation on a copyright owner's exclusive rights.

To preserve the free flow of information, authors are given more leeway when using material from factual works - scholarly, technical, or scientific works.

The purpose and character of my intended use of the material involved is the single most important factor in determining whether my use is fair under U.S. copyright law.

All used images remain the property of their original owners.

ISBN 978-1-66781-143-7

Printed in USA

Dedication

This book is dedicated to the people who made the Merrimack Valley Works an amazing engineering and manufacturing community for over half a century. I think of this book as a scrapbook album, because it's full of memories, photos, and writings that I hope you'll enjoy seeing, remembering, and reading about.

Almost everyone who worked there - the thousands of our friends, families, and neighbors - reminisce daily about the companies that we worked for, Western Electric, AT&T Network Systems, and Lucent Technologies. We can never forget the managers and supervisors, the events that brought us together, the product lines that paid for our homes and the raising of our families, and the incredible co-workers we met and maintained friendships with for decades.

We all have stories, and regrettably, many of the best tales have been lost to the ages. People have passed on, and have been replaced with new lives who will never know the *"we're all in this together"* feeling, and often, the heartfelt pride that we felt when the Merrimack Valley Works did something that couldn't be done.

Given a choice, I honestly don't believe I ever would have retired.

Thank you to everyone who had a part in making this book happen. There are far too many people to even think about mentioning, but if you recognize a photo you took, or an event you took part in, I hope you can look on it in the knowledge that you brought a memory back to many people.

Most importantly, I have to thank my wife Teri who has put up with my years of ruminating about how much I loved my job, and wished it was still here (and not in Malaysia). I've collected so many books, periodicals, photos, negatives, and trinkets, that I don't think there's a room in our house that doesn't have something from the Merrimack Valley Works in it.

But there's always room for more...

Foreword

Charlie Pouliot presents two enlightening volumes of work on the history of the Merrimack Valley Works (MVWs), with a focus towards the impact on both the people and on the surrounding community. The volumes additionally touch on the inter-corporate elements of what was historically known as the Bell System, but that is not the real story being told. Information is drawn from historic articles, publication, clippings and photographs, and has been organized into a series of vignettes presenting stories in and of themselves. Doing this has allowed Charlie to create a historical back drop with just enough technical information to establish a reference frame, while focusing on the people of MVWs. Charlie has added a few of his own personal introspective commentaries on some of the events that touched all of our lives.

MVWs had many programs aimed at improving business, product quality and customer relationships; however, the most impactive programs were those aimed at recognizing its people and teams. These programs provided opportunities for personal enrichment, growth and improvement. Few people are aware or remember that MVWs offered medical services such as, vaccinations, x-ray etc. – out of concern for its people. MVWs was deeply involved with providing support to the local community, for example United Way, Red Cross and Christmas events etc. Through all of the evolutions in the history of MVWs, what is most impressive is the esprit-de-corps that was and still is present among those of us who worked there. The social activities and interaction among colleagues formed the heart and soul of the MVWs. This happened through club activities (there was a club for virtually anything one had an interest in), or support and recognition activities (Engineering Excellence Society, TWIN, WILL, Black Achievers etc.) or family-oriented activities (Special Olympics, Canobie Lake Park Outings, lawn celebration events, etc.) and through personal relationships. In the end, the result was that MVWs people became very much an extended family. Involved and concerned about the lives of their colleagues, families and communities. They were there to help and support both within and external to the work environment.

MVWs commitment to its people was incredible. At one time in my career at MVWs, I technically transferred between different companies within the Bell System. I had been working at my new position for about 6 weeks – when my manager came into the office and asked, "Did your paycheck come through last month?". My reply was "That it had not but that I was sure that it would catch up eventually". His reply, "No way, not how we treat our people" and off he went. About an hour later he reappeared at my office with money in his hand and indicated that he had visited payroll, straightened things out with payroll and that "The money was a draw on what the company owes you!" It was an incredible act, demonstrating with both words and action his concern.

Another backbone of MVWs was its dedication and commitment in times of disaster recovery. These were times when you could feel and sense the entire company come together and focus to achieve what seemed like an impossible task to help restore service. People would do whatever it took -- time, resources, travel, reallocating product shipments without paperwork, reorganizing commitments in their personal lives to restore service to the impacted area. My son told me once that he thought that it really did not matter what needed to be achieved, the point was that the people would band together and move heaven and earth to achieve what needed to be done.

As you read through Charlie's book, your memories will be stimulated. As you proceed, more and more memories will flood into your mind. Some because of the words, some because of the pictures and some out of just reflecting. As you explore the areas that you are not as familiar with, you may be surprised at what you will learn – I was!!

Wayne R. J. Brouillette

Merrimack Valley – 1972 - 2017

Preface

I applied to Western Electric in the summer of 1980, because the place I was working really hard - for $4.50 an hour - wouldn't give me a 0.50 cent raise. A friend I went to high school with, Bruce Reynolds, who was already working at Western, kept telling me to apply.

I finally did apply, took a couple of technology exams (remember the AA01, the DD01, and the Montgomery Tests?), and was called in for an interview. In June 1980, Frank Iuele of Human Resources, told me that I was to be hired as a 209 Product Quality Checker at $1,438 per month. I was to start on June 23, 1980, as Employee number 49528, in the Quality Appraisal (Audit) Department on second shift, working for Supervisor John Russo. I was given a pile of papers to read, and sent on my way, stunned and scared that I was starting work at this extraordinarily massive building. Of course, I got lost many, many, times during those first few weeks. I kept losing my car in the parking lot too.

Everyone reading this page has the "*how I was hired*" story. Everyone will always remember their E number, and everyone laments that, *"you just don't know what you got 'til it's gone."*

For years I've wanted to do this book, and yes, again, much to my wife's annoyance, I collected (literally) a few hundred pounds of photos, negatives, magazines, pamphlets, and computer files of things I thought I'd need for such a book. There are 3,392 photos in this book - give or take a few duplicates or so.

But where to start? How do you take 31 billion minutes of the lifetime of a factory and condense them in to several hundred pages?

What's in your hands is my final idea. It's a scrapbook. Events, photos, and people that I thought were interesting - after all, it is my book ☺. I figured that if I was interested enough to look them up, maybe someone else would too. The stories relate to the companies we worked for. I strove to summarize long stories into timelines, because there are many, many books readily available on the companies themselves. I think I ended up putting together a book that's a Swiss Army Knife® of our piece of the telecommunications industry that was the Merrimack Valley Works.

I hope you enjoy it.

Table of Contents

1 - Introduction

This is my Merrimack Valley Works book. My first goal was to collect an extensive assortment of photos and find a clever way to display them in a book. Then it took a turn, and I couldn't just do a photo book. It just wasn't enough. It wasn't a tribute to the lives of the great men and women that we worked for, and with, for decades. There were general managers who we absolutely know worked hard to keep the business strong and powerful. Managers who would do virtually everything they could to keep the last employee working. And of course, there were section chiefs we'd push in front of a train if at all possible. But I needed to memorialize some great people and incredible successes. I kept finding things that I thought I should add, and as this book was being developed, it grew larger and broader.

In older notes and events, I tried to keep the phrasing and terminology of the day. It's interesting to see how writing styles adapted over time.

This book is for all the people who worked at the Merrimack Valley Works, and who said a million times, *"someone should write a book about that place."* Maybe this will be the only book on the Merrimack Valley Works, or maybe it will be the beginning of a trend by fellow employees.

What was the Merrimack Valley Works?

The Merrimack Valley Works was a massive telecommunications manufacturing plant in North Andover, Massachusetts, not very far from the New Hampshire border. Particulars are within this book, but it was a gigantic place. There were two million square feet of factory floors and buildings, and at one time over 12,000 employees on 3 shifts. The lights were never turned off, and the parking lots were never empty. To many of us, it was so much more than a huge building.

Generations of people worked there, made homes in the area, and raised families. We worked side-by-side for years, found love sometimes, caught each other up on our weekends, shared our kids and activities, and often became lifelong friends outside of work. People were always there to lend a hand if you needed one. In many ways, the building had a life and personality of its own. It clearly was a city unto itself; there were lots of people.

It took Lucent Technologies to finally give us a useful explanation of what we did at the Merrimack Valley Works:

We worked on *"the things that made communications work."*

I miss it.

2 - The Merrimack Valley Works General Managers

Jesse Ault

1943 - 1955   1944: Haverhill Shops Superintendent

1952: Assistant Works Manager,

Haverhill and Lawrence Shops / Western Electric

Superintendent Ault began his telephone manufacturing career on August 21, 1916 in the test set maintenance laboratory of the Western Electric Company's Hawthorne Works in Chicago.

Mr. Ault's experience at the Hawthorne Works included many supervisory positions in the inspection and operating organizations. In 1937, he was made Chief of the Step-by-step Shops, and three years later was promoted to the post of Superintendent. In June, 1942, he was transferred to the Company's plant in Kearny, New Jersey, as Superintendent of the Carrier and Repeater Shops. When the Haverhill Shops was set up as a new manufacturing unit in August, 1943, Mr. Ault was appointed Superintendent.

A native of Indiana, Mr. Ault is a graduate of Purdue University where he earned a degree in Electrical Engineering. Before joining Western Electric, he was connected with the Illinois Steel Company in Gary, Indiana.

Following the opening of the Lawrence Shops, Mr. Ault was named Assistant Works Manager of the Haverhill and Lawrence operations.

In September, 1946, Superintendent Jesse Ault proudly displayed his newly presented 30-year gold service emblem.

In September, 1955, Jesse Ault retired after 39 years of Western Electric service.

Harvey G. (Harvey) Mehlhouse

1955 - 1957

General Manager / Western Electric

Harvey G. Mehlhouse, Superintendent of the Sandia Corporation, was named successor to Jesse Ault, and took over the reins of the Assistant Manager position officially on September 1, 1955.

Mr. Mehlhouse brought to his new position a wealth of company experience - a large portion of which had been in the engineering fields.

Prior to joining Western Electric, he was instructor of mathematics and physics at Naperville, Illinois High School.

Mr. Mehlhouse joined the company in 1929, as an engineer at the Hawthorne Works in Chicago, and became Superintendent of Manufacturing Engineering in 1951.

After Merrimack Valley...

Mr. Mehlhouse was elected a Western Electric Vice President of "Area A" in 1958, and a Director in 1965, when he was named Executive Vice President in charge of corporate staff activities. He assumed his present post in 1967.

Harvey G. Mehlhouse was elected President and Chief Executive Officer of Western Electric, effective December 1, 1969. He succeeded Paul A. Gorman, President since 1964, who will retire on November 30 with more than 40 years of Bell System service.

Mr. Mehlhouse is a Director of Bell Telephone Laboratories, Sandia Corporation, Teletype Corporation, and the MFB Mutual Insurance Company.

W. C. (Clare) Brooks

1957 - 1964

General Manager / Western Electric

W. Clare Brooks joied the Western Electric Company in 1921 as a cost clerk at the Hawthorne Works in Chicago. Following various supervisory responsibilities, he became Superintendent of Industrial Relations in 1946.

In 1949, he was transferred to the Company's distributing organization as Manager of the Indianapolis Distributing House.

A year later he assumed the managership of the Chicago House, and in 1954 he returned to Hawthorn as Industrial Relations Manager.

In June of 1955, he was appointed Assistant Works Manager of a manufacturing organization at Hawthorne - a position which he held until he transferred to the New York headquarters as personal director in May 1956.

In January of 1958 when, Merrimack Valley Assistant Manager H. G. Mehlhouse was elected Vice President of Area A, W. Clare Brooks, formally the Western Electric Company Personnel Director was appointed to the post of Merrimack Valley Works manager.

He was succeeded as Personnel Director by J. Harold Moore, formally project manager of the ADES (Air Defense Engineering Services) project division.

Harry N. (Harry) Snook

1964 - 1969

General Manager / Western Electric

Harry N. Snook, former Assistant Works Manager at the Merrimack Valley Works, was promoted to the position of Works Manager effective March 1, 1964. Mr. Snook succeeds Merrimack Valley Works Manager W. Claire Brooks who retired.

Mr. Snook began his Bell System career on March 24, 1941 as an assistant engineer in the Engineer of Manufacture organization at the Kearny works. Advancing through engineering and supervisory positions at Kearny, he became Department Chief, Staff, on December 1, 1950, and Department Chief, Microwave and Radio Relays, in the Marion, New Jersey shops on May 28, 1951.

On May 12, 1952, after participating in the Company's management training program, he was appointed Assistant Superintendent, Labor Relations at Company Headquarters in New York City. On December 15, 1953, he returned to Kearny as Assistant Superintendent, Manufacturing Engineering, and on September 1, 1955, was promoted to Superintendent, Crossbar, Wired Units and Crystal Shops.

On January 1, 1958, he was named Vice President of Engineering for Manufacture at the Sandia Corporation in Albuquerque, New Mexico, a nonprofit subsidiary of Western Electric operated for the Atomic Energy Commission. He returned to Western Electric on July 1, 1959, as Assistant Works Manager at the Merrimack Valley Works.

A graduate of Lafayette College with a Bachelor of Science degree in Physics, Mr. Snook taught high school in New Jersey and Pennsylvania before joining the Western Electric Company.

He is married to Alva A. Bozarth, and the couple resides in North Andover with two sons, Alfred and Nelson. Mr. Snook is a member of the Board of Directors of the Greater Lawrence Chamber of Commerce, a Director of the Lawrence chapter of the American Red Cross, a Director of the Lawrence YMCA, and a member of the Budget Committee of the Lawrence United Fund.

David L. (Dave) Hilder

1969 - 1977

General Manager / Western Electric

Dave Hilder assumed the position of General Manager of the Merrimack Valley Works on August 1, 1969, when he succeeded Harry N. Snook, who was promoted to Vice President, Manufacturing, Transmission Equipment, with temporary headquarters in Burlington, MA.

Mr. Hilder's previous position was Plant Manager of the Reading Plant.

Charles W. (Charlie) DeBell

1977 - 1980

General Manager / Western Electric

Charles W. DeBell, General Manager, Merrimack Valley Works, began his Western Electric career in April 1941, in the Engineer of Manufacture organization at the Kearny (N.J.) Works. He advanced to Department Chief in March 1947, and was transferred to New York in September 1950, to attend the Company's management training program.

He was assigned to the NIKE Project in May 1951, returning to Kearny as Assistant Manager of wage incentives in July 1952. In June 1954, he moved to New York as a Staff Assistant Manager in the Manufacturing Division's eastern area office and in September 1955, he was placed on special assignment to permit him to enroll in the University of Pennsylvania's Institute of Humanistic Studies.

At the completion of the course in June 1956, he was promoted to Manager of the Step-by-Step shops at the Hawthorne (Chicago) Works.

He was named Manager of the Equipment Shops at the Merrimack Valley Works in April 1958, and advanced to Director of Manufacturing in November 1962.

On April I, 1967, he was promoted to General Manager of the North Carolina Works.

Mr. DeBell is a Director of Bay Bank-Merrimack Valley and a Trustee of the Bon Secours Hospital. He is a member of the Telephone Pioneers of America-Merrimack Valley Works Chapter 78.

Mr. DeBell and his wife, Marian, reside in Boxford, Mass., but will return to his former residence in Winston-Salem N.C. after retirement. They have twin daughters, Gayle (Touchet) and Janice, and a son, James.

Mr. DeBell was born in Winnipeg, Manitoba, Canada. He received a Bachelor of Science degree in mechanical engineering from Purdue University.

William P. (Bill) Dugan

1980 - 1981

General Manager / Western Electric

Bill Dugan returned to the Merrimack Valley Works from Rolling Meadows, Illinois, where he was responsible for the administration of a Western Electric organization that provided distribution, installation, and systems equipment engineering services to telephone companies in four states.

He began his Western Electric career in February 1952, as an engineer at the company's Kearny Works. Two years later, he was transferred to the Merrimack Valley Works where he worked until 1961.

Awarded a Sloan Fellowship in 1967, Mr. Dugan went on special assignment as manager while attending MIT for a Master of Science degree in industrial management.

Bill held various administrative positions at Western Electric's Headquarters in New York City, was Manager of Apparatus Manufacture at the Columbus Works, Ohio in 1968, and appointed Director of Engineering and Manufacture-Electronic Products at the Oklahoma City Works in 1969.

In March 1971, he became Director of Engineering and Manufacture at the Omaha Works and one year later was named General Manager-Service Planning and Administration at Headquarters. He assumed his position in the Central Region in 1979.

Bill is a member of the Society of Sloan Fellows, the University of Nebraska Alumni Association, Sigma Alpha Epsilon Fraternity, the Telephone Pioneers of America, the Board of Directors of Junior Achievement for the Northwest Suburban Area, and the Economic Club of Chicago.

Bill married Brenda Murphy in 1958 in Wellesley. They have four children.

Wayne L. (Wayne) Hunt

1981 - 1982

General Manager / Western Electric

Wayne L. Hunt, former General Manager, Purchasing and Transportation, Purchasing and Transportation Division, became General Manager, Merrimack Valley Works, on May 1, succeeding William P. Dugan who was recently named Vice President of the Transmission East Division.

Mr. Hunt began his Western Electric career in 1957, at the company's newly established Omaha location and became Section Chief of Crossbar Inspection and Testing in 1959.

In 1961, he was sent to the company's pilot plant at Kansas City, becoming Department Chief of Wired Equipment, Inspection and Testing in 1962. Three years later he was promoted and transferred to the Kearny Works as Assistant Manager of Operating, Power and Rectifiers.

In 1968 he advanced to Manager, Service in the Northeastern Region, becoming Manager, New York Communications Products Service Center in 1969, and Manager, Manhattan Service Center in 1970. He was promoted to Director of Division Staff, Manufacturing Division in 1971, and became Director of Engineering and Manufacturing at the Omaha Works in 1972. In 1976, he was named Director of Purchasing, and in 1978, he was promoted to General Manager.

Born in Lincoln, Nebraska, he attended the University of Nebraska, earning a bachelor of science degree in 1954.

From 1954 to 1957, he served as an aircraft maintenance officer in the U.S. Air Force.

Mr. Hunt married the former Donna L. Wetzel, and they have two sons, Jeffrey W. and Gregory L.

Robert E. (Bob) Cowley, Jr.

1982 - 1985

General Manager / Western Electric

General Manager / AT&T Network Systems

During the disability of General Manager Wayne L. Hunt, Robert E. Cowley Jr. had been assigned as general manager of the Merrimack Valley Works.

His appointment became effective on January 15. Cowley comes to the Merrimack Valley Works from Service Lines Planning and Management, Material and Account Management Division in Morristown, N.J., where he was general manager.

Having been an assistant manager here, he is not unknown to many at the Merrimack Valley Works.

He began his Western Electric career in 1943 as a stock handler at the Point Breeze Works (now the Baltimore Works). Upon his release from the Army in 1946, Cowley rejoined the company as a sorter at the Hawthorne Works in Chicago but resigned to attend Cornell University. After graduation in 1951 with a Bachelor of Mechanical Engineering degree, Cowley returned to the Hawthorne Works as an engineer and was promoted to department chief in 1956. Two years later, he was transferred to the Omaha Works where he became assistant manager of engineering in 1962.

Cowley was awarded a Sloan Fellowship in 1963 and was placed on special assignment by the company to attend Stanford University's nine-month program for business executives. Upon completion of the program, he was placed here at the Merrimack Valley Works as Assistant Manager of Operating until he was named Manager of Electronic Switching Systems manufacture at the Columbus Works in 1965.

He was promoted to Director of Engineering and Manufacture at the Oklahoma City Works in 1967 and was named General Manager of the Dallas Plant in 1969. In 1971 he was appointed Associate General Manager of the Oklahoma City Works and became General Manager in 1972. He became General Manager of the Bell System Sales Division's Northeastern Region in 1973 and assumed his most recent position in 1980.

He and his wife, Anne, moved from Berkeley Heights, N.J. to the Merrimack Valley area.

J.E. (Jack) Driscoll

1985   Director of Engineering and Manufacturing

Interim Manager

AT&T Network Systems

Jack Driscoll began his AT&T career in 1957 as an engineering assistant at the former Kearny, NJ, Works.

His 30-year career included assignments at Corporate Headquarters and the Baltimore and Atlanta Works, in addition to Merrimack Valley. Jack assumed his present position as Director of Manufacturing Resource Planning in July of 1986.

He is a past president of the Merrimack Valley Works Chapter of the Telephone Pioneers of America.

John A. (Jack) Heck

1985 - 1988

General Manager / AT&T Network Systems

John A. (Jack) Heck was named general manager, effective Aug. 1, after having served as administrative officer for product management of Cable, Wire and Associated Apparatus, Market Planning - Network Systems Division, at the Atlanta Works of AT&T in Norcross, GA. Mr. Heck succeeds Robert E. (Bob) Cowley, who retired in July.

"I come here with great enthusiasm," he said, acknowledging there are a number of challenges that lie ahead in leading this plant - the largest manufacturing location in the company. Mr. Heck said he was *"extremely impressed"* with the plant and its people, and from the long history of cooperation by the employees and union, he looks forward to *"tackling the challenges that we face in our new competitive environment." "We are very fortunate,"* he said, *"that we have the opportunity to be a part of a business that requires technologically leading-edge products and has growth potential for all of us. Each of us should relook at our jobs and see if there is a better way to do them, to help further improve our competitive edge."*

Mr. Heck, 50, is a native of Baltimore, MD, having attended Baltimore Polytechnic Institute, graduating in 1953, and Georgia Institute of Technology, graduating in 1957 with a bachelor's degree in mechanical engineering. He also attended Johns Hopkins University, New York University and M.I.T.

He joined Western Electric's Baltimore Works in 1959, followed by a series of non-supervisory engineering assignments and management positions. On one of his jobs, he worked out of Western Electric Co., Ltd., in London, England. Mr. Heck holds membership in the American Society of Mechanical Engineers, Toastmasters International and the Optimist Club. He and his wife, Margaret Jane, have four children: Mark Andrew, Ginamarie, Kimberly Ann and John Bradley.

Allan E. (Al) Dugan

1988 - 1990

Manufacturing Vice President / AT&T Network Systems

Allan E. (Al) Dugan has been named to the position of Manufacturing Vice President, Merrimack Valley, replacing Jack Heck, who became Vice President of Product Management, AT&T and Philips Telecommunications B.Y., located in The Netherlands.

Both moves were effective July 1, 1988. Al comes to Merrimack Valley from AT&T headquarters in Southgate, New Jersey, where he was Director of Division Staff.

Prior to his position at corporate headquarters, he was Director of Engineering at the Oklahoma City Works, where he was responsible for the manufacturing engineering of both the 5ESS Digital Switching System and the AT&T 3B Computer family of products.

Al is a native of Rochester, NY, holding a Bachelor of Arts degree in Physics from the University of Toronto, and a PhD in Physics from Pennsylvania State University. He also holds an MBA in Finance and Marketing from Rider College.

Al began his AT&T career in 1967 at the Engineering Research Center (ERC) in Princeton, New Jersey. Initially involved in electron beam inspection and ion implantation research.

In 1973 he led the millimeter waveguide testing group at the ERC Forsgate Laboratory, where he was involved in developing testing methods for AT&T waveguide products. In 1974 Al was named Department Chief of Accounting and Financial Results at ERC. In 1975 he entered the former Western Electric management training program, and upon conclusion became Department Chief of Integrated Circuit Packaging at the Reading, Pennsylvania, Works.

In 1976 he assumed responsibilities for LED manufacturing engineering and silicon materials engineering. In 1977, Al became assistant manager, at the North Illinois Works, where he was responsible for initial introduction of 5ESS switching and 3B computer products. In 1979, he became assistant manager, material management. He was appointed manager of engineering of the Denver Works in 1980, responsible for the manufacturing engineering of AT&T PBX products. He remained in Denver until being named director of engineering at the Oklahoma City Works.

Al has authored several technical papers in the fields of electron and ion beam physics, semiconductor material growth, photoluminescence and optical properties of materials.

John F. (Jack) McKinnon

1990 - 1997

Transmission Systems Vice President

AT&T Network Systems / Lucent Technologies

It is with great pleasure that I return to Merrimack Valley, where I began my AT&T career 28 years ago as a product engineer. Between that first assignment and now I have been to many locations around the country, in different organizations and with varying responsibilities.

It is immediately evident to me that the employees of Merrimack Valley have a lot to be proud of. Your factory is a shining example of how AT&T must operate to remain competitive in the 1990s and beyond.

My door is always open to those with new ideas, and I hope to get to know many of you personally as I continue to become reacquainted with this great facility.

E. F. (JR) Newland, Jr.

1997 - 2000

Product Realization Vice President

Lucent Technologies

It's certainly nice to come to Merrimack Valley during such a strong business cycle. The Valley has always had a reputation of being a best-in-class organization of manufacturing excellence, and I can see why.

We've got a strong and very dedicated group of people who take great pride in what they do. This has led to winning the Baldrige Award and achieving ISO Certification, both of which are of tremendous manufacturing value, and have helped to make Merrimack Valley a valued asset for Lucent.

With the 90s almost behind us, our biggest challenge is to make sure that our provisioning capabilities are a competitive weapon for the years 2000 plus. To be the Global Provisioning Center for all of Transmission, our speed and flexibility will be put to the test. The biggest differentia tor today is who has the fastest response along with the best quality and price. We have already begun framing our strategy for the future, and speed is definitely number one as we head for the year 2000.

World class provisioning and manufacturing excellence are at the heart of the statement "We make the things that make communications work." And at Merrimack Valley, we're going to keep the beat going strong.

Michael I. (Mike) Jones

2000 - 2008   Merrimack Valley Works Integration Center

Vice President & General Manager

Lucent Technologies

- Manufacturing Vice President - September 1999 - October 2001
- Global Integrated Operations Vice President - January 2001 - April 2006
- Supply Chain Vice President - April 2006 - December 2006
- Vice President, Supply Chain - January 2007 - December 2008

Mike Jones has been appointed Merrimack Valley Works Integration Center Vice President & General Manager of one of ONG's three cross-business units.

He is involved in the production, delivery and asset utilization of optical networking equipment. Mike's new business unit offers core competencies in optics, optics assembly, complex systems integration, test, quality, supply chain management and distribution. It will place an emphasis on new product introduction and improved business processes to achieve world-class time to market, on-time delivery and world class asset management.

"Our strength is our people," said Mike. *"We have the required skill set here to move forward to become the world's leading optical integration and test center. We offer an established knowledge base for the development community and our customers to call on to move products from the drawing board into their networks. The most pressing job challenge is determining the migration strategy for going from a vertically integrated manufacturing environment to an integration center,"* Mike said. *"Nailing down what that migration strategy is, making sure it's communicated well and doing it the best way that we can is a top priority for me."*

Mike's day-to-day work includes a number of things. *"There is no typical day,"* he said. *"We interact constantly with Bell Labs, customers and suppliers. Every day presents new opportunities."* So, what does he like best about the job? *"We're in a very exciting and hot market, and we have a lot of challenges in getting products to market faster than ever, but there's an opportunity out there to work with a whole group of customers that we've never had,"* Mike said. *"There's this excitement in the market, and there's never been a better time for the people coming through the business to develop their careers and to move forward within our business."*

3 - Haverhill Shops

In 1891, James Winchell opened the Winchell Shoe Factory on Locust Street. At 84,000 square feet of floor space, it was the largest factory in the city occupied by a single firm.

When the shoe business left Haverhill, this vacant building was just what Western Electric was looking for.

Creating an extension to the Kearny, New Jersey Works, Western Electric established operations in Haverhill in 1943, with originally just 20 employees on loan from Kearny.

The Haverhill Shops grew out of WE's commitment to produce electrical coils for the Bell System and the armed forces during World War II. At the end of 1944, the first year, Western Electric had 2,100 employees and was manufacturing over 3,000 different types of coils, transformers, and other type of communications apparatus, and producing 40,000 coils a week.

The Haverhill plant was originally intended as strictly a "war effort" plant to be phased out later, but the quality of the employees and their manufacturing skills planted the seeds for what became the Merrimack Valley Works.

Mr. Jesse Ault was the Haverhill Shops Superintendent. Wages were approved in 1943 by the New England War Labor Board from a minimum of 50-60 cents per hour, to $1.10-$1.35 per hour. Shift premiums were paid of 5 cents per hour for employees on second shift, and 7 ½ cents per hour for those on the third shift.

As operations expanded, Western Electric enlarged its facilities to include office and manufacturing operations in four former shoe factory buildings in Haverhill:

1	B. F. Grad Building	21-25 Locust Street	8-story	Offices
2	J. H. Winchell Building	13-17 Locust Street	6-story - built 1891	Manufacturing (Razed 1991)
3	C. H. Hayes Building	14-44 Granite Street	7-story - built 1894	Manufacturing and Testing
4	Goldberg Building	31-35 Walnut Street	8-story	Offices and Operating Facilities

In May 1954, the earliest transistors that were designed for commercial use were assembled into telephone equipment made at the Western Electric shop within the Winchell Building.

With the explosive post-war growth in demand for telecommunications services, Western Electric made a decision to expand manufacturing and research capability in the Valley. The original proposed site for a new Western Electric plant was in Haverhill, but the Mayor of Haverhill vetoed the planned location, and the site was shifted to a 157-acre plot of farmland in North Andover.

Plans for the North Andover manufacturing and administration location were announced in September 1953.

In April 1956 - Assistant Works Manager Harvey G. Mehlhouse, announced the latest expansion, of 24,000 square feet at the Lang Building in Haverhill, for offices, stores, and some manufacturing activities.

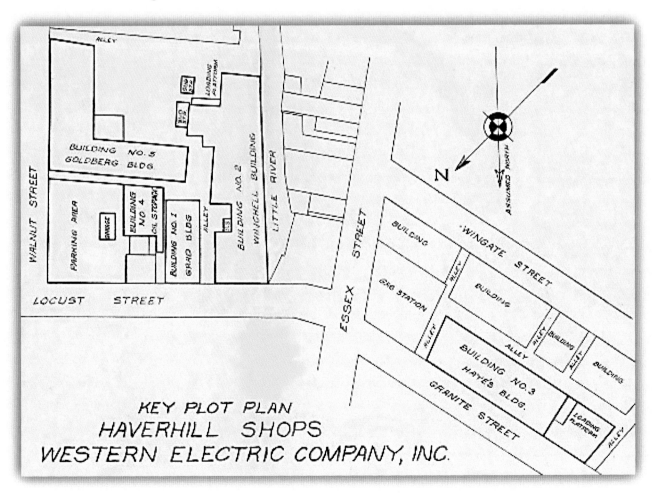

KEY PLOT PLAN
HAVERHILL SHOPS
WESTERN ELECTRIC COMPANY, INC.

Grad Building #1

Hayes Building #3

Winchell Building #2

Goldberg Building #5

Oil Storage Building #4

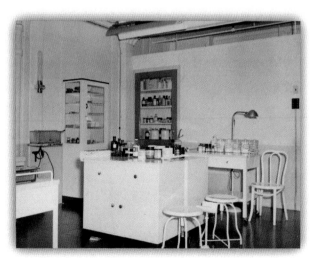

ON A DAILY RUN between Haverhill Shops and the Lawrence Warehouse the trailer truck is snapped as it rounds a bend on the beautiful Merrimack River. "Zeke" Bartlett is at the wheel. This vehicle, the largest owned by the Shops, covers about 1700 miles a month and carries the bulk of the coil parts from the up-river warehouse.

COMMUNICATORS BEING PICKED UP at the press by Danny Cashman. The panel truck is quick and efficient for carrying small, light coil material. Danny has more than three years' service in the Shops.

"HOW'S SHE SPARKING?" "We will soon find out," says "Skip" Faxon. He is using a testing machine on one of the several Company-owned cars and trucks kept in A-1 condition at the garage.

CHARLES KENNEDY of the Test Set Repair and Maintenance Department, 1942, is shown modifying the construction of an SID 100503 Inductance Bridge, extending its range to fit a larger number of coils. This type of test set is used in measuring inductance and effective resistance of coils. There are 11 others like it in the plant. This particular set will be used on the third floor of the Winchell Building for Power Coil inspection. Making top quality equipment for coil manufacture is an important part of Haverhill Shops' job.

OUTDOOR CEREMONY held September 12 when the U. S. Dept. of Labor honored Haverhill Shops with a Certificate of Safety Achievement. While all traffic was stopped, employees filled the street and listened to government representative, William G. Marks, who maintained that only through a high level of employee cooperation and safety effort could such records be reached.

4 - Lawrence Shops

In 1951, Western Electric expanded to include a Lawrence location to accommodate more manufacturing, warehousing, and office operations.

The Lawrence shop was set up in the Monomac Spinning Mill building, built in 1910, on South Union and Grafton Streets in Lawrence, Massachusetts. The Monomac Mill manufactured French spun worsted and merino yarns, on a floor space of five and three-quarter acres, or 300,000-square feet. Monomac suspended operations in the 1950s, and the location was purchased by the Western Electric Company in 1951.

The Lawrence Shops were opened on Nov. 13, 1951 with only one section chief, 13 employees, and a maintenance worker. The plant was opened because business was booming and the original Haverhill Shops had already expanded to its capacity. At its peak, 1,100 people worked at the Lawrence Shops.

In April 1955, a Bell Telephone Laboratories research and development satellite location was created at the Lawrence Shops, with 40 Bell Telephone Laboratories engineers, and 25 Western Electric employees. Peak employment at Lawrence plant was now over 2,000.

A year later in April 1956, Assistant Works Manager, Harvey G. Mehlhouse, announced another expansion of 38,000 square feet in the Pacific Mills Print Works Building in

Lawrence. The additional footage allowed Western Electric to expand its current warehousing operations at that location.

By 1978, after years of gradually transferring its operations and workers to North Andover, Western Electric decided to close the Lawrence plant.

On December 9, of 1979, the D1 / D1D operating shop was relocated from the Lawrence Plant to North Andover. Located on the top floor overlooking South Lawrence, it was the last department left at the plant. The move completed the relocation of all storeroom and operating shops from Lawrence. The last 100 Lawrence employees, many clad in black, commemorated its closing on December 7 with a cake decorated with "Farewell Lawrence". Cutting the cake were Grace Houle, the first person hired at Lawrence, and "A.G." Gagnon, the person who spent the most time working at the plant, 24 years.

Manufacturing Managers, Transmission Equipment, Bill Young and Lance Dockray, and Department Chief, George Emmott were on hand to welcome the Lawrence employees to North Andover.

Remaining in the building was a skeleton crew of Works Security and operating engineers who run the boilers to save the water pipes from bursting.

Corporate Realty now assumed the responsibility of selling the turn-of-the century red brick facility.

In 2009, Ozzy Properties acquired the location, and with a comprehensive renovation, "Heritage Place" is now a professional office complex. It features a two-story atrium with 3,000 square feet of lobby space, a security center, deli, daycare, a new HVAC system, new electric and

Heritage Place

plumbing throughout the complex, high-speed Internet access, and secure parking.

5 - The Merrimack Valley Works - North Andover

The Merrimack Valley Works in North Andover, was one of Massachusetts' largest research and development, and manufacturing facilities ever. It was alongside the Merrimack River, approximately 30 miles north of Boston, in Essex County, and a few miles south of the Massachusetts and New Hampshire border.

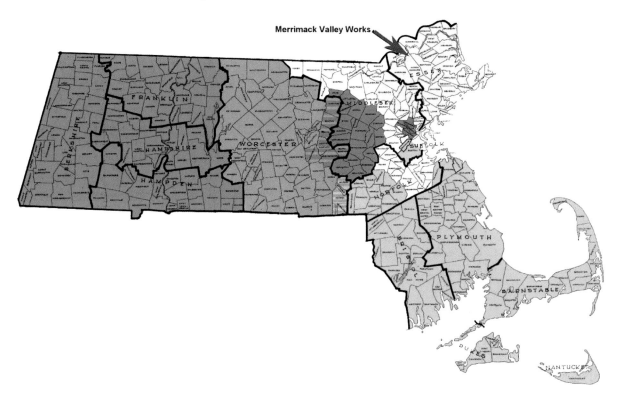

The Merrimack Valley Works rose from the consolidation of Western Electric manufacturing operations established in 1943 in Haverhill, Massachusetts, and in 1951 in Lawrence, Massachusetts. Groundbreaking ceremonies were held in 1953, and construction commenced in November. On August 1, 1956, the Haverhill and Lawrence shops, along with the new North Andover location, became the Merrimack Valley Works under the leadership of General Manager Harvey Mehlhouse.

Throughout the life of the Merrimack Valley Works, it represented the largest concentration in the world of people dedicated to the design, manufacture, marketing, and customer support of transmission systems.

Merrimack Valley broke new ground in the manufacture of man-made quartz crystals, transistors, Lightwave technology products, hybrid integrated circuits, the use of robotics, Picturephones, and the development and use of environmentally friendly processes.

Merrimack Valley Works was in Western Electric's management subdivision "Area C" of manufacturing locations, headed by a Western Electric Vice President. The Allentown, Kansas City, and North Carolina locations were also in Area C.

The Merrimack Valley Works research and manufacturing facility was the economic engine for the town of North Andover for over fifty years, ultimately paying over $800,000 in annual property taxes. At its peak, the plant employed almost 12,000 people - more than the entire 1950 population of the town of North Andover.

After the breakup of the Bell System, Lightwave Transmission Systems manufactured here were the backbone of Lucent's wideband system architecture, which featured the WaveStar family of optical products. Merrimack Valley also manufactured microwave radio systems, digital carrier, digital access and cross-connect systems needed in configuring transmission circuits, and multiplexers, signal processing systems and video messaging and broadcast systems used in multi-media services.

6 - Merrimack Valley Works Manager Photos

MVW Leadership Team 2000

7 - The Merrimack Valley Works Organization

Physical Resources / Statistics / Details

- 169 acres of land
- 25 acres of lawn
- 7 additional acres of land on Holt Road for snow removal
- 38 acres of paved parking lots
- 1,913,000 square feet of floor space
- 2 miles of paved private roadways
- 4.4 miles of major aisles
- 25 acres of lawn
- 7-acre athletic field with 4 softball diamonds
- The front of office building measures nearly a fifth of a mile (1,040 feet)
- The total perimeter of the main building is almost one mile
- 71 rest rooms
- 102 water coolers
- 3,800 telephones
- 8,500 wastebaskets to empty each day
- 20,000 square feet of floor space are cleaned and waxed
- 1,700 gallons of soap and almost 7,000 gallons of floor finisher used each year
- Filtered air for dust-free manufacturing
- Merrimack Valley Works used enough electricity in a year to power 18,000 homes
- Merrimack Valley Works used enough water in a year to supply 2,000 homes
- Merrimack Valley Works used enough fuel in a year to heat 2,600 homes
- Modernized central chilled water plant - 10,000-ton capacity
- Comprehensive security system control and monitoring
- State of the art fire alarm system
- ESD flooring - 75% of facility
- Merrimack Valley Works is second in employment among the Western Electric plants - Hawthorne Works in Chicago is largest

- The cafeteria can seat 1,200 people at a given time, and food services served hot or cold meals to over 5,500 people per day

- The Medical department at one time had three full-time doctors, 1 part-time doctors, 12 nurses, X-Ray technician, laboratory technician, an operating room, a large X-Ray laboratory, and treated 75 employees per day

- 300-seat auditorium with projection capabilities and closed-circuit TV

- A recording studio for production of training programs and in-plant special events

- 150-seat private executive dining room.

- Multi-media conference rooms

- Dual uninterruptable power supply systems with a 900kw standby generator for data center

- Payroll paid (numbers were taken from Merrimack Valley Works periodicals):

  - $67 million   (1969) for over 10,000 employees
  - $88 million   (1971) for over 10,000 employees
  - $93 million   (1972) for over 10,000 employees
  - $110 million (1973) for almost 10,000 employees
  - $148 million (1979) for approximately 7,584 employees
  - $260 million (1981) for approximately 12,000 employees
  - $215 million (1982) for approximately 8,000 employees
  - $288 million (1986) for approximately 9,000 employees
  - $235 million (1991) for approximately 8,000 employees
  - $241 million (1992) for approximately 5,500 employees
  - $318 million (1995) for approximately 4,500 employees

- Property taxes paid to the Town of North Andover

  - $868,949 (1991)
  - $780,328 (1993)
  - $681,480 (1996)

- Professional Trade Services within the Merrimack Valley Works:
  - Carpenters
  - Computer Programmers
  - Draftsmen
  - HVAC Professionals
  - Locksmiths
  - Machinists
  - Master Electricians
  - Millwrights
  - Painters
  - Photographers
  - Pipefitters
  - Plumbers
  - Toolmakers
  - Window Washer

8 - Merrimack Valley Employee Benefits

- AT&T Employee Discount Program
- AT&T Family Care Development Fund
- Athletic Fields on Site (7 acres)
- Auto Loans
- Bell System Savings Plan
- Blue Cross / Blue Shield Medical Plan
- Bonus Program
- Bowling Leagues
- Celebrity Visitors
- Christmas Clubs
- Christmas Parties
- Continuous In-House Training
- Cost Reduction Celebrations
- Credit Union on Site
- Dale Carnegie Training Courses
- Death Benefits - 1 To 6 Year's Salary
- Dental Plan
- Disability Benefit
- Employee Newsletters
- Employee Suggestion Award System
- Extraordinary Medical Expense Plan
- Family Outings
- Fire And Rescue
- Fitness trail around property
- Golf Leagues
- Competitive Pay
- Group Life Insurance
- High School Student Science Tours
- Holidays
- Hospital On Site
- Job Advancement
- Job Posting Program
- Job Security
- Leaves of Absence
- Local Business Discounts
- Local University - part-time programs
- Maternity Benefits
- MVRTA Buses - Haverhill & Lawrence
- On-site X-Ray Technician
- Open House Celebrations
- Overtime Opportunities
- Pensions
- Pioneers of America
- Pioneers Store
- Plant-wide Celebrations
- Professional Development Training
- Red Cross Blood Drives
- Retirement Dinners
- Safety Glasses Store on Site
- Safety Shoe Store on Site
- Savings Bonds
- Security Force
- Sick days
- Social Clubs
- Special Olympics
- Sports Banquets
- Sports Teams
- Stock Options
- Summer On Campus Program
- Technical Library
- Telephone Pioneers Of America
- Telephone Reimbursement
- The Importance of Feeling Important
- Three Work Shifts
- Training Department on Site
- Tuition Refund Program
- Union Representation
- United Fund Campaign
- Up to 6 Weeks of Vacation
- Vacation Clubs
- Very Clean Working Environment
- Vision Care Plan
- Vocational Testing Facilities
- WEValley Recreational Club
- Work Breaks

9 - Merrimack Valley Groups

Employee Business Partners represented groups whose participation in U.S. economic activity had been limited by social factors. EBPs established Charters, Constitutions, By-Laws, and Mission Statements consistent with Lucent Technologies Code of Conduct and to support Lucent's operating style and spirit. EBPs exhibited pro-active partnerships and synergies with each other.

Established Employee Business Partners pro-actively advocated and contributed to Lucent Technologies' diversity initiatives, selected HR processes and business initiatives, and community involvement. EBPs coordinated and sponsored educational events, heritage and cultural celebrations, and provided support to their memberships. Membership was non-discriminatory and open to all Lucent Technologies employees who supported the EBPs' missions. EBPs benefited the business and added value to corporate-wide diversity initiatives. The following is a list of Merrimack Valley's EBPs.

- **4A (Asian/Pacific-American Association for Advancement)** - Advocated the professional development and full utilization of employees of Asian and Pacific Island descent and all Lucent employees.

- **ABLE (Alliance of Black Lucent Employees)** - Enhanced the professional, educational, career and cultural development of communities with people with African descent.

- **EQUAL! -MA (Supporting Gay, Lesbian, Bisexual, & Transgendered Employees at Lucent Technologies)** - The mission of EQUAL! was to advocate a work environment that is inclusive and supportive of gay, lesbian, bisexual, and transgendered employees - enabling all employees to perform to their fullest potential. EQUAL! is a resource serving our customers, shareholders, colleagues, families, and the global community in which we work and live. EQUAL! commits to advancing change that will help people respect and value differences, thus allowing employees to achieve Lucent Technologies vision.

- **HISPA (Hispanic Association of Lucent Employees)** - Maintained a global organization of Hispanics committed to promoting the development, growth, advancement, and general well-being of Hispanics and other Employee Business Partners in order to create a productive diverse workforce in preparation for corporate and community leadership.

- **LUNA (United Native Americans of Lucent Technologies)** - Established a Native American organization open to all employees committed to the cultural development, career advancement, education, understanding, and the general well-being of all employees. Also, to develop our Native American resources as employees, business partners, and customers; support Lucent Technologies in leveraging diversity as a competitive advantage; and support the corporation in developing people and using the rich tapestry of diversity in achieving global business results.

- **WIL-MV (Women in Lucent at Merrimack Valley)** - A group of women and men who promote women's professional growth and development, and personal friendships, as well as mutual support of alliances throughout Lucent Technologies.

Alliance Employee Resource Center

Joseph J. Giampa - Director

Published Mission: "To serve as the highest quality resource for CWA represented employees who want to take charge of managing change in their own lives, and to support those individual efforts by assisting them to realize their optimum career and personal growth and secure satisfying employment in their chosen field."

The Alliance for Employee Growth and Development became an established entity because of the 1986 General Bargaining Agreement negotiations between AT&T and CWA. These organizations share a vision that the growth and development of the individual is the key to success in a competitive worldwide marketplace. The Alliance's mission is to support individual efforts to develop career and personal growth and enhance each individual's employability through continuing learning experiences. The Alliance, in conjunction with the AT&T Merrimack Valley Works and Northern Essex Community College, was established in May 1989. An Alliance Employee Resource Center is at the AT&T site in North Andover, and is staffed with one full-time director, two full-time career advisors and one full-time program assistant. The members of the staff are employees of Northern Essex Community College working under an agreement with the Alliance. This unique Union/Company joint venture has the cooperation and consultation of a board called the Alliance Local Committee which is comprised of two AT&T managers and the presidents of the two Local CWA unions.

Merrimack Valley Works Employee Support

- **Technical Personnel Relations**:

  The Technical Personnel Relations office (TPR) served as an alternate channel of communication when a technical employee did not wish to discuss a particular problem with his or her supervisor.

- **Employee Assistance Program:**

  The AT&T Employee Assistance Program (EAP) offered confidential professional short-term help for personal problems.

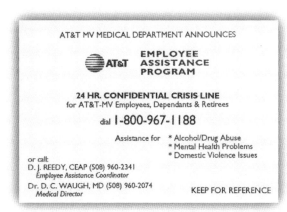

- **Employee Resource Center:**

  In May 1989, the Alliance Employee Resource Center was established. It assisted employees in making informed decisions about education, careers, personal counseling, transferring, and benefit programs. It also offered career assessment, training, life planning workshops and other programs to help employees advance their careers both inside and outside of AT&T.

- **Ombudsperson:**

  The Ombudsperson assisted in the human side of work as a confidential and impartial resource for dealing with employees' complaints, problems, ideas and suggestions.

Merrimack Valley Works - Environmental, Health & Safety Engineering Organization

The following information was reproduced from Western Electric, AT&T and Lucent Technologies reference cards. If you ever wondered why we had such a large and professional Safety department, the list below will answer your questions. Each component of an area of safety required the all-out teamwork and cooperation of the department, as well as any company and/or government agencies.

Emergency Signal Codes:

- Signal 1 - Fire/Evacuation
- Signal 2 - Sprinklers
- Signal 3 - Disorder
- Signal 4 - Medical
- Signal 5 - Other
- Signal 6 - Spill

Environmental - Responsible for:

- ISO 14000 [International Organization for Standardization - a series of standards is to promote effective environmental management systems in organizations]
- Clean Air
- Clean Water
- Hazardous Waste Management
- Pollution Prevention/Reduction
- Process Hazard Review
- Recycling
- Toxic Use Reduction Act (TURA)
- Transportation of Hazardous Materials
- Underground/Aboveground Storage Tanks
- Waste Minimization
- Works Inspecting

Ergonomics - Responsible for:

- Back Injury Prevention
- Chairs
- Cumulative Trauma Disorders
- Lighting/Workstation Design
- Tools

Chemicals and Fire Protection - Responsible for:

- Chemical Control
- Chemical Handling, Storage and Dispensing
- Compressed Gasses
- Egress/Exits and Signage
- Fire Extinguishers
- Fire Protection
- Fire Suppression - Buildings and Machines
- Works Inspections

Industrial Hygiene - Responsible for:

- VPP (OSHA Voluntary Protection Program) (promotes worksite-based safety and health)
- Asbestos
- Blood-borne Pathogens
- Confined Spaces
- Contractor Safety
- Emergency Planning
- Emergency Response Team
- Hazard Communication
- Indoor Air Quality
- LASER/Radiation Safety

- Lead
- Lighting/Noise
- Lock-Out/Tag-Out
- Material Safety Data Sheets (MSDS)
- Personal Protective Equipment
- Respirators
- Toxic Substance Control Act

Other Responsibilities:

- Accident Investigation
- Cranes and Hoists
- Emergency Eyewash/Shower Stations
- Housekeeping/Safety Audits
- Machine Guarding
- Powered Industrial Vehicles (PIVOT)
- Welding and Cutting

And remember, safety glasses with side shields must be worn off main aisles at all times!

10 - Merrimack Valley Works Lexicon

A lexicon refers to a list of words of a language (in this case "Merrimack Valley Works-ese") along with related knowledge.

Academic Olympics and Science Competition:

- The Academic Olympics was a competition sponsored by the Lawrence Partners in Education for students from all the high schools serving Lawrence, MA. They were held each March at various venues in the Lawrence area. The Olympics provided students with an opportunity to express their talents in various fields of study. There were 11 categories: Art, Computer Science, Creative Writing, Culinary Arts, Industrial Arts, Mathematics, Business, Performing Arts, Photography, Science, and Social Science.

- Each category was sponsored by a local business or group. The Engineering Excellence Society at Lucent Technologies sponsored the Science Competition.

- The students' guidelines for the Science Competition were developed by a committee comprising EES members and teachers. Gold, Silver, and Bronze medals are awarded in each of two grade divisions.

- The competition was held at Lucent Technologies, and EES members served as judges and helped the students set up their projects. Upon completion of the competition, the students, judges, and invited guests gathered for an informal lunch in one of the Private Dining Rooms or the Customer Conference Center.

Agere Systems

- Incorporated in 2000, the former Micro Electronics subsidiary of Lucent
- Spun-off in 2002
- Acquired by LSI in 2007

Avaya:

- Equipment manufacturing company spun-off from Lucent in 2000
- Avaya filed for bankruptcy in January 2017

AT&T Incorporated

- In 1995 Southwestern Bell Corporation changed its name to SBC Communications
- Acquired Pacific Telesis in 1997
- Acquired SNET in 1998

- Acquired Ameritech in 1999
- February 2005, SBC acquired former parent company AT&T Corp. for over $16 billion
- SBC took on the AT&T name upon merger closure on November 18, 2005
- SBC began trading as AT&T Inc. on December 1, 2005
- In 2006 AT&T Inc. purchased BellSouth

AT&T Network Systems

- The Western Electric Cabling division became Systemax Solutions
- Spun-off from Avaya in 2002
- Now part of CommScope

Baldrige National Quality Award

The Malcolm Baldrige National Quality Award is the highest level of recognition of performance excellence in healthcare, manufacturing and education. It was developed in the late 1980s by the Department of Commerce to help improve competitiveness of American companies.

On October 14, 1992 at 12:15 p.m., Transmission Systems Vice President Jack McKinnon makes plant-wide loudspeaker announcement that the Merrimack Valley Works has won the National Malcolm Baldrige Quality Award.

Bellcomm

Bellcomm was based near NASA Headquarters in Washington, DC, and formed out of Bell Telephone Laboratories in 1962 to provide technical advice to NASA's Apollo Program Director. The organization rapidly expanded its responsibilities to support nearly all of NASA's Office of Manned Space Flight planning. Bellcomm was closed in 1972.

Bellcore (Bell Communications Research)

In 1997, Bellcore was acquired by Science Applications International Corporation and became Telcordia Technologies, Inc.

Bell System

The Bell System was the system of companies, led by the Bell Telephone Company and later by American Telephone & Telegraph (AT&T), which provided telephone services to much of Canada and the United States from 1877 to 1984. On December 31, 1983, the system was divided into independent companies by a U.S. Justice Department order.

Bonus Program

- The bonus program was a group bonus where everyone shared in the total production of the area, not just what a worker could do on their own.

- The bonus program would pay a percentage of an employee's pay (as a bonus) to the employee, based on the productivity percentage of the employee's workgroup. Western Electric endeavored to keep the bonus between 24% and 27%, and most groups fell within that area.

- If a workgroup started to earn much more, or considerably less than that, there was likely something wrong with the rate of productivity assigned to the job task. Industrial Engineers conducted time studies of how much time it would take a production employee to perform a task.

- A new product job would get a starting bonus of 20% for periods up to 18 months, not based yet on actual time studies. For the next several months after the initial period, the workgroup would be receiving a bonus that would combine what was actually earned, along with a managerial allowance. Ultimately, the workgroup would move to the system with the bonus based solely on productivity.

- Time study engineers would come around to re-evaluate the rates if production associates either worked too quickly or too slowly. If a productivity rate was set too high, the employees would have to live with it. Rates were set on doing one board at a time, even though people frequently worked on three or four boards at a time

- Production associates were required to fill out a document called a "Bogie," which was a personal record of the week's work. Each day, the number of work items was recorded, including time spent waiting for work, setting up to work, and material handling (moving products from place to place in this instance). The week's bogies provide the supervisor information to determine an efficiency rating that gives each associate a sense of how well he or she is doing.

- In 1986, the company ended wage incentives, and implemented the Production Occupation Level Plan.

Cable Forming

Cable forming is changing the shape of a length of wire so that it conforms to a specific layout required by a circuit board, panel, or bay frame. In early manufacturing processes, cable forming was largely done by hand, by laying out a pattern on a board, hammering nails into that pattern, and manually guiding wire around the nails.

Within the last several decades, computer-controlled machines that zip back and forth making the same patterns, have replaced the manual process. At most plants both the manual and automatic processes were done side by side.

Clark Shop

1985 - Located on Terminal Avenue in Clark, New Jersey, approximately 12 miles from New York City, 180 AT&T Network Systems employees of this satellite plant reported to Merrimack Valley Works. The shop is a "one-product final assembly plant," and

has been manufacturing high-quality submarine cable repeaters for 30 years. Current repeater production is for the Undersea Lightguide System (SL = Submarine Lightwave). This digital optical system will use single-mode fibers to carry data at a rate of 280 megabits per second in TAT-8, the eighth TransAtlantic Telephone Cable. Clark repeaters will be spaced at 50-kilometer (about 31 miles) intervals to regenerate the signals and supervise the underwater system. Using digital speech compression techniques, a total system capacity of over 35,000 two-way voice channels can be attained. This capability more than doubles all prior TAT analog capacity. The reliability of Clark's repeaters depends upon the 430 type FICS and SAW filters manufactured here at Merrimack Valley. These and other components must be perfect, since TAT-8 and similar underwater systems are guaranteed to be trouble-free for 10 years, with no more than three repairs over 25 years. AT&T's Clark Shop, which are part of the Merrimack Valley Works, have their own production workers, engineers and technicians, and resident engineers from AT&T Bell Laboratories.

Cliff Robertson

For ten years he was the national TV spokesman for AT&T, even winning an Advertising Age award for best commercial. When he was scheduled to be the keynote speaker at an AT&T stockholders' meeting during a strike, Robertson refused to cross the picket line and would not speak. On May 16, 1987, the official AT&T TV spokesman, Cliff Robertson, made a surprise visit to Merrimack Valley Works, walking through shops, meeting employees and shaking hands.

Closing the Works in 1991

In 1991, the Merrimack Valley Planning Commission investigated what the potential loss of losing the Merrimack Valley Works might cost the region. The study found that a worst-case decline that eliminating the plant's then 7,000 jobs would cost 15 Valley communities $880 million. Lost supply orders for smaller companies in the area would eliminate another 7,700 secondary jobs.

Conveyors

During the life of the Merrimack Valley Works, hundreds of conveyor systems were constructed, dismantled, and reconfigured. Changes in production levels were the basic reason for alternate manufacturing patterns. Newer and faster systems lend themselves to high volume operations.

CWA Local 1366

Limited documentation remains about this union of professional office and factory employees. The Union, Local 1366, of the Communications Workers of America, received its first contract on August 15, 1980, and set up their offices. In 1982, the Local initiated a monthly newsletter called the "Office Spectrum," which informed union members of contract negotiations when in progress, notices on legislation and upcoming issues facing members, grievance information, editorials, and news items regarding the Company.

In November 1983, The *Office Spectrum* listed the following 1366 Officers, Executive Board members, and other essential staff:

- President - Wally Silva
- Vice-President - Fred Welch
- Treasurer - Dick Scruton
- Secretary - Peggy Hurley
- Executive Board Members:
  - Del Cummings
  - Della Eichhorn
  - Joe Alper
  - Mike Miele
  - Nancy Peterson
  - Ron Wilkinson
- Office Spectrum Staff:
  - Editor - Mike Noonan
  - Assistant Editor - Bob Grieco
  - Staff Typist - Rosemary Castle
  - Artist - George Ares
- Correspondents:
  - Claire Turcotte
  - Claire Wentworth
  - Dana Woodbury
  - Joan Collipi
- Local 1366 also listed a Steward staff of 26 employees

Dennis Ritchie

Dennis MacAlistair Ritchie (September 9, 1941 - October 12, 2011) was an American computer scientist. He created the C programming language and, with long-time colleague Ken Thompson, the Unix operating system and B programming language. Ritchie was the head of Lucent Technologies System Software Research Department when he retired in 2007.

- 1983 - Ritchie and Thompson were awarded the Turing Award from the Association for Computing Machinery (ACM)
- 1990 - The Hamming Medal from the IEEE
- 1999 - The National Medal of Technology from President Bill Clinton
- 2005 - the Industrial Research Institute awarded Ritchie its Achievement Award in recognition of his contribution to science and technology, and to society generally, with his development of the Unix operating system.
- 2011 - Ritchie, along with Thompson, was awarded the Japan Prize for Information and Communications for his work in the development of the Unix operating system

Thompson, Ritchie, President Clinton

Department Numbers

In January of 1972, Merrimack Valley switched to the nationally standardized method of numerical identification for the various Bell System sub-groups. Each group at the Works is now identified by a ten-digit "*nameber*".

- The first digit represents the president or executive VP the group reports to
- The second digit is the vice president
- The third and fourth digits are lettered abbreviations for the location (MV)
- The fifth digit - the administrative officer (in 1972, General Manager Dave Hilder)
- The sixth digit - director
- The seventh digit - manager
- The eighth digit - assistant manager
- The ninth digit - department chief
- The tenth digit - section chief.

Wherever a level of management is eliminated in the particular chain of authority, a zero is placed in that position. This new system allows an individual familiar with the code to immediately identify the chain of command above any particular organization. All Works organizations will have 12MV2 as their first five digits.

Digital Signals

- DS0 - Very, very, simply, Digital Signal 0 (DS0) at 64 kilobits, corresponds to the capacity of one analog voice channel carrying a single digitized voice call. The DS0 rate forms the basis for the digital multiplex transmission hierarchy in telecommunications systems.

- DS1 - 1.5 megabits, capable of transmitting 24 voice channels over a T1 line.

- DS2 - 6 megabits, capable of transmitting 96 voice channels over a T2 line.

- DS3 - 46 megabits, capable of high-quality coding and transmission 600 voice channels.

Digital Transmission

High quality voice transmission came to communications when voice channels reached the 64kb range. A short history is highlighted here:

- 1960s - 1.5Mb/s   (T1 carrier)
- 1980s - 417Mb/s & 1.7Mb.7 (FT Series G)
- 1991 - 2.5Gb/s   (FT2000 & OC48)
- 1995 - 20Gb/s   (OLS & NGLN)
- 1997 - 40Gb/s   (OLS 40G)
- 1998 - 400Gb/s   (OLS 400G)

Doctor W. Edwards Deming

W. Edwards Deming was a consultant in statistical studies worldwide. His clients included railways, telephone companies, motor freight carriers, manufacturing companies, consumer research, census methods, hospitals, legal firms, government agencies, and research organizations in universities. All the intercity motor freight in the United States and between the U.S. and Canada, for example, was studied by statistical procedures prescribed and monitored by him. He is best known for his work in Japan, which commenced in 1950 and created a revolution in quality and economic production. Japanese manufacturers created the Deming Prize in his honor, which is awarded annually. In May, 1960, he was decorated in the name of the Japanese Emperor with the Second Order Medal of the Sacred Treasure. He received the Shewhart Medal from the American Society for Quality Control in 1956. He was the author of several books on statistical methods and over 150 papers. Since 1946 he had been a Professor of Statistics at the Graduate School of Business Administration of New York University, and lectured at many universities in this country and abroad.

Duroid

A material used as the base material of a printed circuit board onto which the copper paths, tracks, and subsequent coatings are applied in high frequency designs. A duroid has a long industry presence of providing high reliability with superior performance.

Employee Suggestion Program

The Employee Suggestion Program (ESP) was implemented to find cost reduction opportunities that employees find as part of their daily work routines. The suggestion would be submitted and logged, and the relevant engineers on that product line would be assigned to review the suggestion and research its value. It could be using a different part, eliminating or streamlining a process or test step, or incorporating a great idea.

Ferrite Production

Ferrite, a magnetic material, has been used in transformers and inductors since the launch of the Merrimack Valley Works. Ferrite production was transferred from the Hawthorne Works in 1957-58.

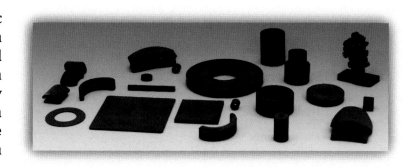

The Flying 15+

When the first FT-Series G system was in development, the *"Flying 15+"* - a group of MV engineers whose jobs varied from trouble-shooting to running parts, worked 24-hour days, and through the Christmas holiday of 1985. They adopted a "Roadrunner" as the team mascot. The team was:

- Bill Augusta
- Bill Erickson
- Bill Leeman
- Bill Talbert
- Bob Burnell
- Bob Litwinovich
- Bubba Williams
- Charlie Marino
- Dave Dixon
- John Hudak
- Keith Diffin
- Mike Flip
- Pete Tokanel
- Sam DiNoto
- Skip Bunker
- Tom Low
- Tom McKenzie
- Tony George
- Tony Iani
- Wes Myers

FT Series G Facts (Fiber Transport Series G)

- An FT Series G system is a high-capacity long-haul Lightwave transmission facility that transmits information through single-mode optical fibers at the wavelength of 1.3μm. It can be operated at either 417 Mb/s or 1.7 Gb/s optical transmission. It interconnected major cities via fiber optic light guide underground cable.

- FT Series G Terminal Equipment could combine 9 DS3 signals - each consisting of 672 voice circuits - and transmit them on a single light guide fiber. Over 6,000 voice conversations could be carried simultaneously on a single fiber.

- The optical signal, could be transmitted a distance of 24 miles before reaching a repeater site where the signal is regenerated. This compares with repeater spacing of only 6 miles, which were common only a few years earlier.

- The repeater spacing can be up to 48km (about 29 miles). In early 1986, FT Series G went into service between Chicago and Philadelphia and between Atlanta and Mosley, VA forming the first part of a long-haul single-mode fiber backbone network across the United States.

- FT Series G had been manufactured at Merrimack Valley Works since 1985, was state-of-the-art technology, and provided highly integrated equipment with modular and flexible architecture.

- During the last three months of 1985, over 8,000 new circuit packs, 550 regenerators, and 200 equipment bays were shipped to meet the January 1, 1986 service commitment.

- By early December 1985, several systems were up and running in the field. Several repeater sites were installed in Ohio and Indiana during a cold spell when outside temperatures were at 20 below zero and barely reached 40-above inside the small 10-by-14-foot repeater huts.

- Production of FT Series G built rapidly in early 1986 to supply several new customers, and to supply AT&T Communications expansion of its all-digital Lightwave network.

- By early 1987, the next phase of FT Series G will include an upgrade to a 1.7 gigabit system, which combines four of the present 417 Mb signals on a single fiber.

- AT&T was proud to announce that the first 1.7 Gb/s Lightwave system in the world was manufactured at Merrimack Valley Works in February 1987.

- Rapid growth resulting in high density traffic is easily accommodated because the FT Series G System can be updated from 417 Mb/s to 1.7 Gb/s without disrupting service to any customer. When it is upgraded there is no need to purchase additional outside plant light guide cable, keeping the costs of adding capacity minimized.

- The FT Series G can transmit 1.7 billion bits of information in a second. That's 24,000 simultaneous telephone conversations - or the amount of information in about 160 novels - in one second, over a single fiber pair.

- The 2,000 route-miles of FT Series G for AT&T Communications, included over 175 equipment bays and 550 regenerators to meet the deadline commitment. Frank Blount, Executive Vice President, AT&T Communications - Networks, expressed appreciation during a December 1986 visit to Merrimack Valley, for the teamwork at MV and in the field. The teamwork resulted in FT Series G being shipped, installed and tuned up for service in an extremely short interval. J. F. Healy, AT&T Communications Vice President - Network Services, returned to Merrimack Valley Works on January 16, 1986 to thank all personally who contributed to this effort.

- AT&T Communications leads all competitors in overall capacity of their intercity Lightwave routes. The new installed capacity - provided by FT Series G - exceeds all previous Lightwave routes combined.

- Signs of rapid advancement in Lightwave technology: FT Series G equipment replaced FTX-180 equipment on several routes which had been in service for less than six months.

- All terminal and repeater equipment was Manufactured at Merrimack Valley and final tested in Department Chief Al Kruschwitz' Lightwave Shop

The Original FT Series G Lightwave Manufacturing Engineering Team

Golden Boy - "The Spirit of Communication"

- The Genius of Electricity ("Golden Boy") Trademark of Western Electric was renamed "The Spirit of Communications" by the local Bell operating companies.

- It was designed by Evelyn Beatrice Longman and weighs over 16 tons, is 24 feet tall, and the wings extend nine feet from the body. Was chosen from the designs submitted in a competition taken part in by eight leading sculptors.

- Miss Longman wanted "The Genius" to symbolize Mercury's speed, the era's continuing sense of mystery about all things "electric," and the modern messenger, the telephone.

- 1916 - The statue was mounted at the top of AT&T headquarters, at 195 Broadway in New York City, and rose to 434 feet above the ground.

- 1983 - AT&T moved to new headquarters at Madison Avenue and 55th Street and installed Golden Boy at the entrance.

- 1992 - When AT&T leased the building to Sony, Golden Boy was moved to Basking Ridge, NJ.

- 2001 - Golden Boy was moved south to AT&T's headquarters in Bedminster, NJ, after sale of the corporation's Basking Ridge facility.

- 2009 - Golden Boy has been removed from the old AT&T headquarters in Bedminster and sent to the new AT&T (formerly SBC) corporate HQ at 208 South Akard St. in Dallas, Texas.

"Hello Charley" Vacation Queen Beauty Pageant

- The name of the beauty pageant originated when a postcard sent to the Hawthorne Works in Chicago was simply addressed to "Charley at Hawthorne." The card found its way to the correct recipient, a popular employee named Charlie Drucker. From then on, all Hawthorne employees were nicknamed "Charley." Winners of Hello Charley were pictured on bumper stickers and luggage tags distributed to Hawthorne employees.

- In 1930, Jean O'Rourke, at Hawthorne, was crowned the first "Hello Charley" beauty queen, inaugurating a fifty-year tradition. Her likeness appeared on "Hello Charley" stickers as Western employees took their mandated two weeks of vacation in July.

When Western employees spotted another car with a sticker, they honked in solidarity. Even on vacation, Hawthorne brought people together.

- The contest started in 1930, was suspended during the depression, and resumed in 1935. It ended company-wide in 1981 when company officials announced the cancellation of the pageant citing the cost of the event, and changes in the role of women that made such programs "no longer appropriate" - a mark of raised social consciousness.

HICs (Hybrid Integrated Circuits)

Hybrid Integrated Circuits (HICs) - Vital in critical circuits, and consisting of solid-state devices (thin-film conductors, resistors and low value capacitors) mounted on an alumina ceramic substrate. They are created through photolithographic techniques (microfabrication using light to transfer a geometric pattern from a photomask to a photosensitive material on the substrate), allowing extremely close control of placement and coupling between circuits.

Lucent GROWS

On October 28 of 1997, Lucent's President and Chief Operating Officer, Richard McGinn, held a company-wide broadcast outlining the new structure and strategies of Lucent Technologies. He outlined the culture and behaviors employees would need to execute the strategies effectively. Those behaviors comprise Lucent GROWS - an effort designed to create an environment in which all employees can do their best and most creative work. Each GROWS Letter signifies a behavior:

- **G**lobal growth mindset
- **R**esults-focused
- **O**bsessed about customers and about competitors
- **W**orkplace that's open. Supportive, and diverse
- **S**peed

Lucent Technologies

- Research and equipment manufacturing company spun-off in 1995
- Merged with French company Alcatel in 2006 to form Alcatel-Lucent
- Acquired by Finland's Nokia Corporation in 2016

Management Titles:

There's a world of difference between a "Engineering Vice President" and a "Vice President of Engineering." If the functional description of the job - engineering, in this case - preceded the title, that meant that the person was one of many with the same job. (Example: Engineering Vice President.) If, however, the title preceded the functional description, that meant that the person was the only one with that particular job, indicating a very senior-level person. (Example: Vice President of Engineering.)

Merrimack Valley Mathematics

- A bit means a "1" or a "0"
- A kilobit (Kb) is 1,000 bits (thousands)
- A megabit (Mb) is 1,000,000 bits (millions)
- A gigabit (Gb) is 1,000,000,000 bits (billions)
- A terabit (Tb) is 1,000,000,000,000 bits (trillions)

Major Western Electric / AT&T / Lucent Works Locations (alphabetically)

1. **Allentown Works** (1948-2002)
   Allentown, Pennsylvania (microelectronics)

2. **Atlanta Works** (1971-2001)
   Norcross, Georgia (undersea cables, later fiber-optic cables)

3. **Baltimore Works** / "Point Breeze" (1930-1985)
   Baltimore, MD (coaxial/marine cables, wire)

4. **Buffalo Plant** (1946-1977)
   Buffalo, New York

5. **Columbia River Switching Equipment Works** (1974-?)
   Vancouver, WA (crossbar switching)

6. **Columbus Works** (1957-2003)
   Columbus, Ohio (switching equipment)

7. **Dallas Works** (1970-2002)
   Mesquite, Texas (electronic switches and power equipment/supplies)

8. **Denver Works** (1970-2001)
   Westminster, CO (Dimension and Horizon business PBX systems)

9. **Engineering Research Center** (1958-1990)
   Princeton, NJ (R&D on manufacturing technologies)

10. **Greensboro Works** (1950-1975)
    Greensboro, North Carolina (military equipment)

11. **Guilford Center** (1970-2006)
    Herndon, Virginia (U.S. federal government business)

12. **Hawthorne Works** (1904-1983)
    Cicero, IL (metal parts, components, thin-film, switchboards)

13. **Indianapolis Works** (1948-1985)
    Indianapolis, Indiana (consumer telephone sets)

14. **Kansas City Works** (1961-1998)
    Lee's Summit, Missouri (electronics, switching equipment)

15. **Kearny Works** (1923-1983)
    Kearny, New Jersey (power supplies and other equipment)

16. **Merrimack Valley Works** (1943-2003)
    North Andover, Massachusetts (transmission equipment)

17. **Montgomery Works** (1955-1987)
    Montgomery, Illinois (telephone parts)

18. **New River Valley Plant** (1980-1990)
    Fairlawn, Virginia

19. **North Carolina Works** (1954-1991)
    North Carolina

20. **Oklahoma City Works** (1958-2002)
    Oklahoma City, OK (payphones, switching equipment)

21. **Omaha Works** (1957-2003)
    Omaha, Nebraska (dial equipment, PBX gear)

22. **Orlando Works** (1981-2005)
    Orlando, Florida (microelectronics)

23. **Phoenix Works** (1968-current as Nokia)
    Phoenix, Arizona (manufacturing of cable and wire)

24. **Pittsburgh Works** (1904-?)
    East Liberty, Pennsylvania (plates/glass)

25. **Plymouth Plant** (1957-1987)
    Plymouth, Michigan

26. **Reading Works** (1952-2003)
    Reading, Pennsylvania (microelectronics)

27. **Richmond Works** (1973-1996)
    Richmond, Virginia (circuit boards and electronic components)

28. **Shreveport Works** (1965-2001)
    Shreveport, LA (telephone sets, payphones)

29. **Winston-Salem Works** (1954-1966)
    Winston-Salem, NC (military & waveguide equipment)

MVFCU - The Merrimack Valley Federal Credit Union

- 1955 - Started as the Communications Workers Employee Credit Union founded by CWA Local 1365, and became the Merrimack Valley Credit Union within its first year.
- Their first offices were at Western Electric, 1600 Osgood Street, North Andover.
- 1980s - The main office moved to 1475 Osgood Street. April 25, 1986, groundbreaking ceremony for new $2 million building to house the MVFCU.
- 1990s - Opened a second branch in Haverhill.
- 2005 - The Credit Union converted to a community charter, expanding membership eligibility to towns in the Merrimack Valley region and New Hampshire.
- 2007 - Relocated corporate headquarters to 500 Merrimack Street in Lawrence.
- 2016 - Opened their sixth branch in Seabrook, NH.
- 2018 - Merrimack Valley Credit Union became a state-chartered credit union.
- 2019 - Merrimack Valley and Bridgewater Credit Union Merge

Partners in Education

- The Partners in Education (PIE) is composed of businesses ranging from small merchants and community organizations to large corporations, joined together for the purpose of enhancing the quality of education in the Lawrence Public Schools.

- Ed Lawler and Joseph Patterson from the Merrimack Valley Engineering Excellence Society last served on the Partners in Education Board of Directors.

Photon Valley, USA

Just as "Silicon Valley" is the area in California where the leading makers of Integrated Circuits are, "Photon Valley" is the area in the Northeast where the world leaders in Optical Network Systems are emerging. There were about 500 such companies. Lucent Technologies Optical Networking factory at the Merrimack Valley Works was leading those companies in defining Photon Valley.

Plant Protection

- Gate 3 - On the Lawrence side of the plant, the Plant Protection Control Center has a public address system that allows immediate dissemination of information throughout the plant.

- Lost and found office of the plant in Guard Headquarters is always a busy place

- Trip schedules are checked as cars leave for Logan Airport to pick up a visiting Western Electric official

- Fire Extinguishers - hundreds of which are throughout the Merrimack Valley Works - are constantly maintained in readiness for use in the event of an emergency. Plant protection guards were responsible to check and recharge dry powder extinguishers.

- At all gates, employee passes must be checked before you can enter the building to report for work. Later, Automatic Turnstiles were responsible for employees entering, and virtually every gate is monitored by cameras in Guard Headquarters.

- The Red "Fire Alert Phone" is constantly at the ready in Gate 3's Control Center. In the event of any emergency, simply by picking up the receiver, a guard is placed in immediate contact with three fire-fighting locations to ensure quick action.

- All vehicles are checked before passing through the Gate 3 entrance by members of the plant protection force.

- Guards are constantly on patrol on the Merrimack Valley Works campus, and make routine report calls to Guard Headquarters from Telephone Fireboxes located throughout the plant as they patrol interior routes at the North Andover Plant.

Printed Wiring Boards

The old "piece part shop," where much of the hardware for the shop was made, was replaced by a printed wiring board shop. The first printed wiring board at the Valley was a single-sided board with copper circuitry on one side. Today we have copper on both sides and copper plating connecting through holes.

The most significant change from the first 25 years, has been how the design on the board is made. The first boards were designed by hand. An employee actually laid black tape on an artwork master. Today, master designs are done with a computer that also tells drilling machines and later processes where components are placed.

Proprietary Information

Proprietary information could have been in oral or written form and was clearly marked as such when in written form. Proprietary information was ANY information developed by AT&T or Lucent Technologies. Such information was intended solely for Company purposes and unauthorized disclosure of such information was strictly prohibited. A clean desk policy was a must at Merrimack Valley. We were told to never leave proprietary information unattended.

QWL - Quality of Work Life

The Quality of Work Life initiative was created to help employees deal with the multitude of changes impacting the workplace. This initiative has three objectives: to improve employee satisfaction, strengthen workplace learning, and to better manage ongoing change and transition. One definition of Quality of Work Life is the solving of problems where they occur, when they occur, by the people who have to live with the solutions. Joint steering committees were established in 1982, and were composed of an equal number of management and union representatives.

QWL Statement of Principles:

Each steering committee established its own charter which included the following nine principles:

1. The essential component of Quality of Work Life (QWL) effort is a process which increases employee participation in the decisions which affect their daily work and the quality of their work life. Specific local concerns and local problem-solving should be the basic of QWL efforts.

2. The goals of QWL efforts are;

   a. to employ people in a profitable and efficient enterprise.

   b. to create working conditions which are fulfilling by providing opportunities for employees and groups at all levels to influence their working environment.

   The pursuit of these goals is guided by the basic human values of security, fairness, participation and individual development.

3. QWL holds as a basic tenet that employees are responsible, trustworthy, and capable of making contributions when equipped with the necessary information and training. Management and the union seek to better acknowledge, employ, and develop the potential of all employees and are committed to providing the necessary information and training to encourage maximum contribution to the success of QWL.

4. QWL efforts must be viewed as a supplement to the collective bargaining process. The integrity of the collective bargaining process, the contractual rights of the parties, and the workings of the grievance procedure must be upheld and maintained. The process of implementing an improved quality of

life at work shall not infringe upon existing employee, union, or management rights.

5. Authorized representatives of the union shall participate in the planning, development, implementation, and evaluation of specific QWL activities which involve union-represented employees.

6. Voluntary involvement by management, the union, and employees is essential to the success of mutual efforts. Participation in specific QWL activities shall be voluntary. Individuals shall have the right to participate in or to withdraw from such activities without penalty.

7. Innovations which result from the QWL process will not result in the layoff of any regular employee or negatively affect the pay or seniority status of any union eligible employee, whether he or she is a participant in the process or not.

8. The success of QWL efforts require a spirit of mutual respect and trust among employees, management, and the union. Each party must give serious attention and consideration to the needs and values of the other parties. Management, the union, and employees must respect one another's legitimate needs and constraints. The success and maintenance of Quality of Work Life requires flexibility and continuing support and leadership from management, unions, and employees at all levels.

9. Quality of Work Life is not a "program": there is no universal or one best approach. It is a process which has great potential, but it can't be the answer to all the problems of employees, the union, or the company.

RBOCs (Regional Bell Operating Companies)

On January 1, 1984, the Bell System was structured into Regional Bell Operating Companies (RBOCs), which also became known as the "Baby Bells." The seven companies were Ameritech, Bell Atlantic, BellSouth, NYNEX, Pacific Telesis, Southwestern Bell, and US West.

RE-USE Organization

RE-USE was a $300 million domestic and international business that grew rapidly. RE-USE shared many of the same customers (Bell Atlantic, AT&T, and SBC) as Merrimack Valley, but they had their own unique set of competitors. RE-USE competitors included HITECH, Diversitech and CTDI, as opposed to traditional Merrimack Valley competitors like Alcatel, Nortel, and Cisco.

A market study at the time estimated that the RE-USE industry was a $1.6 billion industry, and 70-80 percent of the used equipment being sold was Lucent equipment. Lucent didn't want someone else selling Lucent circuit packs, bays, or other products, and many of the parts were simply new product "buybacks" from existing Lucent customers.

When equipment came to the RE-USE department, it was reengineered and configured to meet customers' needs. It was tested and warranted to be electrically and mechanically sound because the remanufactured materials had to pass through the complete and stringent Lucent Quality Assurance processes. Merrimack Valley Works shops that supported RE-USE were compensated for their work. RE-USE started as a transmission solution, but quickly encompassed all Lucent products in transmission, switching and wireless organizations.

The RE-USE department was a resident "Special Customer Operations" organization, mostly housed at Merrimack Valley Works, with 75 employees. The department also had its own Warehouse, Material Management organization, and Engineering and Planning staff. They also maintained Global Provisioning Centers (GPC's) in Phoenix, Kansas City and Charlotte.

This valuable part of the Lucent team improved our service to customers. The more people understood the business, the more people agreed it was good for Lucent. RE-USE was focused on taking market share from the secondary market competitors, and satisfying Lucent customers.

Soldering

In the beginning of 1956, there was very little, if any, automatic soldering. A large part of the work was done with a hand-held soldering iron.

However, by the end of 1956, mass soldering machines were in use that could solder thousands of connections on printed wiring boards in a fraction of the time.

Special Olympics / Special Field Games

A tradition of service to the community has continued by Pioneers over the years. No project better depicts this service than the Special Field Games for special needs children and adults.

The Games started in 1979, bringing together as co-sponsors the Pioneers from Western Electric and Bell Telephone Laboratories, and the Employees' Association of Bon Secours Hospital in Methuen, MA.

The Special Field Games were held at Northern Essex Community College in Haverhill. Local special needs persons took part in relay races, Frisbee and softball toss, soccer ball kick and other events tailored to fit their capabilities. The Games are held to create a greater awareness and understanding by the general public to the needs of special people, and at the same time offer these people the opportunity to experience the pride and satisfaction that can come through competition.

Summer-On-Campus Program

At selected universities, master's degree programs are planned by the AT&T Corporate Education Center and university faculty when employees need advanced technical academic training. To minimize time away from family and job, courses are concentrated in a four or five-week period during the summer, and the work is intensive. Employees who are accepted to the Summer On-Campus Program leave their jobs, their families, and their day-to-day routines to become full-time students. Participating universities waive their normal admissions tests, but students must pass tests at the end of each course.

SUMMER-ON-CAMPUS ENGINEERING PROGRAM 1996
PURDUE UNIVERSITY

Synthetic Quartz Crystal Growing

- Until 1959, quartz crystal used in Western Electric products was imported from Brazil. Large natural quartz crystals of electronic grade are extremely rare in nature, and take millions of years to be formed.

- When the need for high-quality quartz crystals could not be met by nature, a method was developed for growing quartz.

- In 1956 a building for experiments in growing quartz was constructed. The building was a temporary sheet metal building which housed four autoclaves, or growing vessels.

- Bell Telephone Laboratories engineers invented a way to grow the requisite quality of quartz by using a high-pressure growing technique called the *hydrothermal process*. Basically, small and relatively useless pieces of quartz are placed in a pressure container with an alkaline solution of sodium hydroxide, and heated to 750 degrees Fahrenheit, at a pressure of 25,000 to 30,000 psi. Using this process, large crystals of excellent quality could be grown in 33 days.

- All of the cultured quartz that the Bell System used to manufacture quartz crystals and quartz crystal oscillators were grown at the Merrimack Valley Works.

- Quartz is cut into wafers. The wafers are made into crystal units, and the frequency of the crystal is dependent on the shape and the thinness or thickness of the wafer.

- Quartz is used because it is a very stable element that transmits and receives signals at precise frequencies. Crystals are used primarily as oscillators and filters in Merrimack Valley Transmission Equipment.

- Building 37 is the original Quartz growing building. In 1960 the crystal was grown in what is now the crystal cutting building. Fifteen years later the present building was erected which contains 36 growing vessels.

- In the 1960's, the control room in the crystal building looked a lot different than it does today. Back then, a huge board stood before you which had rows of meters keeping track of the temperature inside the growing vessels. The final control room contained one computer system that controlled the temperature inside each vessel, monitored pressure, and had a built-in alarm system.

- Even though this technological breakthrough delivered savings in the millions, Western Electric engineers quickly saved an additional $100,000 annually by replacing a water-soluble lubricant used in cutting slices from a crystal with a special oil that could be filtered and reused.

Take Our Daughters to Work Day®

- This program, launched by the Ms. Foundation in 1993, provided an organized program for girls to visit the workplace to understand the ties between work, education and family. Merrimack Valley had taken part on the fourth Thursday of April, since 1994 with a day filled with informative and fun activities under the direction of the Women of AT&T (WATT) and later, Women in Leadership at Lucent (WILL). Their first program afforded sixty girls (picked by lottery) to take part.

- In 2002, the program accommodated over 100 girls - still picked by lottery since there were always more applicants than spaces.

- In 2003, the Ms. Foundation evolved the program and launched Take Our Daughters and Sons to Work® program. Lucent and Merrimack Valley supported the goals and vision of the endeavor, and was proud of the success and growth over the last nine years.

- In 2003, WILL was asked by Lucent to <u>not</u> participate, and the program did not resume.

TL9000 Quality Management System

Note: At the time, Merrimack Valley Works was known as the Lucent Technologies Northeast Systems Integration Center.

- TL9000 is a telecommunications specific quality system that uses ISO-9001 as a foundation. It adds additional requirements derived from the industry's best practices for the design, development, production, delivery, installation, and maintenance of products and services. TL9000 includes performance-based measurements that quantify reliability and quality performance of these products.

Merrimack Valley migrated through ISO9001 to TL9000:

- 1994 - ISO9001 - A model for quality assurance in design, development, production, installation and servicing

- 2000 - ISO9001 Enhancements:
    - Uses a process management model
    - Customer focused
    - Stresses defect prevention
    - Encourages proactive customer communication
    - Focused on continual performance improvement

- 2000 - TL9000 Enhancements:
    - "Telecommunications specific" for hardware, software and service
    - Uses uniform industry measurements
    - Encourages customer & supplier communication
    - Studies life-cycle management & reliability

Training

Certificates of Completion, Summer on Campus, Skills applicable to the works - Chemistry, Blueprint reading, Software products, UNIX, Troubleshooting, Microprocessors, various product systems trainings, and electrical and electronic technologies. There were also multiple trainings on cultural and social diversity issues.

Transistors

The transistor, developed by Bell Telephone Laboratories in 1947, was the building block of many products at the Merrimack Valley Works. The transistor made our products smaller, more power efficient, and allowed us to engineer more complex and enormously more reliable circuitry. Not only did transistors affect our products, it also changed the processes and production.

From the transistor came integrated circuits, a mixture of transistors and other devices on a single piece of silicon. Eventually new technology led to the computer and the microprocessor - a computer on a single piece of silicon.

The introduction of economical integrated circuits made the change from analog-to-digital equipment attractive in many applications. N and O Carrier systems were analog equipment manufactured at the Works. This equipment has largely been replaced by D1, D2, D3, D4 equipment. The Digital Interface Frame, once the most complex equipment made at the Works, is a digital system used with the 4ESS toll digital switching machine.

Verizon Communications

- In 1997, NYNEX was acquired by Bell Atlantic (taking the Bell Atlantic name)
- In 2000, Bell Atlantic acquired General Telephone & Electronics Corp (GTE) and renamed itself Verizon
- In 2006, Verizon acquired long-distance company MCI

Waste Treatment

- The Waste Treatment Plant at Merrimack Valley, one of the first in Massachusetts, was completed in 1969; a $1.5 million waste treatment plant (also called a Water Pollution Abatement Facility) to combat pollution in the neighboring Merrimack River. Senator Edward M. Kennedy was the principal speaker at the dedication ceremony.

- At no time was it considered that the Merrimack Valley Works was polluting the Merrimack River. When the plant was originally constructed, it included a primary treatment plant which complied with philosophy at the time. With ongoing U. S. legislation for water pollution control, the original facilities became totally inadequate.

- The plant actually is two plants - one to treat an average of 300,000 gallons per day of industrial chemical waste, and one to treat 200,000 gallons daily of sanitary sewage and wastes originating from manufacturing processes and buildings exclusively on plant property.

WaveStar™

WaveStar was the family name for the next generation optical networking products made at Merrimack Valley. It included:

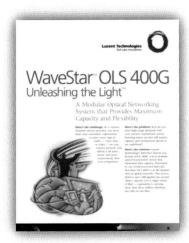

- WaveStar BandWidth Manager
  (a new DACS system)
- WaveStar Access Multiplexer
  (a new multiplexer)
- WaveStar 2.5G & 10G
  (New Lightwave Terminals)
- WaveStar OLS 40G & 400G
  (New Optical Line Systems)

Groups and Websites (as of 2021)

Lucent-Merrimack Valley, North Andover, MA Facebook Group

- Hosted by Beverly D'Agostino, this public group reunites former employees and retirees of the Merrimack Valley Works of North Andover. It contains updates on former employees, a way to stay in touch, see many photographs, and find links to other Merrimack Valley Works information and events.

- `https://www.facebook.com/groups/76457805336/`

The Osgood Street Irregulars!

- Hosted by Phil Baun for friends of Bell Telephone Laboratories at the Merrimack Valley Works, North Andover. The Osgood Street Irregulars website continues to evolve. Phil has spent countless hours collecting and scanning reams of Merrimack Valley Works periodicals, and welcomes any memorabilia of interest to the Merrimack Valley Works community that you are willing to share.

- `http://www.osgoodstreetirregulars.org/index.php`

Western Electric

The former telecommunications equipment-manufacturing company that ceased to have that name as of the 1984 break-up. Through several acquisitions, Western Electric became AT&T Technologies, Lucent Technologies, Alcatel-Lucent Nokia, and now operates as Nokia.

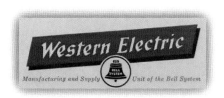

Western Electric's Dictionary

Words like "Plant," "Works," and "Shops," when capitalized, had specific meanings at W.E.

- "Works" are major manufacturing facilities, which comprise many "Shops."

- "Plant" refers to a medium-sized manufacturing facility, encompassing several "Shops."

- "Shop" is used to describe a manufacturing unit under the direction of a manager, that produces one particular product family, like DACS or FT Series G.

Western Electric's Legendary Quality

Until 1983, Western Electric telephones or their components could only be leased by subscribers and never resold, and were repaired by the Bell System operating companies at no charge to the customer. This led Western Electric to pursue extreme reliability and durability in design to minimize service calls. The work of Walter A. Shewhart, in developing techniques for statistical quality control in the 1920s, helped lead to the legendary quality of manufacture of Western Electric telephones.

Equipment designed by the Bell Telephone Laboratories was required to meet "Five Nines" reliability as part of network. "Five nines," commonly taken to mean "99.999%", referred to downtime of less than 5.26 minutes per year.

Western Electric Manufacturing Areas

To meet the challenge so that all parts of Western Electric's total manufacturing effort contribute to the company's overall goals, the Manufacturing Division, under the direction of a Vice President, has four major subdivisions, each headed by a Vice President.

These subdivisions are:

- Vice President-Manufacturing - Area A has reporting to him Baltimore Works, Indianapolis Works, Kearny Works and the Buffalo Plant.
- Vice President -Manufacturing-Area B has reporting to him Columbus Works, Hawthorne Works, Oklahoma City Works and Omaha Works.
- Vice President -Manufacturing -Area C has reporting to him Allentown Works, (and the Laureldale Plant), Kansas City Works, Merrimack Valley Works, and North Carolina Works.
- Vice President -Manufacturing Staff has reporting to him the Division Comptroller and Engineer of Manufacture.

There are specific items produced at each of the locations in the three Manufacturing Areas.

An understanding of the organization of the Manufacturing Division requires a brief discussion of intracompany terminology.

Words like "Plant," "Works," and "Shops," when capitalized had specific meanings at Western Electric, though the reasons may not always be clear and the distinctions do not necessarily apply elsewhere in the Bell System.

In Western Electric usage, "Plant" had a limited meaning. Strictly speaking, there were only two Western Electric Plants (with a capital P). One was in Buffalo, New York and the other was in Laureldale, Pennsylvania.

- "Plant" referred to a separate, medium-sized manufacturing facility, encompassing several "Shops."
- "Shop" was used to describe a manufacturing unit under the direction of a superintendent, that produced one particular product family, like crossbar equipment or cables.
- "Works" were major manufacturing facilities, which comprised many Shops. Western Electric Works were responsible for the great bulk of the company's manufacturing output. Some Works operated satellite Shops with large manufacturing facilities employing sizable numbers of people located physically apart from the Works to which each had reported.

With these distinctions in mind, the structure of the three Western Electric Manufacturing Areas is easier to understand.

Manufacturing - Area A

- Baltimore Works, Baltimore, MD
- Buffalo Plant, Tonawanda, NY
- Clark Shop, Clark Township, NJ
- Fair Lawn Shops, Fair Lawn, NJ
- Indianapolis Works, Indianapolis, IN
- Kearny Works, Kearny, NJ
- Marion Shops, Jersey City, NJ
- Queensboro Shop, Middle Village, NY
- Washington Street Shop, Indianapolis, IN

Manufacturing - Area B

- Clearing Shops, Bedford Park, IL
- Columbus Works, Columbus, OH
- Hawthorne Works, Chicago, IL
- Montgomery Shops, Montgomery, IL
- Oklahoma City Works, Oklahoma City, OK
- Omaha Works, Omaha, NE

Manufacturing - Area C

- Allentown Works, Allentown, PA
- Burlington Shops, Burlington, NC
- Chatham Road Shops, Winston-Salem, NC
- Greensboro Shops, Greensboro, NC
- Kansas City Works, Lee's Summit, MO
- Laureldale Plant, Laureldale, PA
- Lawrence Shop, Lawrence, MA
- Merrimack Valley Works, North Andover, MA
- North Carolina Works, Winston-Salem, NC
- Waughtown Street Shops, Winston-Salem, NC

WEValley Club

- The WEValley Club which organizes social events for the Merrimack Valley Works employees was an outgrowth of the Haverhill and Lawrence clubs. When both clubs came together in North Andover, it was renamed the WEValley Club.

- The purpose of the WEValley Club was to promote social, recreational and educational activities within Merrimack Valley. The club sold tickets (usually at a great discount) for a wide variety of activities - cruises, movies and shows, shopping trips, sporting events, skiing, camping trips and much more.

- In 1956, the club offered a very limited selection of activities such as membership in a bowling league and tickets to a few social events. However, a year after the Merrimack Valley Works was completed, things started happening. In 1957, the Blood Bank was established. In 1960, four softball fields were crafted at the north side of the plant. In 1966, the first family outing was held at Canobie Lake Park.

- Throughout the last 25 years the club officers, directors and representatives have started a variety of activities that have kept Merrimack Valley employees together.

- The club facilitated the delivery of company-related information to MV employees, such as memos from management, benefits bulletins, the Valley Voice, the Other Side of the Window and much more.

- Throughout the last 25 years the club officers, directors and representatives have started a variety of activities that have kept Merrimack Valley employees together.

- The club also sold tickets to athletic, social and community events, and aided in organizing company activities that all employees can enjoy.

11 - MVFCU - Nomination & Election Examples

In 1955, the MVFCU - Started as the Communications Workers Employee Credit Union founded by CWA Local 1365, and became the Merrimack Valley Federal Credit Union within its first year. A credit union is a non-profit cooperative institution made up of members who borrow from pooled deposits. Credit unions offer most of the same services as traditional banks but are owned by members, not shareholders, and are governed by the NCUA (National Credit Union Administration).

1974

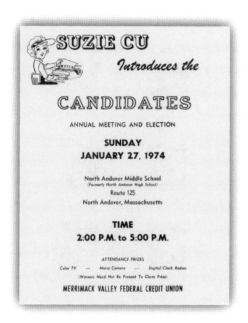

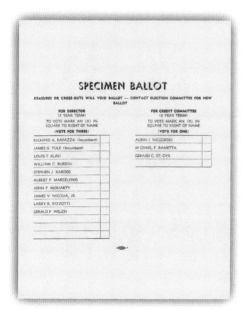

SUZIE CU GOES TO PRESS

MERRIMACK VALLEY FEDERAL CREDIT UNION

Volume 8   MARCH 1974   Issue 2

Our Elected Directors For The Year

Seated left to right: Donald A. Lavallee, Secretary; Richard A. Rapazza, 1st Vice President; William A. Schmidlin, President; John J. Sayers, 2nd Vice President; and Frank Serio, Jr., Treasurer.
Standing: Dominic A. Teoli, Asst Treasurer; Frank J. Talarico, James G. Yule, William C. Burdin, Richard M. Hayes and Leo J. Galeazzi, Directors.

THE ANNUAL MEETING REVIEWED

The annual meeting of the Merrimack Valley Federal Credit Union was held on Sunday, January 27, 1974 at the North Andover Middle School. President William A. Schmidlin presided over the meeting. The total number of ballots cast was 736.

Mr Edward Kneeland, President of Local 1365, C.W.A., AFL-CIO, was appointed as Parliamentarian and as a quorum was present the meeting began.

President Schmidlin reported the many accomplishments that had taken place in 1973. He pointed out that the credit union needs both members who save and members who borrow Therefore, the 6¼% interest paid in dividends quarterly on your savings and the 15% interest refund is to benefit all members.

Mr Frank Serio, treasurer, indicated by his report that despite the unstable economic conditions the

credit union has grown with total assets of $18,009,837, a gain of $3,685,478. Total loans were $15,792,139, a gain of $3,211,605 while shares (or savings) increased to $16,791,002, a gain of $3,509,977

The total of dividends paid to shareholders for the year 1973 amounted to $818,452. In addition, $200,121 was returned to the borrowers in the form of a 15% interest refund.

(Continued on Page 2)

1975

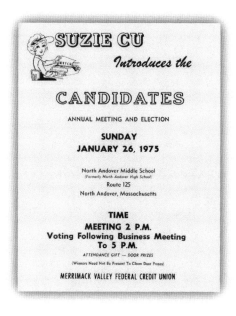

DONALD A. LAVALLEE   JOHN J. SAYERS   FRANK J. TALARICO

LEONARD J. BROWN   JAMES R. CARTER, JR.   JOHN W. CONNORS

NUNZIO DI MARCA   EVA M. JONES   PETER E. LUCCHESI

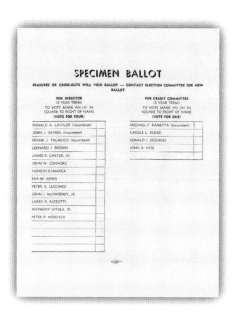

JOHN J. McSWEENEY, JR.   LARRY R. RIZZOTTI   ANTHONY VITALE, JR.   PETER P. WOIDYLA

MICHAEL F. RAMETTA   CAROLE L. BURKE   RONALD J. DESHAIES

JOHN A. HESS

SUZIE CU GOES TO PRESS

MERRIMACK VALLEY FEDERAL CREDIT UNION

Volume 9	MARCH 1975	Issue 2

Introducing "1975 Board of Directors" and Summary of Annual Meeting

Working for our members are from left, front row, Frank Serio, Jr., Treasurer; James G. Yule, 2nd vice president; Richard A. Rapazza, president; Frank J. Talarico, 1st vice president, and Donald A. Lavallee, secretary Second row, from left, directors, Leo J. Galeazzi, John J Sayers, William A. Schmidlin, Peter P Woidyla, William C. Burdin, and assistant treasurer, Domenic A. Teoli.

Sunday, January 26, 1975, Mr William A. Schmidlin, President of the Merrimack Valley Federal Credit Union presided over and welcomed members and guests to the annual meeting which was held at the North Andover Middle School.

Mr Edward Kneeland, president of Local 1365, C.W.A., A.F.L.-C.I O., was appointed Parliamentarian. As a quorum was present, Mr Schmidlin called the meeting to order

Mr Schmidlin proceeded to thank the Board of Directors, the Office Staff and Mr G Harvey Ellis, Office Manager, the Credit Committee the Supervisory Committee and the Educational Committee for their past efforts in performing in a very competent manner

After introducing the Board of Directors, Mr Schmidlin related many of the accomplishments of 1974. He called on Mr Frank Serio, Jr , treasurer to present his report and from all indications 1974 was a most profitable year This upward movement created new highs in both shareholdings and in loans. In order for you to obtain a clear picture of the dollar amount in your Credit Union, please turn to the Financial Report on

page 3. These results are a direct tribute to the stewardship of your Board of Directors.

Mr Michael F Rametta, secretary of the Credit Committee, submitted his report. Reviewed were 10,001 loan applications amounting to $14,168,048. Of these, 78 loans were rejected. Mr Rametta stated that members who are over-burdened financially can request counseling and reminded the members that the guidelines for loan applications are set up by the board of directors.

Mr Richard Parish, chairman of the Supervisory Committee, reported that in addition to the Supervisory Committee the Credit Union operations were reviewed by the Federal Examiners and also the Pontifex Accounting Company to perform semi-annual and annual audits. The Committee was happy to report that there were no significant errors or deviations in the books, procedures, or routines of the Credit Union which would indicate that the Credit Union is serving the members quite adequately

After any old or new business was concluded, and all reports were read and accepted, elections were held. The members voted and door prizes were drawn. The results were announced and the meeting adjourned.

1976

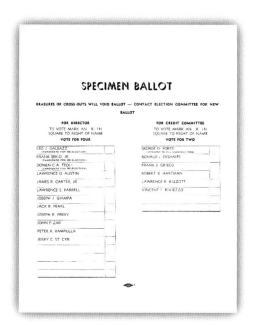

Credit Union News

1600 OSGOOD ST., NO ANDOVER, MASS. 01845

Telephones
- Main Office 681-4181
- Haverh ll Office 372-0111
- Auxi ary Office 681-4185
- Withdrawals 681-5050

Volume 10	APRIL 1976	Issue 1

Introducing Our Board of Directors for the Bicentennial Year

Seated front row, left to right: Donald A. Lavallee, Secretary; Richard A. Rapazza, President; Frank J. Talarico, 1st Vice President, and Frank Serio, Jr., Treasurer.

Standing 2nd row, left to right· Leo J. Galeazzi, John J. Sayers, Joseph J. Giampa, James G. Yule, 2nd Vice President; William C. Burdin and Domenic A. Teoli, Assistant Treasurer.

(Missing when picture was taken — Peter P Woidyla)

Report of Annual Meeting

Sunday, Janary 25, 1976, the annual meeting of the M V F C.U was held. President Richard A. Rapazza presided over the meeting and welcomed members and guests. After the old and new business was conducted, election of officers took place. The four openings on the Board of Directors were filled by· Leo J Galeazzi, Joseph J Giampa, Frank Serio, Jr., and Domenic A. Teoli. Elected to the Credit Committee was George D Forte and Lawrence R. Rizzotti.

The following members won attendance prizes of $25 00 E Bonds at the annual meeting of the M V.-F C.U J P Elias, Roland A. James, Tony Corey, Joe Bolla, Lynne Serio, Jim Fyrer, Eleanor Houston, C. P Sciacca, Ray De-Matteo, P W Mellonakos, Rose Perry, A. E. Camasso, Bill Harter, Frank Chapinski, Rosemary A. Casale, Ted Pelosi, Eleanor K Routhier Gloria Maheu, J W Fields, R. J Baril, Linda Becotte, E. R. Cadorette, Natalie D Grassi, Mike Belmer and Bob Zingali.

12 - Bob Gablosky Collage Samples

Secretaries Week – Spring 1989

Engineer's Week – April 1989

Canobie Lake Park – Fall 1989

Customer Conference Center - November 1989

Bonnie B. Small Award Celebration – September 1990

National Quality Month Celebration with Red Auerbach – November 1990

Malcolm Baldrige Award Celebration – September 1992

Special Field Games – June / July 1996

13 - Building Expansion and Construction Projects

• 1953 - Ground breaking for Merrimack Valley Works in September

• 1956 - Original construction completed on the main building in June

• 1956 - September - Merrimack Valley Works Update: The new Merrimack Valley Works is already being expanded. An additional 480,000 square feet of space is being added to the already 900,000 square foot manufacturing building. This space will be used for the manufacture of carrier and radio relay equipment and switching components.

• 1958 -The construction of the plant had barely begun in 1954 when the skyrocketing production schedules necessitated lengthening the front office building - Building 20 - to the full width of the main manufacturing plant - building 70. The additions were grown from each side of the existing building 20.

• 1958 - Manufacturing building 30 was enlarged by about almost one and a half times as large as originally planned.

• 1958 - Extensions were made to buildings 40 and 41 - and an Electric Substation and Cooling Tower were added.

• 1959 - The Merrimack Valley Works constructed a million-dollar water pollution abatement facility.

• 1959 - A separate 12,000 square foot building for Cultured Quartz Crystal Growing Operations is built. By December, the plant was completed and operational.

• 1961 - The new Quartz building was enlarged to have space to house the department for Ferrite Powder operations. Ferrite powder was used to manufacture magnetic cores for coils.

• 1968 - A pond and two additional cooling towers are constructed.

• 1969 - Bell Telephone Laboratories Building 21 added to the northeast end of Office Building 20 - The three-story, 160,000 square-foot addition, with crossover entrances to Building 20, was estimated to cost $6.875 million in 1967. The first moves were Bell Telephone Laboratories offices on May 3, 1969, with the Bell Telephone Laboratories engineering operations in early July. The addition would also house a 2,500 square foot research library. The North and West parking lots were also expanded to accommodate another 679 cars. All was accomplished on schedule.

• 1969 - In November, a $1.5 million Waste Treatment Plant (also called a Water Pollution Abatement Facility) was dedicated to combat pollution in the neighboring Merrimack River. Senator Edward M. Kennedy was the principal speaker at the dedication ceremony. The plant actually is two plants. Stretched out over five acres, the treatment plant purifies an average of 350,000 gallons per day of industrial chemical waste, and treats 200,000 gallons of sanitary sewage and wastes originating from manufacturing processes and buildings located exclusively on plant property. The waste water is treated through aeration and a series of basins, filters, chemical treatment facilities, and drying beds each day. In addition, the facility purifies well water for industrial use.

- 1969 - In September 1968, Western Electric Corporate President, Paul A. Gorman, announced plans for the construction of a new merchandise warehouse addition to the main plant at the Merrimack Valley Works. The new structure, comprising 132,000 square feet, would be connected to the main plant, and at the west rear (Lawrence side) of the existing building. The addition allows the company to consolidate building and storage functions at the Merrimack Valley Works location. Previously, finished products were stored off-site.

- 1969 - August - Merrimack Valley Works Increases Property Size Western Electric has purchased twelve acres of land adjacent to the North Andover Plant of the Merrimack Valley Works. The parcel of land, which fronts on Osgood Street and Holt Road, will increase the total size of the North Andover tract to 169 acres. The new property will provide the capability of constructing a new access road to the plant. It is anticipated that this road will provide for more effective separation of trucking and pedestrian traffic and add to traffic safety and employee convenience in the vicinity of the North Andover Plant.

- 1971 - Mezzanine within Building 70 constructed for Thin Film Manufacturing.

- 1971 - Chiller Building 44 enhanced for air conditioning of the new Thin Film Mezzanine.

- 1973 - Chiller Building 45 was constructed.

- 1973 - The Electric Substation behind Building 21 was extended.

- 1973 - March - Building 34, the Quartz Crystal Building, is being enlarged in order to accommodate new pollution control equipment. The expansion will be a 26 by 14-foot addition and will extend from the present vestibule to the ferrite loading dock. The pollution control equipment, which the new facility will house, will be used to clean the pollutants from the lapping grit operations in the crystal building.

- 1975 - Waste Treatment Building 50 expanded - The changing character of plant operations has necessitated the expansion of the Industrial Wastewater Treatment Plant. The changes are exemplified by the growth of thin film and printed wiring board chemical operations. The rinse water from these areas and air conditioning blowdown are the principal contributors of wastewater. Besides the volume increase, more stringent laws have been enacted for wastewater treatment by the Environmental Protection Agency and the State of Massachusetts.

- 1975 - Construction of a New Quartz Growing Building at Merrimack Valley - Merrimack Valley Works field construction crews placed 14,000 pounds of sand in each of sixty 15-foot-deep pits to begin construction of additional Quartz Crystal growing autoclaves, (the underground "pressure cookers" for grown quartz). The new building, north of Building 34, will allow MV to more than double the quartz growing capacity. This building, when completed, will have approximately 20,000 square feet of floor space, including a mezzanine area, to house sixty autoclaves and the peripheral equipment needed to grow quartz. The growing cycle will be controlled by two computer systems, with half the autoclaves on each of the computer systems. There will also be a seed cutting area, a seed inspection and assembly area, and a mechanical and an electrical maintenance area in the building.

- 1976 - Quartz Crystal Growing facility expanded for greater-capacity quartz growing, and reuse and staging just north of the existing quartz growing facility, Building 37

- 1979 - Salem, New Hampshire, satellite plant opened on Nov. 26

- 1980 - Georgetown satellite plant opened on April 2

- 1980 - Shawsheen satellite plant opened on April 21

- 1980 - Second mezzanine constructed

- 1985 - Bell Laboratories Ward Hill Location completed. AT&T leased it from developer Al Contarino who received rent in the first year close to his original purchase price of the property. Merrimack Valley Works facilities engineering did all the construction and occupancy work.

- 1985 - AT&T Bell Laboratories occupies new facility at 20 Shattuck Road, Andover with 230 Bell Laboratories developers. Also housed in Andover are 135 Network Systems Product Management employees who formulate marketing and financial strategies for transmission products.

- 1985 - October / November - A construction project at the rear of the Merrimack Valley Works plant added space for storage, extended the truck court area, provided a larger turnaround for trucks, and added a new gatehouse.

  o Phase one was building a mezzanine on the south side over the former truck court providing an additional 6,000 square feet of storage space.

  o Phase two was extending the first floor into the former truck dock area, resulting in trucks docking outside instead of inside. More heaters were installed.

  o Phase three extended the pavement for a larger turnaround area.

  o Phase four provided a new gatehouse for employees using the rear parking lots. The gatehouse is manned 24 hours a day.

- 1986 - Bell Laboratories Andover Product Line Management location completed

- 1987 - April 21 - A new complex of training facilities, assembled by combining 11 mobile classrooms (trailers), is completed and occupied.

- 1989 - October 25 - Customer Conference Center at MV opens. Merrimack Valley's own team of carpenters, millwrights, electricians, pipe fitters, locksmiths, heating / ventilation / air conditioning experts, welders, painters and supervisors turn 30-year-old lobby into showcase for customers.

- 1997 Construction Projects:

  o Ventilation - New Variable Air Volume (VAV) controls were installed. With this new system, each room has a diffuser in the ceiling with a sensor inside. Diffusers will open and close accordingly to adjust the flow of air. Because VAVs have been installed in Building 20 and portions of Building 21, the project is already saving money and making it more comfortable for employees. This project should be complete in early 1998.

  o New Windows - The first phase of a major window replacement project involved updating the Board Room and Vice President's office. The remaining windows in Buildings 20 and 21 will be replaced in 1998.

  o Electrical Upgrades - Over the next year and a half, building 20 will be totally rewired. The 1956 vintage wiring just doesn't have the capacity we need to run all of today's electrical equipment - particularly computers and peripherals. Overhead electrical grids have also been installed in all new shops which offer flexibility as far as rearranging shops.

  o Power House - The Power House is home to four gigantic boilers that produce steam for process work, humidification in our A/C system, and all of the hot water we use. In the past two years, two 1950s boilers were upgraded to meet all 1990s Clean Air Act regulations. The remaining two boilers will be rebuilt over the next two years.

  o Chillers - The chillers and towers in Building 45 provide chilled water for our air conditioning system. They have been completely refurbished over the last few years. Not only are they more efficient, they run on environmentally friendly Freon. This has resulted in a major cost reduction and helped save the ozone layer!

- 1998 - Upgraded Uninterruptible Power Supply (UPS) for the Merrimack Valley Works Datacenter - Dual uninterruptable power supply systems with a 900kw standby generator. The large outdoor facility is alongside Building 20 on the Southeast side and is 40' x 8.0' x 13.5' inside a bricked wall.

- 1996 to 1998 - Major Renovation of the South-East Corner of Building 30 - With months of incredible demolition, renovations, and remarkable new construction, the Merrimack Valley Works received a massive modern serving area, cafeteria, and executive dining areas, an Express Café, a large outdoor cafeteria patio with pergola roof, trees and piped-in music, a beautiful new state-of-the-art auditorium with a butterfly grand entrance staircase

- 1999 - The new OLS area uses the latest grid design, intended to provide flexibility for any use in the future. The grid over OLS consists of approximately:

  - 50,000 linear feet (9.5 miles) of double B-line strut, the green colored structural channel used to support the services

  - 45,000 feet (8.5 miles) of data cable

  - 25,000 linear feet (4.7 miles) of data tray

  - 20,000 linear feet (3.8 miles) of compressed air piping

  - 20,000 linear feet (3.8 miles) of electrical power bus

  - 5,000 new energy-efficient light fixtures

- 1999 - Mezzanine D and the Product Realization Center offices were dismantled; the Multi-Chip Module Clean Rooms, raised floors, and piping were all ripped out; tons of older, unnecessary equipment was scrapped to make way for the open OLS (Optical Line System) floor plan.

- 1999 - Along with the increase in business came a need to upgrade the office facilities. The existing cubicles could not handle the power and data requirements of the equipment needed to support a world class operation. In order to begin the upgrade work in Building 20, one-third of the seats had to be relocated. At the same time, the OLS shop project was displacing an office complex from under the mezzanine. To meet these needs, two portable office buildings had been constructed. "Building 84" opened September 1998 near Gate 6, and "Building 85" opened in late June 1999 off of Building 21. Together, about 260 seats have been added.

- 1999 - May - The Mezzanine "D" complex adds over 80 more seats. The new capacity will allow us to continue the upgrade project, and accommodate support staff until more permanent offices can be finalized. One project converts the former Multi-Chip Module space along the north perimeter of 30-2 into office space early in 2000. More spaces are being considered to bring the remaining staff back into the main building.

14 - The Customer Conference Center

1989 - Merrimack Valley's own carpenters, millwrights, electricians, pipefitters, locksmiths, heating, ventilation, air conditioning experts, welders, painters, supervisors, all had a part in the construction of the new Customer Conference Center at Merrimack Valley. It was a tremendous undertaking, but when the marketing and sales teams bring our customers here, one of the first things they will point to is the workmanship and talent displayed in the conference center itself. Then they will explain that that same attention to detail, that same commitment to quality, is inherent in Merrimack Valley's products. That powerful sales pitch is made possible only through the efforts of the many teams of dedicated people involved in the actual construction of the center.

A decision to build a conference center geared specifically to attract customers to Merrimack Valley was finalized back in the second quarter of 1988. A department, headed by Dom Mazzocco, was formed to look at modernization plans for the entire Merrimack Valley manufacturing and office facilities, but the conference center soon became the principal project. Early players in the game plan included the master architects from Engineering Design & Construction (ED&C), no strangers to Merrimack Valley. Part of the AT&T real estate division, ED&C built the original MV building over thirty years ago. Detailed design work began in January of 1989 and was complete six months later, on June 1 of 1989. Designers went to AT&T conference centers already in Denver, Atlanta and Omaha manufacturing locations and to the Universal Information Systems showcase in Chicago for ideas and feedback from construction crews at those locations.

In July 1989, the lobby and passageway to the shop that had not changed in thirty years became a memory, and by October 1989, the dream was a reality, and ready for a ribbon cutting ceremony that formally opening the doors to the center. The new Customer Conference Center will bring more and more customers to see the workmanship and pride with which our products are designed and manufactured.

Included in the center is a large reception area, a conference room/dining room, an auditorium style studio for product presentation - completely equipped for viewing films and live demonstrations, an office for customer use, and an office with telephones, fax machines, copier, etc.

15 - The Cafeteria / Auditorium Renovation

1996 to 1998 - Major Renovation of the South-East Corner of Building 30 - With months of demolition, remarkable new construction, and extraordinary modernizations, the Merrimack Valley Works received a massive modern serving area, cafeteria, and executive dining areas, an Express Café, a large outdoor cafeteria patio with pergola roof, trees and piped-in music, a beautiful new state-of-the-art auditorium with a butterfly grand entrance staircase. Deb Avery of the Perini Construction Company was the Chief Field Engineer for the remodeling project.

16 - Satellite Locations and Space Leased

- 1943 - Operations Established in Haverhill as Satellite Location of Kearny Works, New Jersey

- 1945 - September - Haverhill Leases 28,000 sq. ft. in the Agawam Dye Works Building on Island Street in Lawrence (formally known as the Kunhardt Mills) for warehousing.

- 1951 - Lawrence Shops Open - In 1951, manufacturing, warehousing, and office operations expanded into the former Monomac Spinning Mill in Lawrence.

- 1955 - October - Merchandise Location Opened in Lawrence - The new warehouse, recently leased by the company for two years, provides 90,000 square feet of space for Western Electric operations. It is in the Pacific Mills Print Works Building - a building adjacent to that in which the Lawrence Warehouse has operated for several years.

- 1955 - November - The Lawrence Shops has leased a parcel of land from the Boston and Maine Railroad to be used as a parking lot. Construction began immediately, and the entrance will be from the corner of Garfield and Falmouth Streets. It is planned to be reserved for office employees, and will accommodate about 125 cars.

- 1956 - April - Western Electric Acquires More Space in Merrimack Valley - The Western Electric Company has further expanded its operations in the Merrimack Valley through the acquisition of 62,000 additional square feet of building space in the area. Assistant Works Manager Harvey G. Mehlhouse, in announcing the latest expansion, stated that the latest space is comprised of 24,000 square feet at the Lang Building in Haverhill, and 38,000 square feet in the Pacific Mills Print Works Building in Lawrence. The Lang expansion is primarily for offices and stores, and some manufacturing activities. The Pacific Mills Print Works Building footage allows W.E. to expand its current warehousing operations at that location.

- 1975 - One Boston Place, Boston, MA - Product Line Planning and Management, the marketing organization for the Transmission Equipment Division, relocates from the Merrimack Valley Works. PLPM basically analyzes the market, then the particular need for a product is pinpointed, a strategy is developed for sales and manufacture, every other aspect that goes into making a product, and finally maps-out the route for new transmission products - long before production begins. They constantly meet with Bell Telephone Laboratories and Western Electric technical professionals to review plans in cost reduction, production, and forecasting, as they relate to marketing plans for a product that will be manufactured at Merrimack Valley Works.

- 1979 - November 26 - Salem I - Salem, NH - A satellite plant opened with 97 Merrimack Valley Works employees on 2 shifts. The newly-constructed 42,000-square-foot building is part of an industrial park, and off Hampshire Road. Production included D4 and LT1 Pre-Wiring, D4 Channel Bank Wiring Section, and D4 Channel Bank Inspection and Test Section. The second phase of the departmental moves took place on Dec. 3, when over 100 employees made the transition. By December 10, 3 shifts were operating with 225 people. By the end of February 1980, the number of workers was over 300. In July 1983, the Salem plant became the model shop for the development of D5 channel banks and controllers. In October 1990, the Salem I plant closed, and satellite operations returned to Merrimack Valley Works. In 1991, the Salem II plant closed, and the last department returned to MV.

- 1980 - April 2 - Georgetown, MA - a satellite plant opened where 40 people microfilm Merrimack Valley Works drawings at a new copy center. The Copy Center reproduces and distributes a variety of papers to Western Electric locations. Microfilm production of tracings (original documents made by draftsmen) and drawings are done here. A tracing file (a process of determining the current and past locations and other information of a unique item or property) is stored at this location which houses about 40 employees.

- 1980 - April 21 - Shawsheen (Andover), MA - a satellite plant opened with 350 employees making cables for Merrimack Valley Works equipment shops. A supply of cables, primarily Mini Cords, Coaxial and Local, are made at Shawsheen for the Miscellaneous section in Equipment Shops. The Echo Canceller and foreign sales are at this plant. There are Miscellaneous Transmission and Apparatus Shops which are also there. The total of about 350 employees working at Shawsheen, soon grew to 500.

- 1985 - AT&T Bell Laboratories, Foundation Avenue, Ward Hill - If you based your familiarity about this Ward Hill AT&T Bell Laboratories satellite location on Merrimack Valley Works periodicals, you'd think it was in the witness protection program. There was barely a trace of the location ever written about it in any of the company publications. Especially odd since even when Merrimack Valley built a new broom closet, there would be an employee celebration with a lobster dinner. I'm told that it was a location for "secret projects," which certainly makes sense in this case.

- 1985 - 3 New England Executive Park, Burlington, MA. - Product Line Planning and Management, and three marketing groups that were formerly at One Boston Place, Boston, MA, shortened their name to PLM (Product Line Management) and have relocated. About 100 engineers and marketing people will work in Burlington.

- 1986 - October 19 - AT&T Bell Laboratories new facility at 20 Shattuck Road, Andover, MA, was officially opened on October 19 with a ribbon cutting/open house ceremony. Product Line Management moved and segmented under the Product Management (PM) umbrella into Product Management Deployment Management and Market Management. Although the facility has been in use since January of this year, the October 19 ceremony marked the completion of construction and full occupancy. The open house which followed included self-guided tours and light refreshments. The building currently houses 230 AT&T Bell Laboratories employees involved with development of secure voice and data transmission terminals, magnetic apparatus, precision analog networks, microwave radio systems, signal processing technologies, digital facilities, and planning and manufacturing data systems. The Andover facility is also the home of 135 Network Systems Product Management employees who formulate marketing and financial strategies, and profit plans for transmission products. In 1993, the well-traveled Product Management group left the Andover location and returned to Merrimack Valley.

- 1993 - Product Management Deployment Management and Market Management close their Andover offices and moves back to Merrimack Valley.

- 1997 - May 27 - Lucent Technologies' Global Provisioning Center (GPC) - 20 Computer Drive in Haverhill opened - Materials from Merrimack Valley Works' building 70 were moved over Memorial Day weekend to the Global Provisioning Center, headed by Operations Site Manager, Wayne MacBain. The warehouse was redesigned, rebuilt, and cutover to a new computer system to support Whole Order Delivery.

17 - How the Merrimack Valley Works

[Originally published in the Valley Voice of February 1972]

The power house provides the essential steam, chilled water, and compressed air for heating, air conditioning and production processes. Steam is generated by four oil burning water tube boilers. These units consume about 3 million gallons of low Sulphur oil per year. In addition to using oil with less than 1% Sulphur, chemicals are added to improve combustion and reduce soot formation, thus reducing smoke and air pollution.

THREE OF FOUR STEAM GENERATORS

The boiler control panel automatically maintains the steam pressure by varying the fuel input to the boilers, thus maintaining the supply of steam to the plant. Fuel and air are proportioned to give optimum combustion efficiencies. Smoke indicators on the panel are activated by a photo-electric device in each boiler flue gas outlet.

The steam is distributed throughout the plant where it is used to heat the incoming air for the ventilation and air conditioning systems in the winter.

BOILER CONTROL PANEL

In the summer, the steam is used in the steam turbine drives for the refrigeration drives for the refrigeration units. Five of these units have a combined capacity of 3,500 tons of refrigeration. This is equivalent to melting 3,500 tons of ice in 24 hours. These units do not produce ice, but actually chill the water to 40 degrees Fahrenheit, after which it is circulated through the cooling coils in the air conditioning units. After the water removes the heat from the incoming air, it is returned to the chiller units where it is again cooled and recirculated.

REFRIGERATION UNIT

Three air compressors each have a capacity of 1,400 cubic feet of air per minute which is compressed to a pressure of 100 pounds per square inch by a two-stage compression cycle. The compressors are individually driven by 250 horsepower motors. After compression, the air must be cooled and passed through water and oil separators. It is then distributed throughout the plant where it is used to power pneumatic machines and tools.

AIR COMPRESSORS

Master Board Outlines Electrical Power Plan

[Originally published in the Merrimack Valley Communicator of May 1960]

While the electrical power distribution at the North Andover Plant of the Merrimack Valley Works is quite complex, a huge master board devised by Orra K. Robinson, Section Chief, Plant Maintenance Department, facilitates the solution of switching problems both before and while repair work is underway.

Actually, an electrified, multicolored "blueprint" of the North Andover Plant's power system, the master board utilizes an intricate network of 43 indicating lamps and 121 switches in a low voltage circuit which allows maintenance men to plan repair work in the safest and most efficient manner. The master board is constantly maintained to indicate the power distribution in use at any given time. Using this master board, maintenance people can see the results of various switchover plans and solve distribution problems in advance of performing the actual repair work.

Electrical power for the North Andover Plant is supplied by the New England Power System. It is received at a sub-station on the plant tract at 23,000 volts. By the use of three 5000 KVA transformers, it is then transferred to the Plant at 4,160 volts. To reduce 4,160 volts for lighting and power applications, there are thirty-one 750 KVA transformers in 17 load centers. By means of 115 high voltage switches in these load centers, the system becomes very versatile for lower voltage distribution. The master board simulates these transformers, switches and the varied network of electrified components.

18 - The Engineering Excellence Society

Few honors give a professional greater pride than having his or her work proclaimed as outstanding by fellow professionals. Each year during National Engineers Week, several Merrimack Valley engineers receive that honor and feel that pride. Induction into the Engineering Excellence Society occurred in a program held in a private ceremony, often at the LANAM Club (**L**awrence-**A**ndover-**N**orth **A**ndover-**M**ethuen) in Andover, MA. Later in the week, at a local banquet facility, and before a crowd of over 1,000 engineers, the individuals deemed outstanding by their peers are introduced.

The Merrimack Valley Engineering Excellence Society (EES) was founded in 1969 to recognize the outstanding accomplishment by members of the Merrimack Valley technical professional community. The Society is composed entirely of recipients of the Engineering Excellence Award. There are 187 members.

EES Society Key

The objectives of the program are:

- To enhance the engineer's stature among other engineers and engineering management at Merrimack Valley, and the community at large.
- To foster pride in a job well done.
- To recognize those individual accomplishments that reflect superior ability and effort.

The Engineering Excellence Recognition Committee (EERC) existed to determine the induction of members into the EES, and to provide peer recognition and acknowledgement of outstanding technical achievement.

Commemoration of that technical achievement was celebrated at an annual event held during Engineer's Week in February each year, where the Engineering Excellence Award was presented to the inductees.

Engineering Excellence was determined by the following criteria:

- Highly respected by peers for expertise, performance, and contributions
- Outstanding engineering service and assistance
- Contribution to advancement of engineering profession
- Successful application and/or implementation of innovative engineering developments, or novel and unique solutions leading to exceptional results
- New developments, special designs or redesigns, quality, production, or operation efficiency improvements, or outstanding cost improvement efforts
- Achievements or contributions of a technical nature which enhance or contribute to the effectiveness of a community

The program is carried out through two separate organizations - the Engineering Excellence Recognition Committee (EERC) and the Engineering Excellence Society (EES).

The original EES booklet, written in 1969 and describing the new program:

> *"The stature of Western Electric [AT&T / Lucent Technologies] has been shaped by dedicated engineering people. If we are to maintain and to enhance our image, to forge ahead, to prosper in the complex world of tomorrow we must continue to meet the technological challenges. There will be among us, certain ones who stand above the crowd; those who perform the unusual, the difficult, those whose contributions can be truly called the cream of technological triumphs. The main purpose of this program is to focus the spotlight of recognition on such persons and to illuminate the importance of engineering as one of the primary functions at Western Electric [AT&T / Lucent Technologies]."*

Engineering Excellence Society (EES)

The Engineering Excellence Society is made up of all recipients of the Engineering Excellence Award. It is chartered to conduct activities designed to enhance the professional environment at Merrimack Valley. Activities of the society included a lecture series that focused primarily on emerging technology, a plant tour for area high school students considering engineering careers, and a scholarship program funded originally by donations from society members, and later, from proceeds from the EES Fashion show.

Jack Heck, Merrimack Valley Works Manufacturing Vice President from 1985 to 1988, spoke about the profession:

> *"We have known about manufacturing in this enterprise for over 100 years, and some will say we are rediscovering it. I want to tell you that you and I are part of one of the most honorable and important professions in the world today - manufacturing technology. And whether you are a product engineer, a product designer, a process engineer, or a part of the team of other disciplines, you are part of an organization that turns ideas into realities."*

The First Engineering Excellence Society Induction

The Society originated in 1969, and the first awards were presented in March 1970 with the following announcement:

Engineers Cited for Excellence:

Six engineers were presented the First Annual Engineering Excellence Awards at the past meeting of Technical Professional Personnel of Western Electric's Merrimack Valley Works. The engineers who were honored on February 24 were:

- *Russell S. Cushing*   Engineering Associate

- *Richard A. Kirsch*   Planning Engineer
- *David W. Rudd*   Senior Staff Engineer
- *Norman F. Smith*   Planning Engineer
- *Edward T. Stocker*   Senior Engineer
- *Robert B. Zingali*   Senior Engineer

The award itself includes a Certificate, Society Keys, inclusion in the listing of the Engineering Excellence Society's plaque, and several additional honors. The actual presentation was made by Harry N. Snook - Vice President, Manufacturing - Transmission Equipment, at the Showcase Cinema in Lawrence in conjunction with National Engineers Week. The presentation highlighted the week which reviewed the progress of the year 1969.

Engineering Excellence Society Scholarship:

Beginning in 1978-1979, the Merrimack Valley Engineering Excellence Society awarded a scholarship to the son or daughter of a Merrimack Valley employee or retiree. This scholarship was open to all MV employees, not just EES members.

The criteria to apply for the scholarship were:

1. The student must be the dependent of a MV employee or retiree.
2. The student must graduate from high school during the current academic year.
3. The student must have been accepted to an accredited college or university in an engineering or science related curriculum.
4. The guideline has been that the degree program to which the student has been accepted must qualify him/her to be hired as a Technical Professional by Lucent Technologies.

The selection committee was composed of EES members. They reviewed all material and reach consensus as to the recipient. The selection was based upon grades, extra-curricular activities, and community service. The society was not privy to applicants' or their families' private information.

Shortly after the announcement, the winner and his/her family are invited to lunch at Lucent Technologies with all EES members who are available to attend. At this time, we award the scholarship check.

Engineering Excellence Society Scholarship Fashion Show Fundraiser

During the early years, the scholarship was funded entirely from donations by EES members. Although donations were still accepted, the major source of funding for the scholarship in more recent years was the annual EES Fashion Show. In 1989, the EES held its first fashion show as a fundraiser to increase scholarship awards. Employees modeled fashions from local retailers.

National Engineers Week / Engineer's Week Celebration

In the United States, National Engineers Week is always the week in February which encompasses George Washington's actual birthday, February 22. It is observed by over 70 engineering, education, and cultural societies, and over 50 corporations and government agencies. The purpose of National Engineers Week is to call attention to the contributions to society that engineers make. There were several events that celebrated Engineer's Week:

- Guided Tours (General Motors, Pease AFB, Seabrook Station, Lowell Historic Park, etc.)
- Guest Speakers (Oceanographers Bob Ballard and Dr. Albert Bradley, Weatherman Al Kaprielian, Astronaut Alan Bean, Dr. George W. Simon, Mountaineer David Breashears, various Company Administrators, and many others.)
- Engineer's Week Banquet / Luncheon at local banquet halls
- Engineer's Award Banquet at the prestigious Lanam Club in Andover, MA.

Andover's Lanam Club was established in 1957 by a group of businessmen and named to reflect the region: L for Lawrence, A for Andover, NA for North Andover, and M for Methuen.

Engineering Excellence Recognition Committee (EERC)

This committee consists of twenty engineers and is chartered to call for nominations from the engineering universe, and to select from those the special few who have distinguished themselves by their technical performance over a five-year interval. The longer interval is called for, rather than a single outstanding accomplishment, to ensure that the people selected can be expected to continue performing in an outstanding manner.

The Merrimack Valley Works Engineering Excellence Society

The Engineering Excellence Recognition Committee at Merrimack Valley, conducted the selection process for candidates to receive induction to the Merrimack Valley Engineering Excellence Society (EES). It was made up solely of voluntary members of the MV technical/professional community, and while sanctioned by management, management could not nominate, influence, or otherwise take part in the selection process.

Each year, the Merrimack Valley Engineering Excellence Society awarded a scholarship to the son or daughter of a Merrimack Valley employee or retiree. This scholarship was open to all MV employees. During the early years, the scholarship was funded entirely from donations by EES members. Although donations were still accepted, the major source of funding for the scholarship in more recent years was the annual EES Fashion Show. In 1989, the EES held its first fashion show as a fundraiser to increase scholarship awards. Employees modeled fashions.

The 31st and final EERC/EES selection process was conducted in 2000. On September 19, 2001, the Engineering Excellence Society closed its bank accounts in order to provide a donation to the current Red Cross Relief Efforts for the September 11, 2001 terrorist attacks on the World Trade Centers in New York City. On September 21, 2001, because of the downturn of the company, the Merrimack Valley Engineering Excellence Society suspended its mission to recognize technical professionals of the Merrimack Valley Works.

In February 1971, the officers of the Engineering Excellence Recognition Committee had formally presented the Engineering Excellence Society Plaque to the officers of the Engineering Excellence Society. The plaque was on the executive office wall at the center aisle on the third floor of building 20. Award recipients were announced at the Annual Meeting during Engineers Week. Those selected became members of the Merrimack Valley Works Engineering Excellence Society and their names were inscribed on the society plaque.

In the mid-90s, at the same time the new cafeteria and auditorium was constructed, a large display case honoring current recipient of the award with photographs and technical biographies, as well as listing all past members, was approved and hung in a prominent location on the hallway wall outside the Express Cafeteria, and across from the new entrance staircases to the auditorium.

The photographs presented here were provided by the Merrimack Valley Public Relations group, or scanned from Engineering Excellence Society Nomination Booklets that had been saved by Society member Larry Fisher, 1978, through the years.

1970

Russell S. Cushing   Richard. A Kirsh   David W. Rudd   Norman F. Smith

Edward T. Stocker   Robert B. Zingali

1971

Carl I. Furlong   Carroll H. George   Robert P. Grenier   Charles W. Higgins

James A. Russo   Herbert G. Witherell

1972

Richard T. Archambault

Ernest A. Gutbier

Nicholas C. Lias

Alfred C. Marzioli, Jr

Richard G. Munroe

1973

Edward J. Biron, Jr.

Albert L. Pepin

Arthur L. Prest

Donald H. Raymond

Phillip M. Scanlon

Peter Tokanel

1974

Clayton E. Goodhue   **Joseph A. Messina**   **Thomas F. Richardson**   **John D. Wormald**

1975

Clayton A. Burton   **Ernest T. Fusi**   **Herman A. McGauley**   **Ralph D. Powell**

1976

George J. Rembis

1977

David E. McDonald   **Joseph A. Salvo**   **Robert L. Vanasse**   **Thomas L. Young**

1978

Joseph W. Chaisson   **Vincent A. Corsaro**   **Edward S. Faber**   **James O. Grieco**

Thomas E. King   **Charles J. Mula**

1979

Lawrence D. Fisher

Theodore J. Nusbaum

Gerald H. Quereux

Robert M. Shearer

1980

Peter P. Filocamo

Gerald J. Koerckel

Frank Kupovics

Burrell C. Lowery

Richard J. Siney

Posthumous

The award was
presented to
his family

Robert P. Gallow

1981

Frank R. Arcidiacono   **Anthony C. DeSimone**   **Kenneth T. Kuster**   **Richard K. Tracy**

Arnold P. Ziemian

1982

F. Edward Crane   **Dennis L. Krause**   **Charles E. Metzger**   **William C. Morse**

Daniel F. Yetter

1983

Arthur E. Carter

Richard J. Lesiczka

Hank M. Moylan

Michael P. Smith

Ronald C. Smith

1984

Anthony L. Cappabianca

David W. Dixon

Richard F. Gordon

David H. Knight

Michael J. Kovach

Stephen Kuzmitski

Emile G. Langlois

Norman L. Major

Frank B. Rose

Earle E. Simpson

1985

G. Ted Dangelmayer

Ken E. Deming

Steven G. LeFoley

Andre W. Yoshida

1986

John F. Barry

Edmund L. Chase

Thomas E. Demers

Phillip S. Dietz

Anne Q. Earnshaw

Gordon V. Hatfield

1987

Steven A. Brown

Kathleen L. DiTroia

Richard G. Dumond

Jack A. Kelsey

Al H. Killiam

Robert J. Lansing

Richard E. LaPlante

Andrew C. Wheelwright

1988

Edward W. Hoffman

Edmund J. Lawler

Daniel J. McAvoy

1989

Melvin H. Bowie

John T. Corcoran

Howard A. Cyker

William W. Dyer III

Stephen J. Kimball

James R. Pruscha

1990

Ralph V. Collipi

Roger W. Dunn

Eric S. Fisher

Arthur J. O'Dea

Terry I. Rankle

1991

Fred F. Abyazi

Ernest Deveres

Richard L. Ferland

Thomas M. Hallworth

Edward Mannion

Peter St. Jean

Jeffrey Smith

Naji N. Wakim

1992

Charles Canali

James E. Gaudette

Robert Roberts

Richard W. Sanders

Michael Sheridan

Michael R. Thuotte

1993

Christopher R. Gayle

Martin K. Gladstein

1994

William C. Cornell

Joseph M. Couto

Phillip S. Dietz

Peter J. Hayden

Edward Holdgate, IV

Phillip S. Kasten

David H. Oesterreich

Iris L. Sindelar

Richard M. Valliancourt

1995

Robert C. Brockway

Keith J. Capulli

Arron L. Frank

Joseph E. Landry

Gerard E. Marchand

Chez Marchwinski

Nicholas J. Molloy

Daniel C. Vanevic

Michael A. Zimmerman

1996

Laurie A. Abyazi

Mary V. Anderson

Norbert C. DeAmato

Marilyn M. DeLeon

Mark E. Dorros

Frances L. Eason

Anthony F. George

Kubrom G. Ghiorgis

Karen E. Leonard

David A. Logan

Laura Magliochetti

Maria A. Montalvo

Curtis A. Siller, Jr

Jeffrey R. Towne

Robert R. Ventura

1997

Matthew J. Gogas

Robert C. Legrow

Joseph Patterson

Thomas T. Wetmore

Akbar Yazdi

Leonard J. Winn

Through a speakerphone from a hospital bed, Quality Director Lenny Winn was awarded Honorary Membership in the Engineering Excellence Society at Merrimack Valley during the 1997 Engineer's Week banquet.

This is the only honorary award ever presented.

1998

P. Stephan Bedrosian

David A. Ierardi

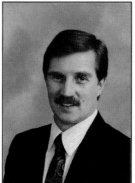
Edward J. Jaworski

Charles J. Pouliot

John B. Schetrompf

William J. Smith

1999

Tom D. Arntsen

Guy R. Belliveau

Mark A. Bordogna

Steven J. Formisani

Steven K. Shumway

2000

Jonathan M. Bradley

Ellen A. Chao

Robert G. Furrow

Robert A. Koehler

Carl A. Rutigliano

Paul M. Vanasse

Robert E. Zampini

2001

Dale B. Bates   **Man Shan Chan**   **Gary Y. Chin**   **Brij B. Garg**

Jeffrey M. Herbst   **Laurie A. King**   **Janet E. Swain**

Engineering Excellence Program Nomination Booklets

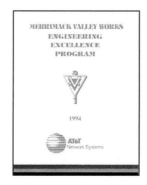

Academic Olympics and Science Competition:

The Academic Olympics was a competition sponsored by the Lawrence Partners in Education for students from all the high schools serving Lawrence, MA. They were held each March at various venues in the Lawrence area. The Olympics provided students with an opportunity to express their talents in various fields of study. There were 11 categories: Art, Computer Science, Creative Writing, Culinary Arts, Industrial Arts, Mathematics, Business, Performing Arts, Photography, Science, and Social Science.

Each category was sponsored by a local business or group. The Engineering Excellence Society at Lucent Technologies sponsored the Science Competition.

The students' guidelines for the Science Competition were developed by a committee comprising EES members and teachers. Gold, Silver, and Bronze medals are awarded in each of two grade divisions.

The competition was held at Lucent Technologies, and EES members served as judges and helped the students set up their projects. Upon completion of the competition, the students, judges, and invited guests gathered for an informal lunch in one of the Private Dining Rooms or the Customer Conference Center.

The following photos are from the final Science competition held at
Lucent Technologies, Merrimack Valley Works

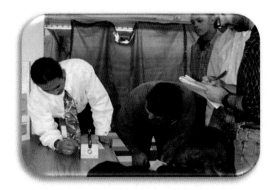

Engineering Excellence Society / Anne Earnshaw Education Award Scholarship

April 1978 - Engineering Society Introduces Scholarship - The Merrimack Valley Engineering Excellence Society established the Merrimack Valley Engineering Excellence Society Scholarship, open to young men and women whose parents are employed at the Merrimack Valley Works. It is awarded on merit to students with an outstanding academic record who will be enrolled as freshmen in engineering or science curriculums at accredited colleges.

May 1994 - Engineering Excellence Society Renames Scholarship for Former Member - Over six years ago, Anne Earnshaw suggested holding a fashion show instead of requesting donations to raise money for the Society's annual scholarship drive. Anne's idea became an annual event, and in the last six years the group has raised over $20,000 for the children of Merrimack Valley employees who are entering engineering studies. Anne was inducted into the society in 1985, was the first woman so honored at the Valley, and became society president in 1991. Each year the fashion show becomes Anne's personal project. In fact, even though Anne retired in 1993, she continued directing the models and keeping the event going. The society members renamed the scholarship the Earnshaw Education Award, in honor of Anne who continued her positive impact on the society and its scholarship program.

19 - Engineering Excellence Scholarship Recipients

Year	Recipient	Will Attend	Major	Parents
1979	Peter Beaulieu	Stanford University	Engineering and Computer Science	Barney Beaulieu
1980	Brian Cordischi	Princeton University	Chemical Engineering	Benny Cordischi
1981	Michael Flanagan	Massachusetts Institute of Technology	Chemical Engineering	Ed Flanagan
1982	Robert J. Wysocki	Electrical Engineering with a computer science minor	Georgia Institute of Technology	Bob Wysocki
1983	Michael Equi	Cornell University	Electrical Engineering	Bob Equi
1984	Kevin Goyette	University of New Hampshire	Chemical Engineering	Phil Goyette
1985	Richard Scatamacchia			Grace & Nicholas Scatamacchia
1986	Not Documented			
1987	Christopher D. McDonald	Cornell University	Electrical Engineering	Patricia & Dave McDonald
1988	Ashwin Sarma	Cornell University	Electrical Engineering	Gopal & Malathi Sarma
1989	Robert L. Morse, Jr.	Princeton University	Electrical Engineering	Bob & Virginia Morse
1990	Sharon Tentarelli	Massachusetts Institute of Technology	Physics	Ken & Liz Tentarelli
1991	James Hill	Rensselaer Polytechnic	Chemical Engineering	Greg Hill
1992	Robert M. Fyrer	Lehigh University	Mechanical Engineering	Jim Fyrer
1993	Beth Ann Ferland	Ithaca College	Biology	Dick & Ellen Ferland
1993	Kenneth C. Ensdorf	Rice University	Electrical Engineering	Walter & Gail Ensdorf
1993	Kim Carroll	Northeastern University	Criminal Law	Lawrence High Student
1994	Peter Hayes	Carnegie Mellon University	Computer Science	Noel & Herbert Hayes
1995	Not Documented			
1996	Not Documented			
1997	Jim Reedy	University of Virginia	Mechanical Engineering	Dave Reedy
1997	Thanh T. Truong	Boston University	Biology	Wa & Chin Truong

Year	Recipient	Will Attend	Major	Parents
1997	Edwin Villafana	University of Massachusetts, Lowell	Electrical Engineering	Lawrence High Student
1998	Eric Sondhi	Rensselaer Polytechnic Institute	Electrical Engineering	Pat & Chandra Sondhi
1999	Aditi Garg	Massachusetts Institute of Technology	Electrical Engineering	Brij & Bala Garg
2000	Dat Truong	Johns Hopkins University	Mechanical Engineering	Wa & Chin Truong
2000	Michael Moriaty	Northeastern University	Mechanical Engineering	Thomas & Mary-Ellen Moriaty

20 - YMCA Black Achievers Program

The first Black Achievers originated in 1971 at New York's Harlem YMCA. In 1975, the YMCA of Greater Boston started its own program to recognize African-American employees who have achieved success in their professional lives. Our mission is to recognize African-American professionals for their career accomplishments, and who in partnership with their employers, commit time and talents to the development of young people. As these successful adult role models link with youth, Black Achievers expose young people to life options and encourage them to set and achieve educational and professional goals. The Black Achievers Branch of the YMCA of Greater Boston operates a year-round program focusing on the development of relationships between recognized Black Achievers and young people in the Greater Boston Area.

African-American professionals in the Greater Boston Community are nominated as Black Achievers by their employers, based upon criteria which include:

- Demonstrated history of achievement in their field
- Progression within the company and potential for further advancement
- Willingness to take part in voluntary community service on behalf of youth

Nominated individuals who are selected to receive the Black Achievers Award are honored at the Annual Recognition Awards dinner held each year in January. Upon accepting the Black Achievers Award, recipients agree to perform 40 hours' volunteer service with young people within the Black Achievers Community Service Program.

Year	Month	Award Recipient	Merrimack Valley Works Department
1989	February / March	Glen Shepherd	Member of Technical Staff AT&T Bell Laboratories, Andover
1990	April / May	Rodney M. Lee Meredith E. Marshall	MTS - AT&T Bell Laboratories, Ward Hill Product Planner for AT&T Network Systems
1991	March / April	Maurice Henderson Bill Hutchinson Al LaFavors Bill McCoy	Diversified Products Computer Business Tools Nationwide AT&T Sales Transmission HICs
1992	February	Pamilia B. Cox E.J. Fletcher Dorothy E. Hynes Avonelle C. James	Wired Equipment Production Leader Digital Loop Carrier Systems UNIX and PC Training Director Software Design and Development

Year	*Month*	*Award Recipient*	*Merrimack Valley Works Department*
1993	January	Kubrom G. Ghiorgis	Lightwave Test Engineering Merrimack Valley Works
1994	March / April	Polycarp C. (PC) Onaga	Engineering Merrimack Valley Works
1995	January / February	Marcia Hamilton Tom Marshall Debra Russ	Vision Circuit Pack Shop DACS Systems Test Area SLC Carrier Product Manager
1996	February	Charles Cohen Saul Desronvil	MCM and Fastech Focused Factory Cable Test Engineering
1997	February	Anita Farrington Joseph Cherestal	Purchasing Specialist in Global Procurement FSA Deployment Manager for NGLN
1998	January / February	Louise Hairston Marcia Hamilton Horace Lawson	Production Associate in Lightwave EO/AA Councilor for the Northeast Region Software Designer for SONET / Alliance of Black Lucent Employees (ABLE) President
1999	January / February	Cardell (Carol) Burgie Janie Rivers Lynda Hansen	Supervisor in the Installer Cable shop Supervisor in the DACS shop Production Associate in Vision / President of Pioneer Chapter 131
2000	January / February	Leslie Mann	OLS Process & Logistics Engineering Staff Merrimack Valley Works
2001	First Quarter	Alfreda Brewer	Supervisor in OLS Master Scheduling Merrimack Valley Works

21 - Tribute to Women in Industry - TWIN

The YWCA Northeastern Massachusetts [formerly YWCA of Greater Lawrence] was founded in 1892 to provide safe housing, job training and support to women moving from rural communities and overseas to work in area mills and shops. Today, a thriving social change agency, they serve over 15,000 women, children and families from throughout Merrimack Valley, Essex County and Southern NH every year. They are an affiliate of YWCA USA, the nation's oldest and largest multicultural women's organization working for social and economic change.

Each year, the Greater Lawrence YWCA presents its Tribute to Women in Industry (TWIN) Award to women in business, professions and industry who serve as role models to inspire and guide young people.

The annual YWCA Tribute to Women [formerly TWIN - Tribute to Women in Industry] awards luncheon celebrates the accomplishments of remarkable women from the Merrimack Valley. The honorees are now among a group of over 1,200 women who have been so honored over the past 36 years!

The Tribute serves as the YW's major fundraiser, supporting over 26 programs for women, children and families throughout the Merrimack Valley, Essex County and Southern New Hampshire.

Below are the recipients of the TWIN award from the Merrimack Valley Works.

September 1985

Honored as "Outstanding Women in Industry" sponsored by the Greater Lawrence YWCA, and awarded at the annual luncheon of Tribute to Women in Industry (TWIN) at the Sheraton Rolling Green in Andover. Paula is the very first TWIN award recipient.
Paula Fines - Department Chair in Transmission Engineering
Melanie Iannuzzi-Glogovsky - Reliability Physics and Process Development Group

May 1987

Louann Basillio - Elected as one of ten "Outstanding Women in Industry" for 1987 at the 4th Annual TWIN Awards Ceremony, for her outstanding professionalism and contributions in the business world. Louann is a graduate of Northeastern University with a BS in Business Administration, and Boston College where she obtained an MBA in Accounting and Finance. Hired in 1980, Louann has held various assignments in materials management and general accounting.

August 1988

Pam Jackson - MV manager of switching & piezoelectric components manufacturing, recently was named one of several recipients of the prestigious TWIN award. Pam's educational and career accomplishments impressed the nominating committee, as did her commitment to serve as an effective role model in the industrial community. At MIT she completed three degrees in five years, receiving Bachelor of Science degrees in Chemistry, Chemical Engineering, and a Master of Science degree in Chemical Engineering.

Spring 1989

Two Merrimack Valley Women Named as TWIN Honorees

Kim-Oanh T. Nguyen - A planning engineer for AT&T Network Systems, working with Surface Acoustic Wave and Precision Crystal devices. Kim holds Bachelor of Science and Master of Science degrees in Chemical Engineering from Kansas State University, and is currently pursuing a Master of Science degree in Electrical Engineering at Boston University. While still in college, Kim published technical papers in her field, presented at the SWE National Student Conference in Anaheim, CA, AIChE Midwest Region Student Conference in Kansas. Kim began her AT&T career at the Kansas City location in 1984 and transferred to Merrimack Valley in 1986.

Wilma Breiland - Supervisor of software design and development for Bell Laboratories at MV, graduated magna cum laude, Phi Beta Kappa, from the University of Vermont with a Bachelor of Science degree in mathematics. She began her AT&T career with Network Systems in 1969 as a software application designer. In 1977, she worked for Bell Laboratories in North Andover, later transferring to Holmdel, N.J. While in Holmdel, she received a Master of Science degree in computer science from Stevens Institute of Technology. In 1985 she returned to Merrimack Valley.

May / June 1991

Diane Ouellette, Film IC Process Engineering and Development manager, was one of several local area businesswomen to receive a Tribute to Women in Industry award. Diane has been with AT&T for thirteen years. After holding various supervisory assignments, she was promoted to function manager in 1984.

June / July 1993

Catherine G. McSweeney, MTS in Software Product Engineering and Manufacturing, was nominated for a Tribute to Women in Industry award. Cathy has been a primary force in the growth of AT&T's Transmission Software Manufacturing Program, designing and implementing processes which are used to introduce and distribute all transmission software products at MV.

May / June 1994

Two Merrimack Valley Works women were recently nominated for the prestigious Tribute to Women in Industry Award

Ruth Pearson, RN - As manager of Nursing operations at MV, Ruth works to provide medical services to 6,000 employees.

Leslie Picard - Having had assignments in Engineering, Project Management, Financial Management and Customer Satisfaction Management allowed her to develop a diverse skill set. Leslie currently leads and coaches 19 QI teams as Customer Satisfaction Manager and Quality Advisor.

May 1995

Women of AT&T (WATT) Hold Very First Conference

Barbara Roselle - Technical Manager in Software Development for International Lightwave Terminals

Elaine Webb - Multi-Chip Module Operating and Engineering Manager, is the only manager of both engineering and production at Merrimack Valley.

May 1996

Three Merrimack Valley Women Named as TWIN Honorees

Karen Beech - Manager, Customer Value Management

Jan Fertig - Head, SONET Realization Center

Mirga Girnius - Member of Technical Staff - At a luncheon honoring women businesses in the Greater Lawrence Area, Mirga Girnius was awarded a Certificate of Recognition for Outstanding Community Service by the TWIN Steering Committee.

May/June 1997

TWIN Honors Three from Merrimack Valley

Tatiana Carvajal - Project Manager for HFC-2000 and Linear Lightwave

Charlene Estes - Export Control Supervisor for the GPC

Mary Simon - Ombudsperson.

May / June 1998

Three Merrimack Valley women were nominated for this year's Tribute to Women in Industry (TWIN) award by the Greater Lawrence YWCA.

Irene Dumas - Senior Public Relations Specialist was selected for being a pioneer, leader and motivator in several successful industrial/educational partnerships.

Luan Giannone - Import/ Export Compliance Planning Manager, was recognized for her commitment to enhancing the lives of people with mental retardation, who live at home with their families, by creating environments in the community and workplace that are open, safe, supportive and diverse.

Claudia K. Richards - Technical Manager in the WaveStar BandWidth Manager Software Development organization, for being an exemplary role model as a strong technical leader, excellent team player, and exceptionally customer focused contributor.

May / June 1999

Three from MV receive TWIN honors at 1999's 16th Annual TWIN Luncheon

Linda Desmond - Product Manager

Jennifer Esty - Technical Manager

Sheila Landers - Human Resources Manager

May / June 2000

Merrimack Valley Has three TWIN 2000 Award Recipients

Colleen Burke-Latour - ISO Compliance Supervisor for Customer Service

Carolyn Collins - Switching & Data Networking Products Director

Susan Godun - Customer Advocacy & Support Manager in MV Information Technology

22 - Take Our Daughters to Work Day®

- This program, launched by the Ms. Foundation in 1993, provided an organized program for girls to visit the workplace to understand the ties between work, education and family. Merrimack Valley had taken part on the fourth Thursday of April, since 1994 with a day filled with informative and fun activities under the direction of the Women of AT&T (WATT) and later, Women in Leadership at Lucent (WILL). Their first program afforded sixty girls (picked by lottery) to take part.

- In 2002, the program accommodated over 100 girls - still picked by lottery since there were always more applicants than spaces.

- In 2003, the Ms. Foundation evolved the program and launched Take Our Daughters and Sons to Work® program. Lucent and Merrimack Valley supported the goals and vision of the endeavor, and was proud of the success and growth over the last nine years.

- In 2003, WILL was asked by Lucent to <u>not</u> participate, and the program did not resume.

23 - Communications Workers of America, Local 1365

- Founded in 1938, CWA got its start representing telephone workers as the National Federation of Telephone Workers. It was renamed the Communications Workers of America in 1947. Today CWA represents workers in all areas of communications, customer contact, high technology, and manufacturing professions in both the private and public sectors, including health care, public service, education, customer service, airlines, and many other fields.

- 1947 - The Haverhill local, known as Local 1360, was part of the National Federation of Telephone Workers, a group that came into being in 1947.

- 1951 - When the company opened the Lawrence shop in 1951, Local 1361 was formed.

- 1956 - Communications Workers of America, Local 1365 is Chartered - When Merrimack Valley Works opened, there was a desire to form a single union local to represent the employees of Western Electric. This task was accomplished after a difficult organizing drive headed by Joe Sweeney and his committee - all from Local 1360. The campaign was successful, and the Communications Workers of America, Local 1365 was chartered on May 15, 1957, to represent the organized labor force. The first election of officers was held in July 1957, and Joe Sweeney was elected as president. The two locals were completely merged by the close of September 1958.

- 1956 - Local 1365's original leased headquarters was at 6 Haverhill Street in what was known as Shawsheen (named for the local Shawsheen River) in Andover. In November 1960, the Local bought its own headquarters at 1627 Osgood St. in North Andover, across from the Merrimack Valley Works.

- November 1956 - CWA Local 1360 (Haverhill) and Local 1361 (Lawrence) waive their Charter rights for the purpose of forming the Merrimack Valley Organizing Committee, Local 1365.

- May 15, 1957 - CWA. Local 1365, Charter Issued with the following Jurisdiction: "Over all employees of the Manufacturing Division of the Western Electric Company in New England."

- June 1957 - "Valley Echo," the voice of Local 1365 began publication, with its first issue featuring congratulatory letters from CWA President Joseph Beirne, Vice-president Ray Hackney, and District 1 Director, Mary H. Hanscom. Michael Halkiotis was editor and Robert Glycart was associate editor. The paper also contained ads for local businesses.

- July 1, 1957 - CWA Officer Ray Hackney praised the Stewards and the membership for the outstanding job done in signing up the non-members. District 1 Director Mary Hanscom praised the Local for its hard work and efforts that have resulted in better service to the membership.

- July 1957 - Local 1365 member Sandy Ramsey competes in the "Miss Universe" contest at Long Beach, California. Sandy is the reigning "Miss Massachusetts."

- July 1957 - Large surplus sparks lay-off rumors.

- August 12, 1957 - Local Officers and Executive Board members elected.

    o President and bargaining committee - Joseph F. Sweeney

    o Vice-President and bargaining committee - Jackie Brouillard

    o Treasurer - Marie Donovan

    o Secretary - Patricia Cressy

    o Charles Haigh was elected to the Bargaining Committee.

    o Executive Board Members:

        - Frances Grazio
        - Vincent J. Lagrasse
        - Arthur Charbonneau
        - Paul Wynn Ryan
        - Harold (Bud) Durgin
        - Evelyn Nielsen
        - Daniel A. Hitchcock
        - Michael T. Halkiotis

- September 3, 1957 - First meeting between Union and Company held to begin contract negotiations. Present agreement expires Oct. 7.

    o Representing the Union: Sweeney, Haigh and Brouillard along with CWA representative Gerry Gaughan.

    o Representing the Company: Bargaining Agent William Mercer, and J.J. Shaughnessy and Harry Youngman of the Labor Relations Dept.

- September 1957 - Forty-one Stewards graduate from Stewards School, which was held at Shawsheen Manor. Jules Pagano, of CWA taught the class. Local 1365 softball team wins Haverhill Industrial League. 14-1 Record.

- October 1, 1957 - CWA overwhelmingly defeated an "Independent Union" in a National Labor Relations Board election which was held to end a dispute over jurisdiction at the Merrimack Valley Plant.

- October 1957 - Contract negotiations between Western and Local 1365 are nearing final stages. The possibility of reaching an agreement early this month is very probable.

- October 1957 - A new contract has been signed between CWA and the Western Electric Company covering the hourly rated Employees of the Merrimack Valley Works. The new agreement calls for wage increases from 6 to 14 cents, pay for four (4) Holidays when they fall on Saturday, a reopener on wages and vacations each year with the Right to Strike on these issues.

- November 1957 - First anniversary of the merger between Local 1360 and Local 1361. (Which joined to form Local 1365)

- November 1957 - The Local President's job becomes full-time position. Nearly 2.000 members unanimously vote for the full-time President.

- November 1957 - Pauline Brousseau defeated Fern Roberts in the Election for Secretary of the Steward Body.

- November 1957 - CWA wins Life Insurance Plan. Terms have been agreed upon for a new group Life Plan, which includes liberalized death benefits.

- December 1957 - Local 1365 inaugurate the "4,000 Membership Drive" to get the membership up to 4,000 members.

- December 1957 - Our Local is negotiating a Toolmakers apprentice program and a Testers training program.

- December 1957 - Santa visits Local 1365 to help inaugurate the Local's "Toys for Tots" campaign.

- December 1957 - Local 1365 has provided over 50 pints of blood to employees and their families since beginning the program in September 1957.

- January 1958 - A 12-member Mexican Labor team was the guest of Local 1365 for a tour sponsored by the U.S. Department of Labor.

- February 1958 -" Valley Echo" discontinued because of financial reasons.

- January 1959 - Newly elected Officers and Executive Board members are sworn in:
    o President - Joseph Sweeney
    o Vice President - Paul Winn Ryan
    o Secretary - Gladys Ouellette
    o Treasurer - Evelyn Neilson.
    o Executive Board:

• Arthur Charbonneau	• Rose M. Dobbin
• James Lagrasse	• Bud Durgin
• Joseph Lacroix	• Harold Roberts
• Michael Halkiotis	• Jackie Jacques

- August 1960 - The Organizing drive continues in "high gear" with 440 new members signed up.

- September 1960 - The "Valley Echo" returns to publication after an absence of two and one-half years.

- September 23, 1960 - Our Local presents our contract proposals to Western:
    o Agency Shop
    o Elimination of dual wage structure
    o Health & Life Insurance

- ○ Paid Blue Cross & Blue Shield plus Major Medical
- ○ An extra Holiday (Veterans Day)
- ○ Vacation: Two weeks after 1 year, 3 weeks after 10, 4 weeks after 15.

- September 25, 1960 - First Annual Stewards Banquet held. Made possible by membership action, the banquet is meant to compensate in a small way for the hard work done by the Stewards throughout the year.

- September 1960 - Norm Obert elected to Executive Board to fill vacancy left by Harold Roberts.

- September 28, 1960 - CWA President, Joseph Beirne visited Local 1365 and praised the Local for the tremendous organizing job it has done. At a reception held in his honor, Beirne said, *"The fact that Local 1365 has done the best job that any local in CWA has done in the past ten to fifteen years, should make every Officer, Steward, and member feel very proud."*

- October 1961 - Local 1365 set a new one-year record with over 2,000 new members. The previous record was 1,700 set during 1956-1957.

- October 1961 - The" Valley Echo" joins the International Labor Press Association.

- October 1962 - The Public Relations program by Local 1365 has been a tremendous success.

- October 1962 - Newspaper and radio ads, billboards, and increased leaflet distribution are some of the methods used to keep the community informed about CWA.

- October 1962 - President Joe Sweeney was re-elected to a third consecutive term as Vice-President to the Mass. State Labor Council.

- January 1963 - Officers and Executive Board Members of Local 1365 CWA for 1963 - 1964 Term:
  - ○ President - Joseph F. Sweeney
  - ○ Vice-President - Frank J. Talarico
  - ○ Treasurer - Evelyn Nielsen
  - ○ Secretary - Betty A. Lewis
  - ○ Executive Board Members:
    - Paul Winn Ryan
    - Arthur J. Charbonneau
    - Charles F. Haig
    - Rita Jean
    - Francis A. Behan
    - Paul A. Marcotte, Jr.
    - Anna O'Connor
    - Richard M. Hayes

Officers and Executive Board Members of Local 1365 CWA for 1963-1964
term: Seated, left to right: Evelyn Nielsen, Treasurer, Frank J. Talarico, Vice-President,
Joseph F. Sweeney, President, and Betty A. Lewis, Secretary. Standing, left to right: Paul
Winn Ryan, Arthur J. Charbonneau, Charles F. Haig, Rita Jean, Francis A. Behan, Paul A.
Marcotte, Jr., Anna O'Connor and Richard M. Hayes.

- April 1963 - Bargaining Goals Set - Local 1365 President Joseph F. Sweeney, returned recently from the CWA Collective Bargaining Police Committee meeting in Chicago, where the 1963 bargaining goals were set. The bargaining goals set by the 59-member policy committee are:

  o Wages - Substantial wage increase.
  o Health Insurance - A company paid for plan providing comprehensive health insurance.
  o Pensions - Elimination of all Social Security deductions from pension calculations.
  o Increase all minimum pensions to $125 a month.
  o Introduction of survivors' rights under the pension plan.
  o Vacations - 2 weeks after 1 year of service, 3 weeks after 10 years and 4 weeks after 15 years.
  o Life Insurance - Payment by Company of total life insurance coverage

- June 1963 - CWA Annual Convention held in Kansas City. Elected to attend: Dick Hayes, Betty Lewis, Joe Gulla, Jackie Jacques, P. Winn Ryan and Charles Nason. President Joe Sweeney will also attend.

- June 1963 - Mike Halkiotis," Valley Echo" editor, attends conference for Labor Editors in Washington.

- June 1963 - Salaried workers at Western Electric form a committee in an attempt to organize a Local of their own. This would ultimately become Local 1366.

- September 1963 - Local 1365 in a dramatic new step towards Community Relations for Labor unions, opened "Community Communications Centers" in downtown Lawrence and Haverhill. The purpose of the "Centers" are to keep the respective communities posted on pertinent bargaining information coming out of the current negotiations between Local 1365 and the Western Electric Company, and to familiarize them with the Local's aims and activities.

- September 1963 - Information about Local 1365 and CWA will also be available to interested citizenry and pamphlets on CWA will be distributed. Pictures and short histories of Local 1365 activities are also on display at the centers.

- July 1964 - Local 1365 became the largest Local in CWA.

- September 1966 - Representatives of the Teamsters Union have been at the Merrimack Valley Works plant of Western Electric Company in North Andover for the past two days, distributing pamphlets urging employees to consider the Teamsters for their bargaining agent. Western employees are represented by the Communications Workers of America, AFL-CIO.

- September 1966 - The pamphlets originated with the Eastern Conference of Teamsters, Industrial Division, and are signed by Thomas Flynn, president.

- September 1966 - North Andover police received several complaints from the Western plant Wednesday and Thursday regarding the presence of representatives of the outside union at the entrances.

- September 1966 - Joseph F. Sweeney, president of CWA Local 1365 at Western, said Thursday he was aware of the action by Teamster representatives. He said there was no scheduled election regarding choice of bargaining agent.

- December 28, 1966 - Contract negotiations are unresolved between CWA and WE. The present contract expires at midnight. Movement of personnel and piecework are major topics.

- January 3, 1967 - Over 5,000 members worked their sixth day without a contract, while negotiations continue. The Local bargaining team is: Don Lansing the CWA representative, President Joe Sweeney, Rose Dobbins, and Richard Hayes

- April 22, 1968 - Pickets set up by striking installers force a strike at the Merrimack Valley Works. Only 50 of the 6,500 reported for work.

- May 2, 1968 - CWA Installers' strike tentatively settled, but IBTW members replaced them on the picket line to protest the Telephone Company use of Western supervisory employees in the Haverhill/Lawrence telephone offices.

- May 9, 1968 - The 6,500 hourly workers at MV return to work after pickets are removed from the plant.

- June 14, 1968 - Negotiations began today for a new contract between Western Electric's Merrimack Valley Works and Local 1365, Communications Workers of America.

- June 1968 - The initial meeting of company and union officials started at 10 a.m. at the Western Electric plant on South Union Street, Lawrence.

- June 1968 - The first task will be to set up a schedule of bargaining hours and agree to the mechanics for future negotiations.

- June 1968 - The present company-union pact will expire July 5. 6,500 production employees at the company's Lawrence and North Andover locations will be affected by the outcome of negotiations.

- June 1968 - Bargaining representatives for Local 1365 are Joseph F. Sweeney, president; Richard M. Hayes, vice president; Rose M. Dobbin, secretary; and Ronald Neilsen, CWA representative.

- June 1968 - Representing the company are John J. Shaughnessy, manager of industrial and labor relations, and Aram E. Chooljian, assistant manager of labor relations.

- July 1968 - A tentative three-year agreement was reached calling for an average increase of 20.55 percent in pay and benefits.

- January 1969 - Local office secretary Bertha Citron leaves after 12 years of dedicated service.

- January 1969 - The Following Officers and Executive Board Members are sworn into Office:

  o President - Joseph F. Sweeney

  o Vice President - Michael L. Grieco

  o Secretary - Irene Y. Lambert

  o Treasurer - Maureen Corbett

  o Executive Board Members:

    - Rita Jean
    - Ronald Prue
    - Richard Rapazza
    - Joseph Perry

    - John George
    - Richard Hayes
    - Anna O'Connor
    - Charles Naso

- December 1970 - Local 1365 becomes a closed shop where the employer agrees to hire union members only, and employees must remain members of the union at all times in order to remain employed.

- February 1970 - Plans have gotten underway to build a new office for Local 1365 and its 6,200 members. The estimated cost is $100,000 and the estimated date for occupancy is March 1971.The old Union quarters were situated in Shawsheen Square, Andover. The new facility will be three times larger, and will have meeting rooms and offices.

- Mid 1970 - Local 1365, in its nearly twenty-five years of organizing, had never been able to organize more than 55% of the possible bargaining unit. During negotiations in 1971, the company agreed to a modified agency shop, under which all new workers who entered the company's employment after the contract (1971) had to join the union, or simply pay union dues. Workers who were on the rolls before 1971 and didn't want to join the union weren't required to.

- Mid 1970 - Prior to 1971 there had been no type of agency shop (the company may hire union or non-union workers, and employees didn't have to join the union in order to remain employed. However, non-union workers must pay a fee to cover collective bargaining costs) at the Merrimack Valley Works.

- January 1971 - The Following Officers and Executive Board Members are sworn into office:

    o President - Michael L. Grieco

    o Vice-President - John George

    o Secretary - Irene Lambert

    o Treasurer - Gertrude Trottier

    o Executive Board Members:

        - Daniel Beauregard
        - Philip Dicalogero
        - Richard Hayes
        - Richard Rapazza

        - Ronald Prue
        - Anna O'Connor
        - Joseph Perry
        - Joseph Belanger

- July 5, 1971 - Local 1365 has rejected a WE/MV contract proposal as being the lowest offered to any Bell System Manufacturing location. 5,800 MV employees are now working without a contract.

- July 20, 1971 - The nationwide strike by telephone workers ended with an increase of 31 percent in wages and fringe benefits over the three-year contract period.

- July 1971 - For Local 1365, the strike came at the ideal time; it began and ended during the vacation shutdown period.

- January 1972 - Local 1365 President Michael Grieco named Chairman of the CWA National Finance Committee.

- January 1973 - The Following Officers and Executive Board Members are sworn into office:

    o President - Michael L. Grieco

- o Vice-President - Edward Kneeland
- o Secretary - Joyce Kneeland
- o Treasurer - Gertrude Trottier
- o Executive Board Members:

  - Daniel Beauregard
  - Michael Rametta
  - Joseph Perry
  - Anna O'Connor

  - Joseph Belanger
  - Charles Nason
  - Peter Casale
  - Phillip Dicalogero

- February 1, 1973 - President Mike Grieco is named as District Representative for CWA. Vice-President Edward H. Kneeland succeeds Mike as President of Local 1365.

- August 1975 - CWA President Glenn Watts Visits Local 1365 while attending a Manufacturing Conference hosted by the Local.

- January 1976 - The Following Officers and Executive Board Members sworn into office:

  - o President - Frank J. Talarico
  - o Vice-President - Peter Woidyla
  - o Secretary - Irene Lambert
  - o Treasurer - Gertrude Trottier
  - o Executive Board Members:

    - Daniel Beauregard
    - Charles Nason
    - Anna O'Connor
    - Joseph Perry

    - Norma Charoux
    - Larry Rizzotti
    - Susan Congo
    - Daniel Tuccolo

- January 1979: The following Officers and Executive Board Members sworn into office:

  - o President - Frank J. Talarico
  - o Vice-President - Daniel A. Beauregard
  - o Secretary - Irene Lambert
  - o Treasurer - Gerald Weisberg
  - o Executive Board Members:

    - Susan Congo
    - Norma Charoux
    - Daniel Tuccolo

    - Joseph Balanger
    - Peter Casale
    - Charles Nason

- Larry Rizzotti
- Frank Grieco

- July 30, 1980 - Local 1365 President Frank Talarico is named to the post of Assistant to CWA National Director John Price.

- July 1980 - Vice-President Daniel Beauregard will serve the remainder of the term as President, with a special election to be held for Vice-President, Secretary, and four members of the Executive Board.

- September 24, 1980 - The Following Officers and Executive Board Members were sworn in as a result of the special election held September 23:

  - Vice-President - Larry Rizzotti

  - Secretary - Norma Charoux

  - Executive Board Members:

    - Alice Cable
    - Jim Macdonald
    - Susan Congo
    - Benny Cordischi

- May 1981 - Thirty-nine Latin American Unionists were guests of Local 1365 as part of an educational exchange between CWA and the Postal, Telephone, and Telegraph Workers of Latin America.

- June 1981 - New Local 1365 publication, the Valley Beacon, begins on a quarterly basis to help improve communication with the membership.

- July 1981 - Local 1365 help host CWA's 43 Annual Convention in Boston, Massachusetts.

- September 1981 - Volunteers from Locals 1365 and 1366 join 400,000 others in Solidarity March on Washington, D.C.

- October 1981 - President Dan Beauregard elected Vice President of the Massachusetts State Labor Council.

- November 1981 - Membership overwhelmingly approves Local 1365 Benefit Plan. The plan is designed to return a percentage of dues annually to each member.

- January 1982 - Newly-elected Officers and Executive Board Members sworn in:
  - President - Daniel Beauregard
  - Vice President - Daniel Tuccolo
  - Secretary - Norma Charoux
  - Treasurer - Gerry Weisberg
  - Executive Board Members:
    - Ron Fantini
    - Joseph Belanger
    - Frank Grieco
    - James Simmons
    - Peter Casale
    - Michael Bistany

- Jim MacDonald
- Susan Congo

- January 1, 1984 - For CWA, the most significant event of this decade was the divestiture of AT&T. The break-up of the Bell System was of great concern to the union. CWA feared that divestiture would bring relocations, personal hardship and rejection, (by the new independent Regional Bell Operating Companies [RBOCs] and their subsidiaries), of contract gains previously won by the union. Personal hardship and relocation did in fact occur, forcing CWA to work hard to preserve the gains that four decades of sacrifice and solidarity had achieved. Job security issues catapulted to the top of the list of bargaining priorities for 1986.

- Mid-1980s - During this difficult period, CWA President Glenn E. Watts often reminded the members that it was AT&T that had broken up, not CWA. The union remained as unified, committed and strong as ever.

- June 2007 - CWA Vice President of Communications and Technologies, Ralph Maly, blasted Alcatel-Lucent's proposed plan to close the North Andover, Mass., facility (the Merrimack Valley Works) unless union-represented workers find, and agree, to accept $6.6 million in cost cutting adjustments:

  "This demand is typical of the new Alcatel-Lucent," Maly said. *"The company says if 250 union-represented workers bear the brunt of $6.6 million in cuts, it might reconsider keeping the operation open. But Alcatel-Lucent seems intent on shutting down its U.S. union-represented facilities and shifting more work overseas anyway."*

  Alcatel Lucent said it plans to shift work from North Andover, which employed 500 employees, to Italy. Maly said that it was CWA and local unions at North Andover that made the product lines there a success. Maly said he would continue to work to keep the facility open:

  "This past quarter, we gave Lucent the best financials that it has received over the past four years, with costs coming in below all budget expectations," said Local 1365 President Gary Nilsson, adding, that, *"Lucent's treatment of union workers at North Andover is a disgrace."*

- 2007 - Local 1365's membership was at 3,000 employees in 1969, peaked at 8,500 in the early '80s, returned to 3,000 in 1993, and the distinguished Merrimack Valley Works ultimately closed with just a few hundred employees still on roll.

24 - Meeting on Circuit Pack Out-Sourcing

In 1998, Merrimack Valley Works produced 1.6 Million circuit packs. In 1999, it is expected that the demand for circuit packs will grow to 3.0 Million. This exceeds are capability in place today. Thus, we are taking several steps both within and external to Merrimack Valley Works to satisfy this demand.

1. **Future Quest 3,4,5**

    These lines will be building predominately OLS 40G and OLS 400G circuit packs. Today, they support many other product lines. Band-Width Manager and OLS 2.5G circuit packs are being moved to the Vision complex downstairs for production.

    FT-2000 circuit pack production will be entirely supported by Solectron. This involves about 40 codes with an average load of 7,000 circuit packs/week. The out-source of this product is being done in 5 phases. When phase 1&2 are complete, 80% of the FT-2000 program will be built externally. This should occur in the April to May timeframe.

    The OLS production is anticipated to be double what the current load is today. Thus, Merrimack Valley Works is making plans to support the "up-side potential" of this product. In the July timeframe, an additional two circuit pack lines are being planned for installation at Merrimack Valley Works to support this load.

2. **Fast Line 1&2, Future Quest 1&2**

    The Vision Process Center on the first floor is overloaded at present. Thus, the Network Multiplexer product line is being completely out-sourced to Celestica for production. This will make capacity available within Merrimack Valley Works for newer product lines that are experiencing growing production demands.

    The Network Multiplexer outsource is being done in 5 phases involving DDM 2000 and DDM 1000. Approximately 40 codes are involved with an average production load of 10,000 circuit packs/week. Phase 1 will be completed in March; all other phases will be completed in April.

    With the removal of Network Multiplexer, Future Quest 1&2 will be utilized to build circuit packs for the SDH product family.

    The circuit packs codes for SDH products are more complicated and of greater density than those of Network Multiplexer. Thus, Fast Line 1 has been upgraded with new facilities to enable it to build SDH products. With this "re-tooling" of the line, the entire production capacity used for Network Multiplexer is now capable of being re-used for SDH products.

    Movement of SDH codes out of the Vision Process Center enables Merrimack Valley Works to support the very large DACS II program that currently exists and the increased demands of the Echo Canceller products. Also, it allows us to handle the Band-Width Manager and OLS 2.5G codes moved from Future Quest 3,4,5.

3. Capability Required to Support the Growing Merrimack Valley Works Circuit Pack Program

To produce 3.0 Million circuit packs annually, Merrimack Valley Works needs to provide a capability of 60,000 circuit packs/week.

When Merrimack Valley Works increased circuit pack production with the addition of the Fast Lines and Future Quest Lines, it was expected that our capability would be on average 40,000 circuit packs/week. We never achieved that level. Our demonstrated capability has been approximately 30,000 circuit packs/week. This has been a disappointment and is one of the reasons we need to supplement our capability through contract manufacturing.

With the upgrades we are making to the Fast Line and Future Quest Lines, and the addition of Production Associates, it is expected that our demonstrated capability will increase. In the February timeframe, we must get to at least 32,000 circuit packs/week. In the March timeframe we must get to at least 35,000 circuit packs/week. To achieve this, Engineering and Operating are driving focused activities on quality improvement and machine utilization to reach these production levels which we know are achievable. "Methods Meetings" are being held to solicit the ideas and energies of Production Associates to help reach the goal.

When the two additional circuit pack lines are installed and made operational, the Merrimack Valley Works capability is expected to be 42,000 circuit packs/week.

Products targeted for Merrimack Valley Works circuit pack production contain more components per unit than those previously produced. Our demonstrated capability to perform Surface Mount assembly has been 40 Million placements/month. To produce the 1999 program, we must reach a level of 60 Million placements/month. Thus, a higher utilization rate of Surface Mount machines is needed to support this level. Additionally, a higher quality level from all assembly operations is needed to prevent In-Circuit Test from becoming a bottleneck operation that limits our production capability.

The large growth in circuit pack demand is driven by an associated growth in demand for systems from Merrimack Valley Works. Thus, plans are being executed to expand Systems Test areas throughout the factory. This consumes large quantities of floor space, limiting the area available for circuit pack expansion.

Because of this, out-sourcing of circuit pack manufacture will continue to be used to supplement our internal production.

25 - The "Hello Charley" / WEValley Girl Contest

Newcomers are often confused during the WEValley Girl Contest by long term employees referring to the queen as the "Hello Charley" Girl. Originally a vacation queen contest, the winner took the name of the greeting that Western Electric employees used when discovering a fellow "Westerner" on vacation. Why "Hello Charley?" The greeting grew from an incident involving Charley Drucker, a benefits service man in the old days of the Hawthorne Works. A pensioner whom he had visited wrote him a letter addressed "Charley, Western Electric." Since the retiree had not remembered Charley's last name, the letter made the rounds until finding the right Charley. Since this letter, people began addressing each other as "Charley Western." Soon the greeting spread throughout the company. Every location has its vacation queen, as we have our WEValley Girl. But to many of our people, it's "Hello Charley" time again.

1930 - "Hello Charley" Girl contest begins in Western Electric's Hawthorne Works, Chicago, Illinois.

1950 - "Hello Charley" Girl contest begins in Haverhill, and becomes the 8th Western Electric location to hold a contest to select a "Vacation Queen." Her face will appear on stickers used to recognize Western Electric people everywhere during the vacation period.

1951 - Twelve Western Electric locations now have "Hello Charley" Girl Vacation Queen Contests.

1953 - Coast-to-Coast "Hello Charley" Girls - The biggest month ever for the "Hello Charley" Girl

Jean O'Rourke – The first Hello Charley Girl - 1930

tradition as the number of Western Electric locations electing queens in the spring and crowned in June reaches 55 this year. The "Hello Charley" Girl Vacation Queen custom is now in its 23rd year.

1969 - Merrimack Valley Works makes changes to the "Hello Charley" Girl Vacation Queen Contest:

- o The title of the contest is changed to "WEValley Girl"
- o A committee, upon completion of its interviews of the nominees, will name ten finalists. From these ten finalists, employees at the Merrimack Valley Works will select a "Queen" and a second and third runner-up, each of whom will stand ready to succeed the "Queen" if necessary.
- o Since there are ten finalists, the girl selected to reign as "Queen" will have nine attendants.

o The "Queen" and her nine attendants will serve as hostesses at various Merrimack Valley Club functions and company events during the ensuing year.

1973 - Though it was never publicly announced, 1973 saw the final "Hello Charley" / WEValley Girl Contest held and celebrated at the Merrimack Valley Works.

Merrimack Valley's "Hello Charley" Girls and WEValley Vacation Queens

1950 - Mary LeBlanc, the 23-year-old record clerk is crowned Haverhill's first "Hello Charley" Girl and Vacation Queen on June 14.

1951 - Marie Paquette named 1951's "Hello Charley" Girl. Marie is bench hand on 3rd floor of the Hayes building, 20 years old, and the oldest of 8 children.

1952 - Claire Gosselin, a clerk in the Engineering of Manufacture files section of the Grad Building in Haverhill, is 1952's "Hello Charley" Girl.

1953 - Kaye Cash of the Coil Shops was crowned "Hello Charley" Girl Vacation Queen before a crowd of 800 people at the Coronation Dance held June 13 at the Central Catholic High School Auditorium in Lawrence. Kay is the fourth "Hello Charley" Girl Vacation Queen elected at our Shops. *Update 1962:* Kaye (Cash) Goudreault was employed as a bench hand in the Small Toroidal Coil department. She left the company in 1958, and is married to George V. Goudreault. Kaye is the mother of three lovely children, Laurie, Thomas, and Paul. They live in the Riverside section of Haverhill.

1954 - Alice Dudash chosen as "Hello Charley" Girl Vacation Queen for 1954 - Alice will reign until the end of the 1954-1955 club year. Her photograph will be used on the 1954 vacation stickers that will be distributed to all employees for use on their luggage and automobiles during the vacation period.

1955 - Sylvia DiPiro was elected "Hello Charley" Girl Vacation Queen on June 10th at the Andover Country Club. Miss DiPiro works in the Haverhill Shops' Purchasing Department. *Update 1962:* Sylvia (DiPiro) Giampa, was employed as a secretary in the Equipment Engineering Organization. She is married to Joseph J. Giampa, a section chief in the personnel department. The couple has two sons, James and John, and resides in Plaistow, New Hampshire.

1956 - Joan Roberts is elected "Hello Charley" Vacation Queen for 1956 - 20-year-old Joan is a secretary in the Inspection Department at the Lawrence Shops. Joan was crowned "Vacation Queen" at the Coronation Ceremonies held at the Canobie Lake Park Ballroom. The four ladies of Joan's court are Ann LaLumiere, Rita Lekas, Marion Dudley, and Pat Legasse. *Update 1962:* Joan (Roberts) Fiorino was employed as a secretary in the Production Control Organization. She is married to Charles J. Fiorino, and the couple and their two children, Catherine and Charles, reside in North Andover.

1957 - Elizabeth Wood was selected as the Merrimack Valley Works 1957 "Hello Charley" Girl Vacation Queen. In February, 1959, "Hello Charley" Girl, Elizabeth Wood, portrayed one of the leading roles in the movie, *"In the Merrimack Valley,"* a 15-minute movie which was filmed in the Merrimack Valley Works and features employees and local area scenery.

1958 - Rachel Goudreault, Engineer of Manufacture secretary, was elected by coworkers to serve as "Hello Charley" Girl Vacation Queen, and will reign over Club social activities. A 19-year-old blonde, Rachel was presented her crown by the 1957 "Hello Charley" Girl, Elizabeth Wood, during coronation ceremonies at the Canobie Lake Park Ballroom. In October 1958, at the Annual Family Outing at Canobie Lake, The Rex Trailer

Show was assisted Rachel, who appeared in Western costume with Rex. *Update 1962:* Rachel (Goudreault) Scruton is married to Richard W. Scruton, and they make their home in Bradford.

1959 - Kathy Tessitore, an attractive mother of two, is elected by coworkers to reign as Vacation Queen. The new "Hello Charley" Girl Vacation Queen is an employee in the Tabulating Department. Her ladies-in-waiting were, Frances Cirome, Patricia Huberdeau, Sheila McLeod, and Lorraine Gaudette. The Coronation Dance was held at the Canobie Lake Park Ballroom in Salem, New Hampshire. In August, 1959, several Merrimack Valley folks were featured in WE Magazine, and "Hello Charley" Girl, Kathy Tessitore, has her photograph in an article "Queens All."

1960 - Cammy Pennisi is the 1960 "Hello Charley" Girl. Cammy, a flashing 22-year-old brunette clerk in the voucher department was crowned at a colorful coronation ceremony highlighting the annual "Hello Charley Girl" Dance at the Canobie Lake Park Ballroom. Miss Pennisi was the 11th "Hello Charley" Girl to be elected to the honor at the Merrimack Valley Works. The other finalists in the 1960 competition were Ann LaLumiere, Barbara Campana, Dorothy Cordischi, and Pat Marcoux.

1961 - Priscilla Smith is the Merrimack Valley Works "Hello Charley" Girl and Vacation Queen for the summer of 1961.

1962 - Merle Archambault, a 19-year-old brunette who lives in Methuen, is a clerk typist in the Small Toroidal Department, and was selected by her coworkers as 1962's "Hello Charley" Girl Vacation Queen. The new Queen's Court consisted of Bernadette DeBoisbriand, Gail Cleary, Julie Roy, and Sue Blunt.

1963 - Donna Drew was presented with the floral crown of a "Hello Charley" Girl as employees and friends looked and cheered her on.

1964 - Janice LaFleur was announced as this year's "Hello Charley" Girl in May. 1,500 attend ceremonies at the annual dance. Janice is an employee in the Merrimack Valley Works Reproduction Department.

1965 - Barbara Stott named 1965 "Hello Charley" Girl. 1,500 MV employees and friends attended the formal dance at the Canobie Lake Park Ballroom. Shown here receiving her crown from 1964's "Hello Charley" Girl, Janice LaFleur.

1966 - Barbara Vedrani was selected as the "Hello Charley" Girl Vacation Queen for 1966. 19-year-old Barbara is from Amesbury, and works in the Technical Service Department. Shown here receiving her crown from Merrimack Valley Works General Manager, Harry N. Snook.

1967 - **Mary Ellen O'Rorke** is honored as 1967's "Hello Charley" Girl at coronation ceremonies that highlighted the annual "Hello Charley" Girl dance, held this year at the Sheraton Rolling Green Motor Inn.

KAREN	MARIE	PAULA	TERRY	TINA

1968 - For the first time, five finalists will share the 1968 "Hello Charley" Girl title - one Vacation Queen for each day of the week. The Vacation Queens sharing the crown are **Karen Clarke**, a 21-year-old blonde, **Marie Becotte**, petite brunette mother of four, **Paula Cahalane**, green-eyed blonde, **Terry Fay**, brown-eyed brunette mother of one, and **Tina Daggett**, a blue-eyed blonde. They will each reign over all MV activities occurring on their assigned day. No vacation stickers were issued this year.

1969 - Carol Leavitt, a tester at Merrimack Valley Works, was crowned the first "WEValley Girl" in colorful ceremonies that were held for the first time in the North Andover plant. The program was videotaped for viewing during lunch periods.

1970 - Pam Czerepak, a member of the drafting organization, is crowned 1970's WEValley Girl. The two runners-up, were Simone Mooers and Deborah Fleischmann. The top ten finalists in the competition at the Merrimack Valley Works were: Nancy Malloy, Simone Mooers, Peggy Murray, Pamela Czerepak, Laurie Colella, Marcia Buckley, Eileen Vigneault, Eileen Grudenski, Joy Erickson, and Deborah Fleischmann.

1971 - Sue Kots is crowned 1971's WEValley Girl. Helene Croteau, was selected first runner-up and Lorraine Bomba, was second runner-up. Sue is shown here receiving her crown from Merrimack Valley Works General Manager, Dave Hilder, and 1970's WEValley Girl, Pam Czerepak.

1972 - Graciela Gou was crowned 1972's WEValley Girl on June 27, congratulated by General Manager Dave Hilder, driven through the Works at the head of a procession, and captured on videotape for closed circuit television broadcasts. Graciela is a Bench Hand in the D2 Carrier Channels Assembly and Wire Section. Originally from Cuba, where her family still lives, she now lives in Andover with her aunt and uncle.

1973 - Beth Davis was Crowned 1973's WEValley Girl on July 5 by General Manager Dave Hilder and 1972's WEValley Girl, Graciela Gou. The annual ceremony was held in the Works auditorium where guests waited for the announcement of the winner of the plant-wide balloting. Beth is a Clerk-Typist in the Indices and COMCODE Control Section. The 1973 nominees for this year's WEValley Girl contest were Beth Davis of North Andover, Joyce Cargill of Lawrence, Mary Blaikie of Amesbury, Donna Moreau of Methuen, and Francine Watson of Haverhill. Beth was the last WEValley Girl.

**WEValley Girl
Election Ballot**

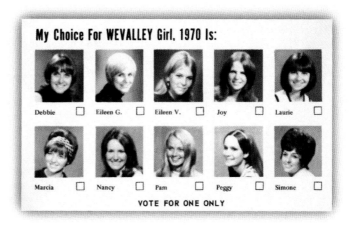

My Choice For WEVALLEY Girl, 1970 Is:

Debbie ☐   Eileen G. ☐   Eileen V. ☐   Joy ☐   Laurie ☐

Marcia ☐   Nancy ☐   Pam ☐   Peggy ☐   Simone ☐

VOTE FOR ONE ONLY

Hello Charley Vacation Stickers

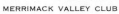

Hello Charley & WEValley Girl Memories

26 - Employee Suggestion Award Recipients

The Employee Suggestion Program (ESP) was used to discover cost reduction opportunities that manufacturing employees would come across as part of their daily work routines. The suggestion would be submitted and logged, and an engineer on that product line would be assigned to review the suggestion, research its future value, and decide its adoption or non-adoption. It could be using a different part, eliminating or streamlining a process or test step, or simply incorporating a really great idea. There were literally thousands of award recipients.

It's important to note that all of these suggestions unquestionably led to improvements in the products manufactured, and processes followed, at the Merrimack Valley Works. All recipients and their families, and all employees, should be extremely proud of their involvement, and understand the value of their significant contributions to the community of the Merrimack Valley Works.

Below is a listing of recipients of awards that were listed in Merrimack Valley periodicals. This is by no means an exhaustive list of all Merrimack Valley Works award recipients. It's truly just a small fraction of all the awards that were given to Haverhill / Lawrence / North Andover / Merrimack Valley Employees over the years.

Year	Month	Award Recipient(s)	Award
1969	March	Thomas D. Mahoney	$320
1969	April	Agnes P. Lauretta	$590
		Herbert Hargraves	$585
		Anthony J. Hickey / Phillip M. Reed, Jr.	$350 (shared)
1969	July	Aime J. Gosselin	$495
1969	August	Barbara Vaughan	$2,115
		Agnes P. Lauretta	$965
		William J. York	$230
		Basil DiPietro	$105
1969	September	Michael Bedrosian	$410
		Joseph Gonthier	$225
1969	December	Charles Riley	$945
1970	January	Carroll O. Smith	$2,050
		Michael J. Begley	$960
1970	May	Shirley Cyr	$610
1970	July	Paul Dort / Chester R. Dzioba	$630 (shared)
		Merion P. Gill	$360
1970	August	Aime Gosselin	$225
1970	September	Arthur Evans	$865
1970	October	Andrew La Pierre	$1820
		Gregory J. Scuto	$1,335
1970	November	Jennie Johnson	$565
		John Daigle / Frank Devine	$315
1971	January	Francis Lavallee	$2,290
		William McLaughlin	$1,885

Year	Month	Award Recipient(s)	Award
1971	February	George R. Delselva Don Hurrell	$695 $305
1971	March	Joanne Gianitti Ed Fleming	$360 $230
1971	April	Arthur Boisselle Ralph Lakin	$1,570 $385
1971	May	John Stewart John Donahue Norm Carleton	$1,655 $600 $390
1971	October	Michael Miele	$345
1971	November	Charles Lindquist, Jr. Doris Blouin	$815 $705
1971	December	James Meehan Alvin McArthur	$390 $265
1972	February	Joseph Monayer	$1,245
1972	April	Bill Owen / Steve Radzwill Joan Joaquin	$325 (shared) $430
1972	May	Biago DiPietro	$885
1972	July	Ken Bloomfield	$160
1972	Sep / Oct	Robert McCarthy Linda Droese	$2,125 $275
1972	December	Robert Krafton	$495
1973	February	Harry Johnson	$320
1973	March	Mrs. Alba Bocuzzo William Lyons	$1,000 $345
1973	May	Michael Halkiotis	$1,735
1973	September	Gerry Martin	$1,760
1973	November	Vernon Evans	$50 savings bond
1973	December	Martin Kelley	$590
1974	January	Ron Boisselle	$385
1974	February	John Ricci Natalie Nimmo Roland Benoit Robert Hart	$765 $420 $300 $295
1974	April	Ken Bloomfield Frank DePanfilis / Bea Rogers / Ellen Marchisio	$900 $600 (shared)
1974	May	Joe Dobrowolski Frank DePanfilis	$900 $820
1974	June / July	Robin Orr	$355
1974	September	Alexander "Ted" Taylor	$690
1974	October	John Haigh Beatrice Rogers / Ellen Marchisio / Frank DePanfilis	$975 $530 (shared)
1974	November	Josephine Sudol Walter Lupa	$370 $185
1974	December	Pauline Goivin Lillian Maciel Shirley Cyr	$175 $160 $150

Year	Month	Award Recipient(s)	Award
1975	January	Beverly Carvalho George Howe Joseph Morin Bob Leriche Norm Guerin	$735 $355 $345 $320 $315
1975	March	Bill Kibler Frank DePanfilis Bruno Turchi	$910 $905 $325
1975	May	Judy Shaia Olive Ward Helen Foster Joseph LaCroix	$300 $290 $290 $225
1975	June / July	Joe Dobrowolski Girard Mailloux / Gerald Nordengren	$300 (supplemental) $395 (split)
1975	August	Joyce Cargill	$320
1975	November	Wayne Holland Louis Hatem / John Karoliszyn Josephine Sudol	$1,080 $555 $480
1976	January	Bill Kibler Bob Krafton	$2,410 $220
1976	April	Bob Desharnais Larry Faye / Mike Halkiotis Shirley Cyr $400 AI Gallant	$3,560 $850 $400 $275
1977	January	Ernest Courcy Clyde Tozier Girard Mailloux Mary Zaremba	$1,395 $410 $355 $215
1977	March	Albert A. Abraham Doris Gurley Anthony J. Rinaldo Carol J. Butler Henry C. Welch Arlene Earnshaw	$295 $235 $235 $225 $205 $200
1977	April	Tom Pallano Lawrence W. Faye Michael T. Halkiotis Norma Swift	$475 $275 $275 $225
1977	May / June	Cecile A. Cote Steve Bird John A. Coppola	$1,215 $985 $220
1977	July	James E. Abbott Albert E. Leblanc	$655 $510
1977	August	Lawrence H. Cogswell	$245
1977	November	Ray Marquis Robert Pothier Mary Zaremba William Kibler	$1,025 $675 $560 $555
1977	December	B.A. Dipietro	$605

Year	Month	Award Recipient(s)	Award
1978	February	F. Wesley Bishop Salvatore Genualdo	$1545 $1460
1978	March	Harry Kimball Herbert Skinner	$1,245 $375
1978	July	Dick Barlow RonaJd Dupont Michael Kentopian	$9,245 $680 $450
1978	September	Cliff Dolfe / Ralph Sawyer Arthur Gray Frank Chapinski Frank Depanfilis	$3,985 (shared) $1,095 $732 $375
1978	October	James Abbott Joanne Flagg Edward Watson	$415 $180 $125
1978	November	Roger Gaumond Josephine Sudol Donald Richardson Frank Depanfilis Beatrice Rogers	$1,305 $905 $895 $277 $277
1978	December	James Gallagher Richard Hayes Virginia Czerepak Audrey Meader Raymond Belanger	$1,410 $1,245 $1,010 $960 $670
1979	January	Louis Hatem John Karoliszyn	$245 $245
1979	March	Cliff Dolfe Ralph Sawyer	$1375 $1375
1979	April	Edward Goyette Norma Poulin Louis Hatem John Karoliszyn	$345 $275 $205 $205
1979	September	Robert Gorton Frank Depanfilis Richard Hayes Joseph Berube Lawrence Student Richard Barlow	$2,180 $1,815 $1,245 $387 $387 $290
1979	October	Francis J. Lavallee Thomas J. Thomson	$330 $215
1979	November	Salvatore (Sam) P. D'Antonio Frederick P. Welch	$2,850 $230
1980	January	Joseph F. Casey Robert H. George Walter S. Kostrzewa Richard J. Rurak	$350 $242 $242 $195

Year	Month	Award Recipient(s)	Award
1980	May	James Abbott	$810
		Richard Mazzaglia	$455
		Bob Gulezia	$415
		Marcelle Belanger	$345
		Arthur Fairbrother	$325
		F. Wesley Bishop	$285
		Alva Clark / James Davis / Francis LeVallee	$770 (shared)
1980	July	Mark Porro	$1970
		Leonard Connolly	$600
		John Karoliszyn	$600
		Edward Richard / George Spencer	$462
		John Howell	$335
		Raymond Marquis	$330
1980	November	Russell Pike	$1305
		Michael Bistany	$785
		Raymond Duchemin	$727
		Albert Gauvin	$727
		Clifford Dolfe	$410
		Ralph Sawyer	$410
1980	December	Michael Kentopian	$975
		Clifton R. McIntire	$455
		Alan M. Dunn	$245
		Dennis M. Robichaud	$245
		Alfred O. Gagnon	$217
		William L. Worrall	$217
1981	January	John F. Whitney	$595
		Robert A. Boucher	$255
		Richard C. Wengel	$255
		F. Wesley Bishop	$225
1981	February	Velma M. Glover	$250
		Melvin W. Maddox	$235
		Irene F. Baublis	$225
1981	March	Antonion J. Talarico	$835
		James E. Abbott	$495
		Robert J. Zannini	$235
1981	Summer	William Boddy	$1,210
		Ernest J. Courey	$505
1981	Fall	Gerry J. Mailloux	$2,270
		William L. Boddy	$1210
		Spike Vermeulen	$775
		Richard L. Farr	$480
		Joseph P. Filomia	$465
		Barbara S. Cole	$375
		Henry J. Smith	$250
1981	October	Joseph G. Curtis	$1,885
1981	November	Scott D. Arena	$1,545
1981	December	Joseph Comeau / Leo Glynn / Marlene Hannagan	$1,000
1982	February	Richard L. Farr	$4,000
		Philip A. DeMarco	$3,740
		Gennaro D'Ambrosio	$1,670
		John J. Howell	$975

Year	Month	Award Recipient(s)	Award
1982	March	David N. Blumberg Philip A. Demarco	$3,020 (2 awards) $620
1982	May	Kenneth F. Caron	$1,180
1982	June	William L. Boddy Dwight E. Milner Joseph F. Casey / Peter O. Fredrickson	$375 $265 $242 (shared)
1982	July	Grace E. Conway Anthony J. Huck / Nicholas W. Sarcione	$250 $232 (shared)
1982	August	David J. Mariano / Michael A. Soucy Constance M. Wright	$297 (shared) $280
1983	Jan / Feb	Ray Germain / Jim Malcuit Dick Clarke James A. Elliott Ellen G. Follansbee Charles W. Hayes Bernard T. Hebert	$1,685 (shared) $590 $500 $345 $345 $345
1983	March / April	Max Maldonado / Tom Mahoney Mike Butler Jeanne Ninteau Tom LaCroix Ellen Follansbee	$2,360 $1,030 $865 $690 $690
1983	May / June	Mark Rivet Brian Levasseur	$625 $580
1983	Sep / Oct	Cathy Steinnen Alvin B. McArthur James Stiles	$1,845 $1,560 $1,035
1983	Nov / Dec	Dick Lamprey Bill Boddy / Hollis Anderson / Mark Stack	$1,385 $1,245 (shared)
1984	Jan / Feb	Tuyethong T. Tran Dick Levitan	$2,100 $1,520
1984	Mar / Apr	Richard C. Berube Frank Bayliss, Jr.	$1,925 $1,230
1984	Sep / Oct	Chanel Fredette Brenda Conkel John C. Banks Shirley Elie	$2,725 $980 $740 $645
1984	Nov / Dec	John O'Hara / Dom Giorgio Mike Passamonte John Robinton	$2,120 $1,810 $1,295
1985	Jan /Feb	Bob Zannini Robert W. Nault Wally Brewer	$10,000 (maximum) $1,545 $1,365
1985	Mar / Apr	John Coppola / Bill Arsenault / Donna Luciano Cathy Steinnen / Jim Wilson Kevin Sirois Al Ragust Mary Spina	$2,726 (shared) $1,900 $1,340 $1,200 $1,025

Year	Month	Award Recipient(s)	Award
1985	Summer	Phyllis Desmet	$2,825 (4 awards)
		Richard Wansker	$2,030
		Wes Straw	$1,965
		Paul Begin	$1,905
		John E. Castillo	$1,870
		Carlos Oliveira	$1,650
		Frances Bottai	$1,345
		Robert McCarthy	$1,345
1985	September	Douglas Packard	$8,580 (2 awards)
		Claire Poirier / Emily F. Dizazzo	$6,420 (shared)
		Charles J. Lafond / Victor Duphily, Jr.	$2,825 (shared)
		Robert L. Ackerson	$2,550
		Robert R. Girard	$1,715
		Trudy R. Newcomb	$1,041
1985	Oct / Nov	Richard B. McPharlin	$2,555
		Christine T. Tuccolo	$1,805
		Joseph F. Casey	$1,410
		Roland Gatchell	$1,135
1985	December	Robert T. McCarthy	$3,255
		Wesley Straw	$2,930
		Alphonse T. Levesque	$2,005
		Domenic Georgio / John J. O'Hara	$1,930
		Christine T. Tuccolo	$1,805
		Katherine Morrow / Susan Hartford	$1,460
		Robert W. Nault	$1,250
		Michael E. Riordan	$1,220
		Mason R. Todd	$1,005
1986	Jan / Feb / Mar	Edward Mannion	$7,655
		John J. O'Hara / Domenic Georgio	$3,860 (shared)
		Dennis Gauvin	$2,580
		Richard J. Rurak	$1,745
		Roland L. Gatchell	$1,420
		Bernard F. Godbout, Jr.	$1,330
		Mary E. Temple	$1,255
		Robert A. Blais	$1,165
		Harold W, Seber / Donald L. Olmstead	$1,115 (shared)
1986	Apr / May / Jun	Mike Dombrowski / Jim Malcuit / John Scafidi	$10,000 (shared)
		Christian F. Gannett	$1,654
		Paul Lambert / Kevin T. Linehan	$1,592
		Joseph L. Girard	$1,445
		Dale A. Martin	$1,325
		Eileen J. Marchand / Gayle E. Morris	$1,040
1986	July	Janet E. Arthur	$635
		Habouba EI-Kazzi	$430
		Charlotte S. Dodge	$300
		Daniel M. Kissel	$300
1986	September	Robert A. (Bob) Gibson	$3,115
		Maureen L. Parent	$2,095
		Cheryl A. Pipitone / Carol A. Titus	$625 (shared)
		Victor E. Perreault	$450
		Dennis P. Anderson	$375

Year	Month	Award Recipient(s)	Award
1986	October	Maureen Moschetto	$2,820
		Robert J. Zannini	$1,510
		Thomas A. LaCroix	$1,510
		Garry J. Godin	$1,045
		Frank J. Azzarito	$1,045
		Gayle Morris	$1,040
		Eileen Marchand	$1,040
1986	November	Charles W. Senter	$2,610
		Richard J. Marshall	$1,560
		Roland L. Gatchell	$1,560
		Richard F. Warner	$547
		Joseph C. Kozdra	$547
		Patti A. Weinhold	$530
1986	December	Lucille B. Tallini	$2,115
		Robert J. (Bob) Zannini	$1,510
		Francine Lehmann	$1,152
		Michael R. Raymond	$1,152
		Cathy A. Harrington	$585
1987	January	Robert R. Desjardins	$7,155
		Lucille B. Tallini	$2,115
		Mark S. Jillson	$1,810
		Byron E. Kitsos	$1,765
		Steven R. Marcouillier	$1,720
1987	February	Karen L. Christie	$1,805
		Bruce A. Robinson	$840
		Michael P. Costas	$560
1987	March	Byron Kitsos	$1,765
		Craig A. Boiselle	$1,045
		Joan L. Goyette	$650
		William L. Boddy	$520
1987	April	Mason R. Todd	$3,005
		Daniel G. Menard	$2,720
		Brian S. MacLaren	$1,795
		Byron E. Kitsos	$1,300
1987	May	Daniel G Menard	$2,720
		Glenn S. Smith	$2,415
		Charles W. Senter	$2,075 (2 awards)
		Byron E. Kitsos	$1,755
		Lori Ambrosio	$1,065 (2 awards)
		Ioannis Papageorgiou	$535
1987	June	Stephen M. Wholley	$10,000
		Michael H. Crowley	$4,405
		William E. Owen	$1,270
1987	July	Glenn S. Smith	$3,605
		Tadeusz Kolodziej	$890
		Jerry G. Kotval	$890

Year	Month	Award Recipient(s)	Award
1987	August	Jeanette G. Morgan Hyung D. Kim Gordon P. Smith Howard W. Bailey Edmund T. Smith John T. Harmon	$3,333.34 $3,333.33 $2,327.50 $2,327.50 $950 $950
1987	September	Robert R. Davidson Richard F. Mazzaglia	$1,160 $565
1987	October	Rene M. Thibault Anis S. Azzi William L. Boddy	$1,040 $755 $650
1987	November	Arthur G. Luedtke William E. Owen Cynthia A. McKinley Dorothy Levesque	$2,325 $982.50 $930 $907.50
1987	December	Irene C. Dumas William J. Welch David P. Naylor	$5,960 $2,156 $1,490
1988	January	William J. Lahey Ralph J. Reed III	$415 $400
1988	February	Donald K. Goldthwaite / Scott A. Hill Donald C. Hurrell Robert F. O'Brien Robert M. Blomgren	$4,700 (shared) $2,775 $1,215 $1,130
1988	March	Richard F. Mazzaglia Joseph C. Kozdra Susan L. Gagne Noele Y. Rizkallah	$2,090 $1,500 $1,047.50 $1,047.50
1988	April	Harry Apostolides Byron E. Kitsos David P. Kane Earl R. Tessimond Richard A. Prescott Lynn J. Ternet Christine M. Rapazzo Renee Roumeliotis	$10,100 $935 $767.50 $767.50 $702.50 $702.50 $500 $500
1988	May	Frank A. DiMauro	$1,165
1988	June	Carl D. Kirsch Jerome J. Nicolosi Mark D. Hazell Frank T. Knowlton	$2,145 $1,070 $992.50 $992.50
1988	July	Gregg E. Cote Carol A. Vincent	$505 $505
1988	August	Donald M. Buja Paul D. Hudson Dennis M. Sinclair Leo V. Clarke	$2,005 $2,002.50 $1,692 $965

Year	Month	Award Recipient(s)	Award
1988	September	Pauline A. Bourque David P. Bourque James A. Roberts David M. Morse George W. Lunn Edmund T. Smith	$3,433.33 $3,383.33 $3,333.34 $1,917.50 $1,892.50 $1,860
1988	October	Frederick S. Crosby, Jr Robert J. Zannini Daniel P. Chretien Richard J. Maddox	$1,190 $1,015 $990 $880
1988	November	Aura Alba Charles W. Senter	$2,430 $1,195
1988	December	Glenn H. Gehly Paul D. Hudson Kenneth F. Paradis Mark D. Bean William R. Hartung	$5,765 $1,505 $1,210 $650.83 $600.83
1989	January	Charles Q. Gilmore Robert J. Zannini Brian H. Martin Charles E. Murray	$1,475 $980 $967.50 $690
1989	February	Kenneth F. Paradis Garry R. Snook David C. Auger Aline E. Menasian	$1,475 $1,455 $1,030 $720
1989	March	Scott A. Hill James R. Malcuit Daniel E. Mannion Harold W. Seber Earle J. Frazier	$6,915 $2,375 $1,770 $1,645 $1,415
1989	April	Henry M. Smith Joseph W. Buck Marie J. Martin	$2,415 $1,037.50 $1,037.50
1990	February	Chuck Senter	$9,900
1990	June	Greg Head Peggy St. John	$1045 $710
1990	September	Dora Bouchard Bob Murphy Dan Gudinas	$5,490 $1,955 $1375
1990	October	Dan Kissel Jeffrey Page Michael M. Brown Deborah W. Gatchell Kevin A. Robichaud Roger A. Chandonnet	$10,000 $6,010 $2641.67 $2641.67 $2641.67 $1,465
1990	November	John J. Zappala / Norman A. Hamel Ronald C. Barton	$3,760 (shared) $1,000

Year	Month	Award Recipient(s)	Award
1990	December	Bill Welch / Glenn Welch	$10,000 (shared)
		Charles W. Senter III	$2,760
		Manuel H. Feliciano	$2,205
		Fannie L. Latham / Peter A. Beauregard	$1,822
		Jules R. Bauters	$1,495
		Jeffrey Page	$1,095
1991	January	Donald J. Descoteaux	$1,780
1991	February	Robert D. Rennie	$3,330 (2 awards)
		Stephen F. Yannalfo	$1,310
		Peter A. Beauregard	$1,255
		Leo A. Dubois	$1,150
1991	March	Ken Santarelli	$2,000
		Robert J. LaPierre	$1,645
		Wayne A. Shiends	$1,540
		Manuel D. Ariceto	$1,460
		John F. Page	$1,290
1991	May	Jamie L. German	$3,640
		Carolyn J. Gagnon	$1,291
1991	September	Charlene R. Fox	$10,000 (maximum)
		James F. Cloherty	$2,000
1991	October	Cheryl A. Pipitone	$2,631
		Linda C. Consentino	$2,242
		Betty D. Phelps	$1,989
		Raymond C. Bouchard	$1,912
		Weldon S. Almon	$1,862
		Peter A. Beauregard	$1,117
1991	November	Jeannette C. Gagne	$3,710
		James F. Cloherty	$2,483
		Wayne A. Sheilds	$2,115
		Richard K. Chang	$2,000
		Reynaldo Perez / Mark R. Rivet	$1,369
1991	December	Debra Cutrona / Beverly Anderson / Ann Owen	$2,707
		Frederick S. Crosby, Jr.	$1,751
		Donna M. Ketchen	$1,730
		Rodney Ratcliffe / Kevin Lekarcyk / Bill Lee	$1,600
		Scott E. Quinney / Barry J. Rembis	$1,000
1992	January	Donald L. Bodwell	$784
1992	February	Marie M. Banton	$3,654
1992	March	Evelyn M. Fazel	$8,447
		Charles W. Senter, III	$2,600
		Wayne A. Shields	$1,496
		Leslie J. Hamlett	$1,266
		Kathryn M. Dyke	$1,082
		Evelyn B. Royer	$1,005
1992	April	Thomas C. Hovan	$2,000
		Kristina M. Sakash	$1,796
		Mark D. Hazell	$1,585
		Donald C. Hurrell	$1,333
1992	May	Arthur F. Smith	$2,103
		Theresa M. Perry	$2,000
		John P. McCormack / Wallace J. Brewer, Jr.	$1,202 (shared)

Year	Month	Award Recipient(s)	Award
1992	June	Evonne E. Miles	$5,328
		Phyllis M. Matteo / Paul M. Collins	$2,000 (shared)
		Betty J. Thibodeau	$1,455
		Hung T. Tran	$1,095
1992	July	Robert J. Zannini / William E. Plummer	$3,101 (shared)
		Stephen A. Fairbrother	$1,203
1992	August	Sandra Keefe	$2,000
		Glenn Smith	$1,542
		Bill Welch	$1,542
1992	October	Cheryl Pipitone	$1,158
1992	November	Harold Burke	$3,665
		James Dow / Raymond Fredette / Emilio Venturi	$2,170 (each)
1992	December	Gregory Head	$5,414
		Luann Derochers	$2,463
		Sandra Keefe	$2,000
		Bill Welch / Glenn Smith	$3,085 (shared)
		Roger Daniel	$1,650
		Cheryl A. Pipitone	$1,159
1993	January	Charlie Alexander	$2,449
		Jacqueline Gudinas	$2,040
		Joe Duchemin / Donald Frechette	$1,989 (each)
		Dimitrios Tzortzis	$1,522
1993	February	(Names not indicated)	$2,755 (shared)
1993	March	John Zappala	$1,958
		Peter Beauregard	$1,120
1993	April	Aldo Contratino	$1,880
1993	May	(Names not indicated)	$865
1993	Fall	Ed Ledwich / Les Hamlett	$1,815 (shared)
		Rodney Ratcliffe / Kevin Lekarcyk	$3,230 (shared)
		Lisa Breen	$1,687
		Raymond Germain	$1,849
1994	Jul / Aug	Kathleen Loughlin / Betty Staryk-Houle / Robert Foster	$12,000 (shared)
1994	Nov / Dec	Doris Jaskunas / Jane Orth	$1,543
1995	Jan / Feb	Basilia Alba	$2,500 (revised)
1995	Mar / Apr	Roger Garneau	$1,400
1995	May / Jun	Stanley Wojicik	$10,000
1995	Jul / Aug	Bruce Garrett / Chris Wilkinson / John Sielicki	$5,058 (shared)
1995	Sep / Oct	Glenn Boucher / Roger Giard	$2,131 (shared)
		Karen Wunderlich	$1,920
1995	Nov / Dec	Bill Ravgiala	$6,442
		Jack Hume	$3,863
1996	First Quarter	Charlie Kennedy	$10,000 (maximum)
1996	June / July	Wally Brewer / John McCormack	$4,217 (shared)
1996	Sep /Oct	Kevin Lekarcyk / Bill Sullivan	$3,735 (shared)
1996	Nov / Dec	David Jenkins / John Zappala / Joyce Glidden	(Not stated)
1997	May /June	Ann McIntosh	$10,000
1997	November	Joe Iannalfo / Bruce Weymouth / Mike Santo	$1,200 (shared)
		Joe Currier / Dennis Anderson	$880 (shared)

Year	Month	Award Recipient(s)	Award
1998	January / February	John Gage Pat Murphy Joe Papalardo / Bob Buxton / Dick Jackman Peter Abcunas / Mark Roche / Steve Andrukaitis	$4,400 $600 $600 (shared)
1998	Spring	Modesto Espinosa Richard (Larry) Marsolais Bob Waardenburg	$6,400 $2,100 $1,753
1999	March / April	Kevin Robichaud / Craig Catton	$11,000
1999	July / August	Paul Perrault	$600
1999	Fall	Kevin Robichaud	$4,747
2000	January / February	Paula Reynolds Bill Ellis Vernon Chambers	$7,300 $2,125 $1,600
2000	January / February	Bill Kane / Chris Obert / Steve Schloth Nancy Bodwell / Bob Harris / Steve Fairbrother Jim Davies	$ 14,000 (shared)
2000	March / April	Carol Tattan Frank Tasca	$1,000 $800

27 - Western Electric

Western Electric's fundamental business was to provide the Bell System with a reliable source of high-quality communications equipment.

Western Electric had six functions as a company:

1. Manufacturing
2. Systems Equipment Engineering
3. Installations
4. Distribution
5. Repair
6. Purchasing.

Western Electric had seven Objectives of Management:

1. *Service, Quality, and Cost* - Good service, high quality, and reasonable costs
2. *Earnings* - The business must be kept financially healthy.
3. *Treatment and Performance* - Fair treatment of the customer. Pleasant performance is the role at all times, in all circumstances.
4. *Balanced Consideration* - Consideration of the customer, employee, public, and shareholder, must be balanced and fair to all.
5. *Research and Development* - Constant and adequate effort on research and development for progress in product, quality, and employment conditions.
6. *Long-range Planning* - Must never be overlooked in the solution of current problems.
7. *Stature as Management* - Integrity and dignity by all is vital to successful management.

Western Electric had nine Divisions:

1. Manufacturing
2. Service
3. Administration
4. Engineering
5. Defense Activities
6. Legal and Patent Division
7. Finance
8. Personnel and Public Relations
9. Organization Planning

Why was the Merrimack Valley Works location selected?

Representatives from plant design and construction flew over prospective sites in helicopters to see if the properties fit the company's requirements for the 1950s:

1. What were the surrounding residential areas like?
2. Did roads offer adequate access?
3. Was their railroad access for the shipment of heavy materials?
4. What is the local labor market like?
5. What is the tax situation?
6. What is the local community?
7. What are the areas educational opportunities?
8. Are there political advantages like influential senators?
9. What is the state's sales pitch for locating there?

28 - Western Electric Company Bullet History

- 1856 - George Shawk, a skilled craftsman and telegraph maker, purchased an electrical engineering business in Cleveland, Ohio. On December 31, 1869, he entered a partnership with Enos M. Barton, and later sold his share to inventor Elisha Gray.

- 1856 - The New York and Mississippi Valley Printing Telegraph Company merged with the New York and Western Union Telegraph Company with the goal of creating one great telegraph system with unified and efficient operations. The merged company was named the Western Union Telegraph Company, and Western Union was born.

- 1869 - Western Electric was founded by Enos Barton and Elisha Gray, and is created as a principal manufacturer of equipment for Western Union.

This building on St. Clair Street in Cleveland housed the original Gray and Barton shop in 1869. Circle indicates the space occupied.

- 1871 - October 8 - Mrs. O'Leary's cow kicked over a kerosene lamp and twenty-seven hours later, 18,000 Chicago buildings worth $196-million had been destroyed. The citywide fire devastated 2,000 acres, but halted just two blocks from a small firm that made telegraph equipment and electrical devices. The firm, then known as Gray and Barton, swung into action and immediately began replacing vast amounts of telegraph and electrical equipment throughout the city. By its efforts, the company earned a reputation for dependable performance under emergency situations, and went on to become the manufacturing and supply unit of the nationwide Bell System - Western Electric.

- 1872 - Barton and Gray moved the business to Clinton Street, Chicago, Illinois, and incorporated it as the Western Electric Manufacturing Company.

- 1873 - Western Electric hires its first Black employee, William Smith, in Dallas, Texas.

- 1873 - Western Electric hires its first woman employee, Sarah Adlum, in Chicago, Illinois.

- 1876 - on February 14, Alexander Graham Bell filed a telephone patent application.

- 1878 - AT&T General Manager (President), Theodore Vail, established the Bell System as a nationwide integrated telephone service dominated by AT&T affiliates and urged Western Electric to make telephone production a priority over power-generating equipment.

- 1878 - The First Woman Telephone Operator - Emma Nutt, a 29-year-old proper Bostonian, took her place in the lexicon of 19th century news by joining the Telephone Dispatch Company as the nation's first woman telephone operator. The manager of the Boston exchange of the Company

The world's first commercial typewriter manufactured by Remington Brothers in 1874. Co-designed by Western Electric.

(later the New England Telephone Co.), hired Emma on September 1st on an "experimental basis." So successful was the experiment with a woman operator, that in just seven years, all the Boston telephone operators were women. Emma Nutt retired on a pension in 1911 after a 33-year career. She died in Cambridge in 1926 at the age of 77.

- 1879 - Elisha Gray's Western Union telephone patent competed against American Bell, but Bell's patent was upheld and Western Union withdrew from the telephone business.

- 1881 - Bell Telephone Company, incorporated as American Bell Telephone Company, and acquired Western Electric.

- 1882 - Alexander Graham Bell's company buys a majority interest in the Western Electric Co., securing a sole supplier for telephone apparatus for over a century of business.

- 1885 - American Telephone and Telegraph subsidiary formed with Theodore N. Vail as president.

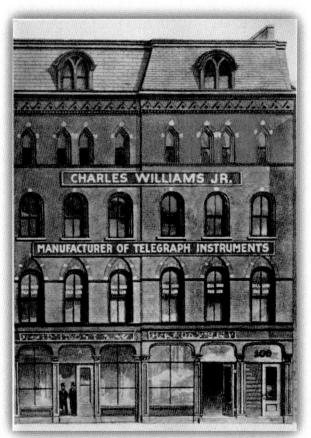

Boston instrument shop where Bell made the first telephone. Bought by Western Electric when it entered the Bell System in 1881.

- 1899 - Western Electric was the first company to join in a Japanese joint venture with foreign capital when they invested in a 54% share of the Nippon Electric Company, Ltd.

- 1912 - March - The first employee magazine was "Western Electric News - Published Once a Month for Employees," commencing with Volume 1, Number 1, under company president Harry Bates Thayer. Its purpose was to provide a forum where ideas could be exchanged, company events and activities could be recorded, and to provide technical and commercial information of value to the employee.

- 1913 - Western Electric developed the first high-vacuum electronic tube.

- 1914 - The Hawthorne facility was Western Electric's sole production facility, causing plants in New York and Chicago to close their doors. Over the following 70 years, the Hawthorne Works, including over 100 buildings, would produce

The Hawthorne Works

telephones, cable and every major telephone switching system, including the equipment necessary to make it work.

- 1915 - Transcontinental service begins.

- 1915 - The assets of Western Electric Manufacturing were transferred to a newly incorporated company in New York, New York, named Western Electric Company, Inc., a wholly owned subsidiary of AT&T.

- 1916 - Western Electric invents the loudspeaker.

Early in the 1900s, telephone installers used the new "horseless carriage" to deliver Western Electric wall sets.

- 1917 - Western Electric developed the first air-to-ground radio communications, which allowed World War I pilots to talk to ground stations and other pilots. W.E. Radios also linked tanks, and enabled warships to contact other warships and shore stations. New electrical listening devices helped to detect enemy planes and guns. When telephone wires were cut in wartime, W.E. made portable radio telegraphs to help the allies maintain communications.

- 1920 - Western Electric sold their appliance business that produced vacuum cleaners, sewing machines, washing machines, fans and dishwashers.

- 1920 - Alice Heacock Seidel was the first of Western Electric's female employees to be given permission to stay on after she had married. This set a precedent in the company, which previously had not allowed married women in their employ. Miss Heacock had worked for Western Electric for sixteen years before her marriage, and was at the time the highest-paid secretary in the company.

- 1921 - The Willis-Graham Act allowed AT&T, as the company who had designed, built, installed and maintained the national network, "Natural Monopoly" status, exempting them from antitrust penalties. By the end of the 1920s, AT&T - after buying up smaller local telephone companies - stood as the world's largest corporation.

- 1921 - Western Electric's development of the loudspeaker was a by-product of the development of the high-vacuum tube. Western Electric public address systems were used at the 1920 presidential conventions, and at Warren Harding's inauguration. On Armistice Day (November 11) in 1921, Harding dedicated the Tomb of the Unknown Soldier before 100,000 people at Arlington National Cemetery. The address was sent by telephone to New York and San Francisco. In both cities, Western Electric loudspeaker systems carried Harding's speech.

- 1923 - Atlantic City's Boardwalk was turned into an auditorium on Saturday, January 27th. The occasion was entertainment by the National Exhibitors. Through the projectors (speaker horns) of the Western Electric Public Address System mounted along the boardwalk, those over 2,000 feet away heard everything as clearly as if they were 50 feet of the entertainers. Amplification of entertainment is only one of the services a Western Electric Public Address System provides. It has a place in the quick, accurate distribution of information in the city Police, Fire, and Education departments.

- 1924 - Walter A. Shewhart, known as the father of statistical quality control, develops the Quality (statistical) Control Chart in Western Electric, which spark a revolution in quality control.

Walter Shewhart

- 1924 - Western Electric developed permanent public address systems and Western Electric engineers perfected long-distance speech transmission.

- 1925 - Western Electric worked with competitors to perfect a talking motion picture system. Western Electric's Vitaphone system was used in 1927 to record "The Jazz Singer." This was the first full-length feature film with dialog recorded on a 16" disc.

WE Vitaphone

- 1925 - Western Electric also managed an electrical equipment distribution business, furnishing customers with non-telephone products made by other manufacturers. This electrical distribution business was spun off from Western Electric in 1925 and organized into a separate company, Graybar Electric Company, in honor of the company's founders, Elisha Gray and Enos Barton.

- 1925 - January - Western Electric formed a subsidiary to handle the company's non-telephone business. Electrical Research Products Incorporated (ERPI) developed and distributed studio recording equipment and sound systems to Hollywood studios. The equipment was leased rather than sold, just as the Bell System leased telephone equipment. ERPI equipped 879 movie theaters in 1928, and 2,519 in 1929. By 1932 only 2% of the theaters in America were not wired for Western Electric sound. ERPI abandoned the theater business in 1937, but the company continued to produce sound equipment for movie studios until 1956 when Western Electric abandoned most non-telephone business.

- 1926 - Western Electric issues the first Bell System telephone with a handset containing both the transmitter and receiver in the same unit. Previous telephones had been of the candlestick type, which featured a stationary transmitter in the desktop set or the wall-mounted unit, and a hand-held receiver to be placed to the user's ear.

- 1929 through 1933 - Employment levels at AT&T and Bell Telephone Laboratories each fell about 32% during the depression while Western Electric lost over 75% (87,000 to 21,000 employees). AT&T had to keep services going, but Western could postpone building more equipment. Little wonder that Western Electric came to be known as the Bell System "shock absorber."

- 1930 - At the Hawthorne location in the early 1920s, someone sent a postcard addressed to "Charley, the Western." Amazingly, it reached its destination - a popular employee named Charley Drucker. Wags (wives and girlfriends) began to call Western Electric "Charley Western." In 1930, Jean O'Rourke was crowned the first "Hello Charley" beauty queen, launching a fifty-year tradition. Her likeness appeared on car bumper stickers that were available for the mandatory two-week July vacation, and employees honked in solidarity when one was spotted.

- 1931 - Sound-on-film eliminated Vitaphone, however, Western Electric also manufactured MovieTone projectors, speakers, and recording equipment for Sound-on-film. The MovieTone sound system is an optical sound-on-film method of recording sound for motion pictures that guarantees synchronization between sound and picture.

- 1930s - Unemployment forced customers to give up telephones that they could no longer afford. Western Electric bore the brunt of the Bell System's crisis and sales fell by 50% and 80% of workers were out of jobs. Western Electric was forced to use the finest craftsmen in the United States to build common household items like fans, hot plates, irons, bookends, and ashtrays.

- 1930s - During the depression, the President of AT&T, Walter Gifford, continued to pay stockholders dividends. His belief was that his commitment to investors would build loyalty when good times returned.

- 1932 - March - "The Western Electric News - An Illustrated Magazine Devoted to the Interests of Western Electric Men and Women," is temporarily discontinued. *"Now that the Company is in the midst of a serious decline in its business, which carries with it the necessity of adopting further measures of economy, the conclusion has been reached that for the time being, the men and women in the business will be willing to forego the monthly visits of the News. The Editors hope that this period of suspension will not be long."*

- 1933 - The company's revenue fell from a high of $411 million in 1929 to less than $70 million. The Hawthorne plant's employment fell from 43,000 workers in 1930 to about 6,000 by 1933.

- 1933 - Western Electric made layoff allowances for employees with families to support. Working with the assumption that married women had their husband's income to fall back on; the company used marital status as the most common exception to the seniority rule. By the same logic, single men were at greater risk than married men. Beyond these policies, managers had some leeway regarding whom to let go.

- 1933 - The "Make Work Program" is started. The company paid its employees to make "articles in general demand" from furniture to cigarette lighters to keep them employed, and then it distributed the goods at cost through the company stores.

- 1933 - Studies from 1924 to 1933 at the Hawthorne Plant inspired the development of the field of industrial psychology:

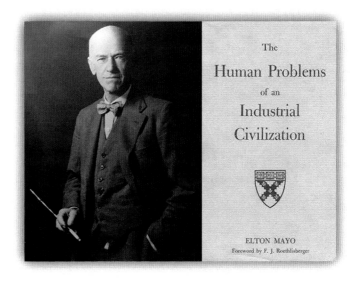

  o Elton Mayo conducted the research of the effect of lighting changes and work structure changes, such as working hours or break times, on manufacturing productivity.
  o The series of Hawthorne experiments revealed an emphasis on the importance of communication, the need to understand employee behavior and ideas, and the importance of participation through teamwork.
  o The "Hawthorne Effect" is the inclination of people who are the subjects of a study to change or improve their behavior only because it is being studied, and not because of changes in the experiment parameters or motivation.

- 1936 - The model 302 telephone, the first Western Electric instrument that combined the desktop telephone set with the subscriber set and ringer in one unit. It became the mainstay of American telephone service well into the 1950s. It was followed by the model 500 telephone starting in 1950, which became the most extensively produced telephone model in the industry's history and ultimately discontinued in 1986.

- 1936 - During the Great Depression, some of WE's Kearny Shops made a lot of items not normally associated with the telephone business. Such as a mahogany coffee table made in the Kearny woodwork shop. Back then, wood was used to build switchboards and phone booths, and after years of the depression, a minimum of available work dwindled into no work at all, so Kearny Koffee tables, ash trays, ping pong tables, etc. were actually sold to a few people during the depression years.

- 1936 - Prior to unions, Western Electric employed "counselors" to hear and filter employee complaints and grievances. At the Hawthorne Works, the counseling program grew from 5 counselors handling 600 people in 1936, to 55 counselors handling 21,000 people in 1948.

- 1936 - On April 17, 1936 the headline screamed flood across 12 states - Thousands marooned from Pittsburgh through New England. New England hardest hit and traffic is paralyzed. Never had the Bell System faced such widespread disaster. Never did it organize for relief so quickly. In one-week, Western Electric's shipped record shipments to the stricken areas. Total flood shipments for the emergency topped 2,600 tons.

Washington Square – Haverhill, MA

There're many acts of individual heroism. In one week, Western Electric supplies 160 million conductor-feet of cable, 50 million conductor-feet of rubber covered wire, 27,000 telephones, 750,000 pounds of copper line wire, and 23 sections of central office switchboard.

- 1938 - The New England hurricane on September 21, 1938, ultimately took 700 lives, destroyed half a billion dollars' worth of property, silenced half a million telephones, flooded central offices, and washed-out railroads and highways. Sweeping into action, Western Electric shipped nearly 23,000 tons of material to devastated areas. Within three weeks, the demand for many of the items exceeded the average monthly requirements for

Hurricane of 1938 – New York Times

the entire Bell System. With this material, over 2,300 skilled telephone employees from all over the country soon had the telephone system working again.

- 1941 - Press Release: *Busier Than Ever* - This country has the best telephone equipment in the world and this equipment has extra margins for growth and emergencies. Both the growth and emergency are here. The margins are being used. The Bell System has two things that help a lot these days. It has experienced manufacturing facilities and a dependable, nation-wide distributing organization. Both are handled within this System by Western Electric, makers of your Bell telephone and its related apparatus. This has been a good policy for a generation. Never have its benefits been so clear as right now when the country is under pressure. The Bell System is doing its part in the country's program of national defense.

- 1941 - President Roosevelt enacted Executive Order 8802, calling for the integration of government contractors. After the order, Western Electric began to hire blacks, but did so slowly. In 1942, of 50,000 workers, 103 were black. In 1943, the number increased to 7,000.

- 1941 - Western Electric's African American presence in the company amounted to a handful of workers at distribution centers. Not one African American worked in any of the company's three major plants. Western Electric first hired African Americans at its plants during World War II. One such employee was Kearny employee Ruby Dee who went on to be a screen actress best known for "A Raisin in the Sun" with Academy Award winner, Sidney Poitier.

Ruby Dee (Left) "A Raisin in the Sun" 1959

- 1942 - Mirrophone, Magnetic Tape Recorder - Bell Labs had been researching magnetic recording for some time before the development of the Mirrophone which used magnetized metal

tape to record a 1-minute continuous loop. It was used in language development.

- 1942 - Western Electric removed signs designating race, and partitions that separated black and white sections of the bathrooms.

- 1943 - The company moved a black woman into the inspection department at the Point Breeze facility in Baltimore, and twenty-two white women demanded her removal. The women went on strike and the Point Breeze Employees Association (PBEA) - the employer-sponsored labor union - supported them. After several meetings, the company denied their request for separate facilities. The women then returned to work without a change in conditions. But later, the PBEA submitted a petition seeking racially segregated toilet facilities. The company rejected the petition and PBEA called a strike vote. It came to 1,802 for, and 1,144 against a strike. The black group assembled, and telegraphed President Roosevelt and the War Labor Board requesting that they take over the plant for the duration of the strike threat. After several futile discussions between the PBEA and The War Labor Board, the PBEA called a strike. President Roosevelt then issued Executive Order 9408, authorizing government takeover of the plant. This was largely symbolic, and the plant was under the possession of Brigadier General Archie A. Farmer, but the plant was actually run by Western Electric managers. On March 23, 1944, full control of the plant returned to the company, and Western agreed to build additional lockers and toilets to segregate the plant.

- 1943 - September - "The Kearnygram," a magazine for the employees of the Western Electric Kearny Works, announced: "A New Plant Leased in Massachusetts." Another manufacturing location for the Western Electric Company was acquired last month through lease of the Winchell and Grad buildings in Haverhill, Mass., on the Merrimack River, in the northeast corner of the Bay State. Many of the machines and tools needed will be moved to Haverhill from the Kearny Works. The company will employ from 1,500 to 2,000 people from the Haverhill area.

- 1943 - Western Electric comes to Haverhill and starts making coils for voice communication. It takes over a former shoe factory on Locust Street and later expands to another factory on Granite Street.

- 1944 - On this, the 75th Anniversary of the Western Electric family, in coping with the production problems of the war, has derived strength and inspiration from the inheritance handed down by the thousands of former employees whose careers have enriched the Company's history. Our abilities and energy, now devoted to the war efforts of our country, are the extension of their work; our feeling of pride, fellowship, and common loyalty is the fruition of their ideals.

- 1944 - Western Electric was supplying more equipment every two weeks than it had during the entire 4 years of World War I.

- 1944 - Western's greatest volume of important secret defense work was on radar, or "radio distance finding." Radar offered both offensive and defensive capabilities. It made weapons more accurate and therefore efficient, requiring fewer shots to score a hit. It also allowed defenses to detect planes in any weather, day or night.

- 1944 - During World War II, Western Electric's Personnel Director, Walter Dietz helped develop a program called Training Within Industry (TWI), which helped prepare individuals to learn how to perform jobs different from the ones they had held before the war, or to enter the workforce for the first time. TWI was later applied throughout the world.

- 1946 - President Harry S. Truman awarded the U.S. Medal of Merit to Western Electric President Clarence Stoll. Under his direction and outstanding leadership, his company produced over 30% of all electronics and communications equipment, and over 50% of all radar manufactured in the U.S. during the war.

- 1947 - Bell Telephone Laboratories invents the transistor.

- 1947 - The first transistor type, called "point contact," was invented at Bell Telephone Laboratories in December by John Bardeen and Walter Brattain.

The invention of the transistor was made public in June 1948 at a press conference held by Bell Telephone Laboratories in New York City.

- 1947 - TRANSVIEW Design: Still another Pioneering step in FM by Western Electric - Since the very beginning of broadcasting,

Western Electric has been noted for pioneering new ideas in transmitter design, which have later become standard practice in the industry. Stabilized feedback - the high-efficiency amplifier circuit - mounting all electrical components on the central vertical structure, achieving maximum accessibility - Synchronized Frequency Modulation are typical Bell Laboratories / Western Electric contributions. And today, Western Electric's TRANSVIEW design FM line sets the pace for tomorrow. *"You'll like the full-length glass doors, which provided an unobstructed view of all tubes at all times. You'll like the striking modern appearance, and the attractive station call letters. Most of all, you'll like the low inter-modulation, the low harmonic distortion, and other features that put this new line of FM transmitters far out in front in performance as an appearance."*

- 1949 - Western Electric's reputation for sound management was so stellar that President Truman requested that Western Electric manage Sandia National Defense Laboratories. As a non-profit service to the government, Scandia Labs in New Mexico operates a vital installation for the Atomic Energy Commission. The development and design of nuclear weapons that will provide the United States with a strong deterrent to aggression. Their mission is to develop  strategic and tactical weapons; provide manufacturing engineering for production; surveillance of the condition of nuclear weapon stockpiles; and the training of military personnel in assembly and use.

- 1949 - The justice department pursued antitrust lawsuits against the AT&T Bell System, forcing the company out of all non-telephone businesses.

- 1950 - Hawthorne is now represented by the International Brotherhood of Electrical Workers (IBEW). Shop stewards became the recipients of employee complaints. The counseling program was over.

- 1950 - The second transistor type, called "grown junction," was developed at Bell Telephone Laboratories in 1950, based on the theoretical work of William Shockley. The Nobel Prize in Physics 1956 was awarded jointly to William Shockley, John Bardeen and Walter Brattain "for their researches on semiconductors and their discovery of the transistor effect."

- 1950 - At the start of the Cold War, Western Electric was selected to build the SOSUS anti-submarine sound surveillance system.

- 1951 - Dr. Joseph M. Juran publishes the Quality Control Handbook. Still the most widely used reference work for quality managers.

- 1951 - At the Allentown Works location, Miss Bonnie B. Small was convinced that Walter Shewhart's abstract ideas in statistical quality control - alone - were of little help in the factory. She decided to translate these ideas into practical methods using the control chart as a tool. When she left Allentown, there were 5,000 control charts used in the plant, and performance had dramatically improved. Miss Small then shifted to the assignment of promoting control charts throughout the company.

- 1952 - 10/31 - While campaigning for the 1953 U.S. Presidency, General Dwight D. Eisenhower specifically diverted his motorcade through Cicero, Illinois to briefly stop at the Hawthorne Western Electric plant and speak to employees.

- 1952 - Western Electric's involvement with defense projects grew from the Nike [the Greek goddess of victory] guided missile program [a line-of-sight anti-aircraft missile system] beginning in 1950, to discussions of one of the biggest military engineering jobs in history, the Distant Early Warning Line (DEW Line), a 3,000-mile system of radar outposts across the Arctic to detect approaching bombers. AT&T's new president, Cleo Craig, turned down the defense department's request for Western Electric to construct the "northern radar fence" and associated communications equipment and facilities over the next two years. Craig cited that the

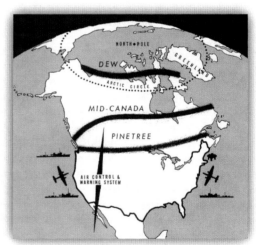

From north to south: The Distant Early Warning (DEW) Line, Mid-Canada Line, and Pinetree Line.

company was overburdened with demands of public telephone systems, heavy defense obligations, and antitrust threats. Advocates for the Bell System intervened. On December 1954, Western Electric was awarded the DEW Line contract, and it was developed with a partnership between Bell Telephone Laboratories and the Massachusetts Institute of Technology. The Arctic segment of the job was completed on schedule in July 1957, the 700-mile westward communications segment in the spring of 1959, and the 1,200-mile eastern segment in November 1961.

- 1953 - The company buys five parcels totaling 157 acres of farm land adjacent to Route 125 in North Andover for what will become the Merrimack Valley Works.

- 1953 - On November 2, groundbreaking ceremonies were held for the Merrimack Valley Works (Merrimack Valley Works) state-of-the-art manufacturing plant at 1600 Osgood Street, North Andover.

- 1955 - In May, Ellen Dyer sets up secretarial office at new Merrimack Valley Works North Andover building still under construction. She was the first Western Electric person occupying the building.

- 1956 - March / April - WE Magazine, Vol. VIII, No. 2 - "The New W.E. - New plants, new Jobs, new people - and a new spirit." The New Merrimack Valley plant nears completion as Western Electric announces construction plans for a new plant in Omaha.

- 1956 - The Federal government restricts Western Electric to the manufacture of telecommunications equipment of the type Bell companies requires. Prior to 1925, Western Electric products included vacuum sweepers, hair dryers, sewing machines, and foot massagers.

- 1956 - Haverhill's Western Electric moves to its new Osgood Street, North Andover, location.

- 1956 - The Nobel Prize in Physics 1956 was awarded jointly to Bell Telephone Laboratories Scientist/Engineers William Shockley, John Bardeen and Walter Brattain "for their researches on semiconductors and their discovery of the transistor effect."

- 1956 - By way of a 1956 consent decree, the Bell System was ordered to divest all non-telephone activities - except those involving national defense. Western also had to give up its interest in Northern Electric of Canada.

- 1956 - First Trans-Atlantic cable laid.

- 1956 - The Hush-A-Phone vs. United States ruling allowed a third-party device to be attached to rented telephones owned by AT&T.

- 1956 - The Western Electric Statistical Quality Control Handbook was first published, and has been the shop floor authority for quality control throughout the world ever since.

- 1958 - Western Electric established the Engineering Research Center (ERC) near Princeton, New Jersey. The ERC was one of the first research organizations solely dedicated to manufacturing-focused, rather than product-focused science. Four hundred engineers worked to bring new manufacturing technologies into the company's production environment. Their developments included computer-driven mathematical models and related statistical quality-control systems to improve production flow and logistics, novel metal-forming techniques, circuit board assembly automation, fiber-optic waveguide manufacturing techniques, application of LASERs for industrial processes and cleanroom robotics for semiconductor production.

- 1959 - The Touchtone telephone was trial tested, and introduced in 1963. Combined with the ESS (Electronic Switching System), the keypad sped up direct-dialed long-distance calling.

- 1959 - Princess phone introduced. It was a compact telephone designed for convenient use in the bedroom, and contained a light-up dial for use as a night-light. Many millions were sold.

- 1960 - NASA awards Western Electric a contract for over $33,000,000 for engineering and construction of a tracking system for the Project Mercury program. As part of this effort, Western Electric engineers trained remote-site flight controllers and Project Mercury control center and operations personnel.

- 1960 - BMEWS - Ballistic Missile Early Warning System - Western Electric Company has a prime contract to provide the all-important rearward communication system from the BMEWS bases to NORAD (North American Aerospace Defense Command) at Colorado Springs - a system of advanced design, reliability and quality. BMEWS systems are in Alaska, Greenland, and England. If a missile attack is detected to be aimed at the United States, Canada or Britain, BMEWS radar would feed information about them to computer systems which would determine key facts such as location, speed, trajectory, possible impact areas and launch points. In split-second time, this information would be relayed to headquarters of NORAD, and relayed to the headquarters of the Strategic Air Command (SAC) at Omaha.

- 1962 - Telstar was the world's first satellite to relay television & telephone signals. It was launched by NASA into elliptical orbit on top of a Thor-Delta rocket on July 10, 1962 from Cape Canaveral.

- 1963 - The Data Phone was manufactured by Western Electric for use by the Bell Telephone System. It was an early commercial modem (acoustic coupler). Bell Telephone Laboratories invented the first computer modem (modulator -

demodulator) a few years earlier in 1958. A modem converts digital signals to electrical (analog) signals and back, allowing communication between computers. Bell Telephone's Data Phone service was offered to businesses who needed to send data over traditional phone lines at the cost of normal telephone rates, and was touted as being able to send messages 16 times faster than audio messages. Customer data (Inventories, payroll, orders, sales figures, production data, etc.) was input into the Data Phone via <u>punched card</u> or tape from their local computer.

- 1963 - Western Electric 202 E Data-Phone Telephone - Computers can talk by telephone too - More and more, "machine talk" is being transmitted over the same communications facilities that carry your everyday telephone conversations. The Western Electric Data-Phone set helps make it possible. It converts machine language - from punched cards, paper tape, or magnetic tape - into tone language for transmission over the nation-wide telephone network. It is the versatility and reliability of this communications network that permits machines to "talk" with each other no matter what the distance between them. They can, because the entire Bell Telephone network was designed and built to common standards by people with a common purpose - ever-better telephone service.

- 1963 - Western Electric 202 E Data-Phone Telephone - Western Electric makes data sets for the Bell System's Data-Phone service. Inventories, payrolls, bills, etc. can be transmitted at speeds up to 2,700 words a minute. Doctors even use it to send electrocardiograms. If you skipped lightly over that figure - 2,700 words a minute - take a minute more to consider it. In order to send and receive signals at such a rate, each part must not only work, but work perfectly every split second. Reliability is the name of the game. Western Electric has been building reliability into telephone equipment since joining the Bell System team in 1882. This experience, gained from working together over the years, is one of the reasons Bell Telephone companies are able to provide your home or business with the world's most dependable communications service.

- 1963 - Teamsters arrived in Baltimore, Maryland to organize the Western Electric Point Breeze plant - later known as the Baltimore Works. This was the beginning of the teamster's campaign to organize the Telecommunications industry. The week of the vote, teamster leader Jimmy Hoffa spoke at Point Breeze. In the days leading up to the vote, police stayed at the home of the head of the Communication Equipment Workers Inc. (CEW), Robert Bach. CEW had represented the

Jimmy Hoffa

plant since 1949. Bach had reportedly received an anonymous phone call offering bribes if he would step down, and threatened with violence if he did not.

- 1967 - Western Electric designed, built and installed a communications system linking space flight personnel during interplanetary missions. The system was installed at the Jet Propulsion Laboratory's Space Flight Operations Center in Pasadena, California.

- 1968 - The Federal Communications Commission allowed the Carterfone and other devices to be connected directly to the AT&T network, as long as they did not cause damage to the system.

- 1969 - Western Electric was one hundred years old on November 18, 1969. Looking back over a century of incredible change, the company's history may be separated into three distinct periods. From its inception in 1869 until it joined the Bell System in 1882, it was primarily a small shop engaged in producing electrical devices. After joining the Bell System, it took the lead in diversifying and broadening communications in America but continued its activities in the electric equipment field. After 1925, it limited its role to that of the manufacturing and supply unit of the Bell System, its chosen course for the future.

- 1969 - The Engineering Excellence Society was founded to recognize outstanding engineering accomplishments by members of the Merrimack Valley engineering community.

- 1970 - The Western Electric Columbus Works grew from 6,000 employees to over 13,000 in 18 months.

- 1970 - The first practical Ion Implanters to make integrated circuits were developed at the ERC and later implemented at Western Electric's chip-making factories.

- 1972 - Astronaut John Glenn and Western Electric Present "Here Comes Tomorrow: Fearfighters." Doors that unlock by touch through fingerprints, TV cameras that monitor city streets, policemen who fly, and cameras that see in the dark, are just some of the technological advances that will make life safer in the 1980's. Here Comes Tomorrow: The Fearfighters, a television special on the ABC-TV Network, will discuss and show these new safety devices. The program, sponsored by Western Electric, will have Colonel John Glenn, the first astronaut to orbit the earth, as its host.

- 1972 through 1974 - New electronic production required a new type of worker, prompting Western Electric to establish a program for retraining its work force. Four-thousand employees from Merrimack Valley's seven-thousand-member work force underwent job retraining to prepare them for new skills needed in the manufacture of new products.

- 1974 through 1975 - During the time of the time of the great layoffs, personnel layoff procedures for non-union employees were based on merit. This practice became important to corporate equal-opportunity goals. Most minority workers would fall to the "last-hired, first fired" case. In the early twentieth century, length of service was the determining lay-off factor.

- 1974 - Columbia Closes In River May - On January 10, Western Electric announced that it will cease all manufacturing at its Columbia River Pilot Plant on May 1. Approximately 570 people will have been laid off by that date. B. W. Northrup, the plant's General Manager, said the company is closing the leased facility with extreme regret but must do so because of the recession, which has substantially reduced Bell System demand for the switching equipment made there.

- 1975 - At Merrimack Valley Works, 2,532 people were laid off because of the economic downturn that hit telephone companies, causing them to cut orders.

- 1975 - Western Electric published The Western Electric Engineer, later known as The Engineer.

- 1975 - Western Electric was the prime contractor for the Safeguard anti-ballistic missile system.

- 1976 - Western Electric introduced their first digital switch, the #4ESS *toll-switching* system. The system reflected an investment of $400M and five years of development. AT&T did not announce official plans to develop a *local* digital switch until 1977. This was because of the imbedded base of cost-effective analog switches, and despite the future of telecommunications clearly being digital. The Northern Telecom DMS-10 digital switch did not compete with the analog Western Electric switches, but a year later, their DMS-100 did.

- 1977 - LASER processes developed by Western Electric's Engineering Research Center in Princeton, New Jersey, have already repaid the company's investment many times over in money saved through cost reduction and cost avoidance. The LASER Studies group uses high-powered carbon-dioxide LASERs - among others - to develop new and better manufacturing procedures.

- 1978 - Celebrating its 100th birthday this year, the telephone directory has played a unique but taken-for-granted role in American history. It began when callers looked up a number on a single sheet, and gave it to the local switchboard operator. Today's comprehensive phone directories and direct dialing show a considerable evolution. The birthday is a significant event for 13,000 Bell System directory employees.

- 1980 - In the last two years, scientists at Western Electric's Engineering Research Center have cut costs by over $156 million. Breakthroughs include: a new soldering technique that makes 20,000 connections in less than 60 seconds; a computer program that makes technical drawings in ¼ the time of manual methods; an automatic system that sorts telephone parts by color; a process that measures the production of optical fiber 1,000 times per second - keeping the diameter accurate to 30-millionths of an inch; and a system that takes 30 seconds to align tiny integrated circuits that are 200 times thinner than the thinnest human hair.

- 1980 - The Merrimack Valley Works averaged 40-70 new hires a week.

- 1981 - Western Electric unveils its #5ESS system for local switching.

- 1981 - February - Western Electric designs a "vandal-resistant" pay phone booth called the "Sentry Rugged II" - either a pedestal or wall-mount.

- 1981 through 1983 - Over 12,000 workers are employed at the Merrimack Valley facility.

- 1982 - January 8 - The settlement of United States v. AT&T, a 1974 US Department of Justice antitrust suit against AT&T. Under the settlement AT&T agreed to divest its local exchange service companies, in return for a chance to go into the computer business. AT&T's local operations were split into seven independent Regional Bell operating companies (RBOCs) or "Baby Bells".

- 1983 - Obituary: Ma Bell Dies at 107 - Ma Bell died at the stroke of midnight, Saturday, December 31, 1983. She succumbed to the forces of technological change and the public's desire for competition. She was 107 years old. Funeral arrangements were made by the U.S. Department of Justice's antitrust team led by William Baxter. Officiating was Judge Harold H. Greene. Eulogies were given in almost every newspaper and journal in the country and felt in the hearts of more than a million dedicated, service-oriented people who worked for her. She had no disease; there were no failures in any of her systems. She was remarkably healthy for her age. Yet, the nation spent a year preparing for her death. Her last will and testament were read on Wall Street several weeks before her passing. Survivors include eight children who will share her $152 billion in assets. She ran an organization that was a cross between a profit-making business and a social service agency. And no one did it better. The fruits of her efforts were the best in the world. Guided toward a belief that everyone should have a telephone at the lowest possible price, she achieved her primary objective in life: universal service. It is through this accomplishment and the legacies of her other achievements that she will be remembered. [Traffic Topics IBEW Local 1944]

- 1984 A ruling by Judge Harold H. Greene of the U.S. District Court in Washington, D.C., breaks up the Bell system. Western Electric officially becomes a unit of AT&T.

- 1984 - January - Western Electric announces the planned closings of the Hawthorne, Kearny, Point Breeze, Indianapolis, and Baltimore Works locations. Western Electric Chairman Don Procknow said that the company simply had far too much capacity for new technologies, required Clean Rooms that the old plants did not have, and old multistory buildings hindered workflow.

- 1984 - AT&T Technologies, Inc., a new company, assumed the corporate charter of Western Electric, which was split into several divisions that focused on specific customer needs.

- 1986 Hawthorne Works Demolished - After the plant closed in 1986, most of the industrial complex was torn down and the site was cleared for a shopping center that adopted the factory's name. The tower was retained as a decoration to crown the Hawthorne Works mall, and two buildings were converted into a business center. But only one factory building remained untouched: a six-story structure at 26th Street and Cicero Avenue, a graffiti-marked building down the block and across the street from the plant's former main offices. On Sunday, April 17, 1994, the owners, DiMucci Development, demolished the 26th Street building to clear space for new stores and parking lots.

- 1986 - The 2500-series telephone, released in 1969, was upgraded to employ dual-tone multi-frequency (DTMF) signaling for transmitting digits to the central office, and replaced the rotary dial phone. DTMF technology is referred to by the trademark Touch-Tone.

- 1986 - The Indianapolis Works telephone plant closed, and US production of AT&T single-line home telephones ended.

- 1987 - The Merrimack Valley Works was busy manufacturing numerous distinct product lines:

  o USEC, 5B EC, ADR6/11, BCM 3200, BCMX, D4, D5, D5 Generic II, DACS, DACS CNC, DACS Enhancements, DACS II, DACS Remote Unit, DCT, DDS, DDS Enhancements, DIF, DIF Enhancements, DIF Generics, Echo Cancellers, Export DACS, FT Series G (417), FT Series G (1.7), FT3C, FTX180, LT2, Metrobus, SM Lightwave, SRDC, T1G, TD90, D1/D3, A5/A6, L4/L5, T1/T2, DXS, and E2A.

- 1990 - The Engineering Research Center (ERC), now integrated into AT&T Bell Laboratories, was closed.

- 1990 - AT&T's Corporate Education Center (CEC) was closed.

- 1991 - AT&T discontinued telegraph services.

- 1991 - AT&T acquired NCR Corporation (National Cash Register), hoping to benefit from the personal computer and Unix server markets, but was unsuccessful.

- 1992 - The Merrimack Valley Works wins the 1992 Malcolm Baldrige National Quality Award for engineering efficiency and quality.

- 1993 - MV announces it has totally eliminated use of all ozone-depleting substances, more than 2 1/2 years ahead of worldwide ban.

- 1994 - Merrimack Valley goes cigarette smoke-free. Areas outside the plant have been designated for employees and visitors who still wish to smoke. Some office areas have designated smoke rooms.

- 1994 - AT&T combines three units, including the Merrimack Valley Works plant in North Andover. Under the restructuring, AT&T's transmission unit is combined with the switching business unit and operating systems unit.

- 1994 - AT&T purchased the largest cellular carrier, McCaw Cellular, for $11.5 billion and started its cellular division with 2 million subscribers.

- On September 20, 1995, AT&T announced that it was restructuring into three separate publicly traded companies: a systems and equipment company (which became Lucent Technologies,) a computer company (NCR) and a communications services company (which would remain AT&T.) It was the largest voluntary corporate break-up in the history of American business.

- 1995 - At the time of the spinoff, Lucent employs 6,250 employees at the Merrimack Valley Works.

- 1995 - Western Electric comes to an end when AT&T changes the name of AT&T Technologies to Lucent Technologies.

- 1996 - While the Bell Laboratories name went to Lucent Technologies, the researchers who supported communications services stayed with AT&T as the staff of the new AT&T Labs.

- 1996 - Lucent Technologies became independent on September 30, 1996.

- 2013 - The stylized *"Western Electric"* brand name survives as the trademark of the Western Electric Export Corporation, a privately owned high-end audio company in Rossville, Georgia.

29 - The Eastland Disaster

[This story relates a tragedy in Western Electric history. It is not related to the Merrimack Valley Works, but it is of interest and I thought it should be included here.]

On July 24, 1915, Eastland and four other Great Lakes passenger steamers were chartered to take employees from Western Electric's Hawthorne Works to a picnic in Michigan City, Indiana. This was a major event in the lives of the workers who could not take holidays. Many of the passengers on Eastland were Czech immigrants (220 of them perished).

The Seamen's Act of 1915 had been signed into law by President Woodrow Wilson, because of the Titanic disaster three years earlier, requiring retrofitting of lifeboats on Eastland, and many other passenger ships. The additional weight may have made Eastland dangerous by making it more top-heavy. Eastland was already so top-heavy that it had special restrictions concerning the number of passengers that could be carried.

On the morning of July 24, passengers began boarding Eastland on the bank of the Chicago River about 6:30 am, and by 7:10 am, the ship had reached its capacity of 2,572 passengers. Many passengers were standing on the open upper decks, and Eastland began to list slightly to the port side (away from the wharf). The crew attempted to stabilize the ship by adding water to its ballast tanks, but with little success.

Sometime during the next 15 minutes, a number of passengers rushed to the port side, and at 7:28 am, Eastland lurched sharply to port, and then rolled completely onto its port side, coming to rest on the river bottom, which was only 20 feet below the surface. Many passengers had moved below decks on this relatively cool and damp morning to warm before the departure. Hundreds of people were trapped inside by water and the sudden rollover, and some were crushed by heavy furniture, including pianos, bookcases, and tables. Although the ship was only 20 feet from the wharf, and despite of the quick response by the crew of the nearby ship, Kenosha - which came alongside the hull to allow those stranded on the Eastland to leap to safety, 844 passengers and four crew members died in the disaster.

The bodies of the victims were taken to various temporary morgues in the area for identification. The Western Electric Company provided $100,000 to relief and recovery efforts of family members of the victims of the disaster.

Marion Eichholz, the last known survivor of the capsizing, died on November 24, 2014, at the age of 102.

Writer Jack Woodford witnessed the disaster and gave a first-hand account to the Herald and Examiner, a Chicago newspaper. Woodford writes:

> *"And then movement caught my eye. I looked across the river. As I watched in disoriented stupefaction a steamer large as an ocean liner slowly turned over on its side as though it were a whale going to take a nap. I didn't believe a huge steamer had done this before my eyes, lashed to a dock, in perfectly calm water, in excellent weather, with no explosion, no fire, nothing. I thought I had gone crazy."*

A grand jury indicted the president and three other officers of the steamship company for manslaughter, and the ship's captain and engineer for criminal carelessness, and found that the disaster was initiated by "conditions of instability" caused by any or all of overloading of passengers, mishandling of water ballast, or the construction of the ship.

During the hearings, principal witness Sidney Jenks, president of the shipbuilding company that built Eastland, testified that her first owners wanted a fast ship to transport fruit, and he designed one capable of making 20 mph and carrying 500 passengers. Defense counsel Clarence Darrow asked whether he had ever worried about the conversion of the ship into a passenger steamer with a capacity of 2,500 or more passengers. Jenks replied, *"I had no way of knowing the quantity of its business after it left our yards... No, I did not worry about the Eastland."* Jenks testified that an actual stability test of the ship never occurred, and stated that after tilting to an angle of 45° at launching, "it righted itself as straight as a church, satisfactorily demonstrating its stability."

The court reasoned that the four company officers were not aboard the ship, and that every act charged against the captain and engineer was done in the ordinary course of business, "more consistent with innocence than with guilt." The court also reasoned that Eastland "was operated for years and carried thousands safely", and that for this reason, no one could say that the accused parties were unjustified in believing the ship seaworthy.

The Eastland was pulled up from the river, renamed the Willimette and converted into a naval vessel. It was turned into scrap following World War II. All lawsuits against the owners of the Eastland were thrown out by a court of appeals and the exact cause of the tipping and subsequent disaster has never been determined.

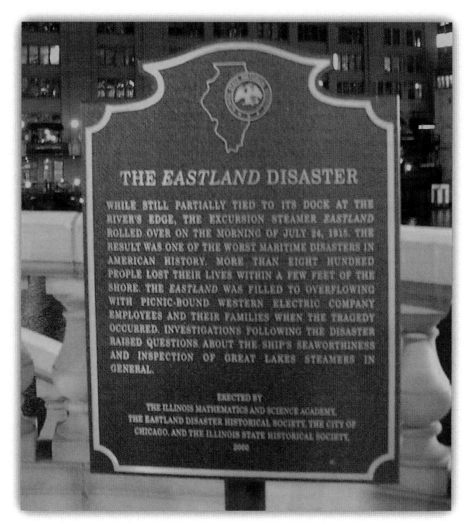

30 - AT&T Bullet History

1889   1900   1921   1939   1964   1969

- 1925 - On January 1st, 1925, AT&T officially created Bell Telephone Laboratories as a standalone company owned half by AT&T, and half by Western Electric. The Labs would research and develop new equipment for Western Electric, conduct switching and transmission planning, and invent communications-related devices for AT&T.

- 1940 - World War II greatly impacted the Bell System. First telecommunications, and especially their related services, were so crucial to the management of war that the Bell research, development, and manufacturing arms instantly became among the most vital of national resources.

- 1942 and continuing until 1945 - Bell Telephone Laboratories and Western Electric devoted themselves largely - almost entirely - to military work. The domestic telephone network had to be somewhat disregarded as to plant modernization and even maintenance. Yet at the same time, war brought on enormously increased demands on that network. Servicemen calling home from distant bases, businessmen conferring with government or military authorities about contracts and deliveries, military units communicating with each other - all these meant telephone calls, and many of them long-distance. So many as to make the demand for service not just unprecedented, but previously unimagined. The very news of Pearl Harbor caused an immediate 400% increase in volume.

- 1945 - One outstanding weapon of this war is the rocket, now used by our fighting forces on land and sea and in the air. Scientists at Bell Telephone Laboratories had an important part in the technical development of this American weapon. One of their contributions was the "ribbon frame" camera which takes 120 pictures a second on a continuously moving film. It has proved of great value in studying rockets and shells in fight. The ribbon frame camera is only one of many Bell Telephone Laboratories developments which are being turned against the enemy. Our Laboratories are now wholly devoted to the war. When it is won, they will go back to their regular job - helping the Bell System give you the best telephone service in the world.

- 1946 - In May, the laboratory models of the first experimental microwave-radio system (TDX) were being tested. At the same time, the development groups started more detailed planning of the new system to be called TD2.

- 1948 - Bell Telephone Laboratories completed development of the TD2 repeater, antenna, power plant and all other items. Equipment delivery was scheduled to begin in the last quarter of 1948, with installation to start in early 1949, working from east to west so that the eastern systems could be tested as the western systems were being installed.

- 1950 - The TD2 New York to Chicago route was opened to service on September 1, and the Los Angeles to San Francisco route a few weeks later. The entire coast-to-coast route was completed in time to carry President Truman's opening address before the Japanese Peace Treaty Conference from San Francisco to New York on September 4, 1951. The design of TD2 had become a reality.

- 1956 - As a result of a 1949 U.S. Department of Justice antitrust suit against AT&T, the company is ordered to divest all international operations, and is not allowed to market computer technology and must focus only on the national phone network. AT&T is still allowed to retain ownership in Bell Telephone Company of Canada, however AT&T's Western Electric unit is forced to sell the stake held in Northern Electric (later to become Nortel), to Bell Telephone of Canada. AT&T is also no longer permitted to purchase any new shares in Bell Telephone Company of Canada.

- 1956 - The first erosion to the AT&T monopoly occurred in 1956 where the Hush-A-Phone vs. United States ruling allowed a third-party device to be attached to rented telephones owned by AT&T.

- 1958 - July 29 - NASA created - The U.S. Congress passes legislation establishing the National Aeronautics and Space Administration (NASA), a civilian agency responsible for coordinating America's activities in space. NASA has since sponsored space expeditions, both human and mechanical, that have yielded vital information about the solar system and universe. It has also launched numerous earth-orbiting satellites that have been instrumental in everything from weather forecasting to navigation to global communications. NASA was created in response to the Soviet Union's October 4, 1957 launch of its first satellite, Sputnik I. The 183-pound, basketball-sized satellite orbited the earth in 98 minutes. The Sputnik launch caught Americans by surprise and sparked fears that the Soviets might also be capable of sending missiles with nuclear weapons from Europe to America. The United States prided itself on being at the forefront of technology, and, embarrassed, immediately began developing a response, signaling the start of the U.S.-Soviet space race.

- 1960 - Synthetic Quartz - Large natural quartz crystals of electronic grade are extremely rare in nature. During World War II, the demand for crystal units went from a few thousand to millions per year. Bell Telephone Laboratories devised a way to grow the required quality of quartz in a laboratory using a high-pressure growing technique called the hydrothermal process. Basically, small, relatively useless pieces of quartz are placed in an alkaline solution of sodium hydroxide in a pressure container, and heated to 750 degrees Fahrenheit at a pressure of 25,000 to

30,000 psi. Using this process, large crystals of excellent quality could be grown in three weeks. Mass production of man-made crystals was conducted at the Merrimack Valley Works.

- 1962 - T1 Carrier is deployed at Illinois Bell - the first common-carrier digital communications system in the world. Using Pulse Code Modulation (PCM), where it converts an analog signal to a train of coded pulses, it marked the beginning of the historical age of digital communications. It represented two major accomplishments. First, it only requires an extremely short pulse - permitting other information to be multiplexed between the pulses, and second, the coded samples can be exactly reconstructed along a communications line.

- 1962 - The T1 Carrier System was the name of the entire system. The original 24-channel terminal was called the D1 channel bank.

- 1962 - TD3 was announced in April, taking advantage of all of the innovations in technology available. TD3 met all objectives and worked very satisfactorily, but some components were very expensive. Experience was gained on TD2, and performance was improved and costs reduced on TD3.

- 1962 - The US Government asked Bell Telephone Laboratories to direct systems planning for the Apollo project. To do this, the Bellcomm Corporation was formed, luring employees largely from Western Electric and other Bell System locations. In 1969, six months ahead of President Kennedy's deadline, Neil Armstrong took that first small step for man. The Bell System shared the nation's pride in that accomplishment. Bellcomm was disbanded in 1972.

- 1963 - Mobile Radio comes of age - Manually controlled land-mobile service was in place in several hundred cities and towns nationwide, but offered service only to an extremely small fraction of the driving public. Research was directed to increasing capacity which was saturated in major cities. The objective was to make calling convenience and quality as good as direct-dialed landline calling.

- 1967 - The L4 Coaxial System - 3,600 two-way voice circuits, much smaller, used less power, and were far more reliable than 1953's L3 Coaxial system. Main-station buildings, at 150-mile intervals along the L4 route, were built as hardened underground buildings. These bomb-resistant buildings were designed and equipped to operate for several weeks completely sealed off from the outside world in the event of a nuclear attack.

- 1967 - The Apollo One tragedy might have been avoided if a Bellcomm recommendation had been followed. Bellcomm scientists had advised against using a pure oxygen environment in the Apollo capsule for danger of fire. Astronauts Gus Grissom, Ed White, and Rodger Chaffee died when their Apollo capsule burst into flames during a testing exercise on January 27th.

- 1968 - The FCC allowed the Carterfone [a device that connects a two-way radio system to the telephone system, allowing someone on the radio to talk to someone on the phone] decision allowed third-party equipment to be connected to the AT&T telephone network.

- 1969 - July 20 - American astronauts Neil Armstrong and Edwin "Buzz" Aldrin became the first humans ever to land on the moon. About six-and-a-half hours later, Armstrong became the first person to walk on the moon. As he took his first step, Armstrong famously said, *"That's one small step for man, one giant leap for mankind."* The Apollo 11 mission occurred eight years after President John F. Kennedy announced a national goal of landing a man on the moon by the end of the 1960s. Apollo 17, the final manned moon mission, took place in 1972.

- Late 1960s - Hybrid Integrated Circuits (HICs) - Performance and small sizes of new devices were best realized when they were assembled as HICs. They were vital in critical circuits, and consisted of solid-state devices (thin-film conductors, resistors and low value capacitors) mounted on an alumina ceramic substrate. They are created through photolithographic techniques (microfabrication using light to transfer a geometric pattern from a photomask to a photosensitive material on the substrate), allowing extremely close control of placement and coupling between circuits.

- 1970 - TD3A is announced. A huge improvement on TD3 using the best and least costly components.

- 1972 - Sometime during the final week of 1971, the Bell System reached a milestone of particular significance - 100 million telephones in service. It marked the achievement of a goal set by AT&T's first president, Theodore N. Vail, back in 1908 - universal telephone service in the United States. At that time, there were four million subscribers, and by the end of World War II, there were 25 million phones in the Bell System. Finally, that figure has quadrupled, and it is estimated the total will approach 150 million by 1980.

- 1970 - AT&T Advertisement - Thousands of telephone people stuck to their jobs in the face of the worst hurricane to ever hit the U.S. mainland - Camille. Many lost their homes and personal belongings. Some had even graver losses. Still, they reported in at their telephone jobs to see how best they could serve. We are not claiming anything special for telephone people. Just that they are human beings - and very much a part of your life. [*Hurricane Camille was the second most intense tropical cyclone on record to strike the United States, and the most intense storm of the 1969 Atlantic hurricane season. It strengthened to a Category 5 hurricane before it reached landfall in Mississippi.*]

- 1972 - Lifting By LASER - A tiny glass particle being held aloft by the light energy of a LASER is researched by Bell Telephone Laboratories. The experiment demonstrates optical levitation for the first time and is expected to provide new techniques for studying optical communications by manipulating small particles without using mechanical support.

- 1972 - The Federal Communications Commission's Common Carrier Bureau said last week that Bell System companies apparently "have moved close" to Equal Employment Opportunity Commission suggested standards in their recruiting policies. In connection with the EEOC's request that the FCC issue a summary decision against the Bell System concerning alleged sex discrimination in recruiting material.

- 1972 - The L5 Coaxial System - Initially 9,600 two-way voice circuits, and three times the bandwidth of the L4 system, later increased to 10,800 voice channels, and L5E (expanded) brought the number of voice circuits to 13,200.

- 1973 - TD3D is announced. Incorporating better testing and maintenance capabilities, using a new solid-state transmitter, and doubling the capacity of the original TD2.

- 1974 - Bell Telephone Laboratories spends over $500 million on nonmilitary R&D, or about 2 percent of AT&T's gross revenues. Western Electric spent even more on its internal engineering and development operations. More than 4 cents of every dollar received by AT&T in 1974 went to R&D at Bell Telephone Laboratories and Western Electric.

- 1974 - The United States Justice Department opened the case "United States v. AT&T". This was prompted by suspicion that AT&T was using monopoly profits from its Western Electric subsidiary to subsidize the cost of its network, a violation of anti-trust law. A settlement to this case was finalized in 1982, leading to the division of the company on January 1, 1984 into seven Regional Bell Operating Companies, commonly known as Baby Bells.

- 1974 - DDS - Data transmission over purely digital facilities began as the Dataphone® Data communications Service (DDS). DDS service to five cities started in December 1974. By the end of 1975, a backbone network of 24 cities was interconnected, and preparations were underway to expand the network to 100 cities.

- 1975 - Termination of AT&T's service agreement with Bell Canada, and to the subsequent relationship between the two companies.

- 1976 - Northern Electric changes its name to Northern Telecom.

- 1976 - 4ESS Digital Electronic Switching System is introduced.

- 1979 - Bell Telephone Laboratories develops the 1A digital voice storage system for electronic central offices - now universally known as voicemail.

- 1982 - AT&T agrees to divest itself of their 22 Regional Bell Operating Companies (RBOCs), and retain long-distance, research and manufacturing.

- 1983 - More than half of all exchange trunks (a single communications channel between two points) were digital. By 1984, more than three-quarters, and at the time, all trunks were expected to be digital by 1990.

- 1983 - AT&T reorganizes the 22 RBOCs into seven holding companies; US West, NYNEX, Pacific Telesis, Ameritech, Bell Atlantic, BellSouth, Southwestern Bell (Later to become SBC Communications). AT&T will keep Bell Telephone Laboratories, Western Electric and Long lines (long-distance services).

- 1983 - A sign hung in many AT&T locations:

"There are two giant entities at work in our country, and they both have an amazing influence on our daily lives... one has given us radar, sonar, stereo, teletype, the transistor, hearing aids, artificial larynxes, talking movies, and the telephone.

The other has given us the Civil War, the Spanish-American War, the First World War, the Second World War, the Korean War, the Vietnam War, double-digit inflation, double-digit unemployment, the Great Depression, the gasoline crisis, and the Watergate fiasco.

Guess which one is now trying to tell the other one how to run its business?"

- 1983 - AT&T is spending about $1 million to "de-identify" about 9,500 buildings - that is to remove all traces of the Bell symbol that is being replaced (except for the seven companies that AT&T will spin off). Erecting the first wave of signs with the new Globe symbol will cost about $9 million; a further $10 million or more will be eventually spent on signs. Then there's about $1.250 million to be spent for symbols and stripes on 30,000 sedans, wagons, and vans. AT&T's current ad campaign to introduce the new AT&T Globe symbol is costing the company about $10 million. Other costs - replacing stationery, business cards, etc. - are yet to be estimated. The Company will even scrap some 50,000 hard hats because it's easier to replace them than repaint them. Purging the bell symbol will take a long time.

- 1984 - On January 1st, 1984, the Bell System breakup officially went into effect. AT&T and Western Electric - now one combined company - were severed from the local phone companies (such as New England telephone and Southern Bell). Most AT&T Bell Laboratories employees stayed with AT&T, and a significant number - about 10% - went to a new research institution called BellCore which was established to serve the research and development needs of the new baby bells.

- 1984 - The RBOCs are broken off from AT&T and are now independent.

- 1985 - AT&T Bell Laboratories at Murray Hill, NJ, will donate 1,000 feet of copper that has roofed the auditorium since 1940, to patch the badly deteriorated sections of the Statue of Liberty's skin during the statue's restoration. The copper is the correct thickness, and has aged to the correct color to match the existing skin of the statue.

- 1986 - A group of AT&T manufacturing officials visited Japan to study the Japanese reputation for superior quality. The purpose of the visit was to bring home some lessons that AT&T could apply in America. Members of the group visited five factories with examples of Total Quality Management (TQM). They found that quality was not just a responsibility of the inspection group. The Japanese did not believe that you could "inspect quality" into the product, they were more concerned with the quality being built into the overall process. Their host was the Nippon Electric Company (rebranded in 1983 as NEC), who had been the creation of a Western Electric joint venture in 1899. When NEC's Tokyo plant was destroyed by earthquake in 1923, Western Electric oversaw the construction of a plant that was actually a duplication of the Western Electric Hawthorne Works, including the tower. Management consultants W. Edwards Deming and Joseph Duran, visited Japan in the 1950s to introduce quality methodologies. In 1986, AT&T was asking the Japanese to re-educate them in the Deming/Duran techniques.

- 1988 - AT&T began a corporate-wide re-evaluation of quality, adopting the "Baldrige criteria." Between 1981 and his death in 1987, US Secretary of Commerce, Malcolm Baldrige urged American companies to look beyond short-term competition and focus on excellence. After his death, Congress established a National Quality Award in his honor.

- 1990 - AT&T officially changes its legal name from the American Telephone & Telegraph Company to AT&T Corporation.

- 1990 - AT&T makes an unsolicited attempt to buy NCR (formerly National Cash Register) for $6 billion, as AT&T Chairman, Robert Allen believes that telephony and computers are a perfect fit. NCR flatly refused. Five months later, after a bitter battle, AT&T finally had a deal for $7.5 billion.

- 1990 - To help fund the NCR deal, AT&T sells its 19% share in Sun Microsystems for $700 million.

- 1992 - AT&T introduced the VideoPhone 2500, the world's first color videophone that could transmit over analog telephone lines. Unlike the earlier Picturephones, the VideoPhone 2500 employed digital compression methods to enable a significant reduction of the bandwidth required for full-motion video transmission. A lack of sales led AT&T to discontinue the VideoPhone 2500 in 1995.

- 1994 - AT&T purchases McCaw Cellular for $12.6 billion and enters the wireless market as AT&T Wireless.

- 1994 - July - Whitney Houston becomes the AT&T "True Voice" spokesperson.

- 1995 - June - AT&T hires Lars Nyberg from Phillips Electronics as CEO of NCR. Three months later, NCR is renamed Global Information Solutions (GIS), and announced plans to fire 20% of the unit's workforce.

- 1995 - September - AT&T announces that GIS - the computer maker - would no longer manufacture computers.

- 1995 - With the forthcoming Telecommunications Act of 1996, (which will allow any communications company to compete in each other's market), AT&T management foresees that AT&T Technologies, Inc. will be regarded more of a competitor than a trusted supplier of communications equipment, so announces the "Trivestiture", an initiative by AT&T Corporation to spin-off AT&T Global Information Solutions (NCR Corporation), AT&T Technologies, Inc. (Lucent Technologies, Inc.) with AT&T Corporation remaining a communications services company.

- 1995 - AT&T Announces that will split into three distinct businesses: AT&T, a communications company; Lucent Technologies, former Western Electric and AT&T Network Systems business; and the NCR computer business. By 1996, all businesses are independent of each other.

Bob Allen Announces Trivestiture

- 1996 - Bell Atlantic merges with NYNEX, and NYNEX name is dropped.

- 1997 - AT&T attempted to merge with SBC Communications. Regulators in Washington were anxious that they were trying to rebuild the "Ma Bell" monopoly. The FCC immediately stopped the merger.

- 1997 - Pacific Telesis is acquired by SBC Communications for $17 billion.

- 1998 - Ameritech is acquired by SBC Communications for $62 billion in stock, the second-largest merger in U.S. history.

- 1998 - Northern Telecom changes its name to Nortel Networks.

- 2000 - Bell Atlantic merges with non-Bell company GTE, and the combined company is called Verizon Communications.

- 2000 - US West is acquired by Qwest Communications for $44 billion in stock.

- 2000 - Lucent Technologies spins off their Business Communications and connectivity solutions unit, creating Avaya; the Microelectronics Group, renamed Agere; and sells off the Consumer Products Group to VTECH Holdings, which assumes the exclusive rights to use the AT&T name on consumer phone products.

- 2000 - Cingular Wireless is founded by SBC Communications and BellSouth, with SBC controlling 60% and BellSouth the remaining 40% of the venture.

- 2000 - September - the 19% share in Sun Microsystems that AT&T sold for $700 million, is now worth over $35 billion. That loss - on paper - is staggering.

- 2000 - AT&T Wireless becomes a separate company from AT&T Corporation, but still retains the AT&T name under licensing agreement with AT&T Corporation.

- 2004 - Cingular Wireless acquires AT&T Wireless for $41 billion and the combined company takes on the Cingular name.

- 2005 - SBC Communications acquires AT&T Corporation for $16 billion.

- 2006 - Lucent Technologies merges with Alcatel in a $13.4 billion stock swap.

- 2006 - Agere is acquired by LSI Corporation for $4 billion in stock.

- 2006 - Verizon acquires MCI Inc. for $8.44 billion.

- 2006 - SBC Communications acquires BellSouth for $86 billion and consolidates the Cingular and yellowpages.com venture under the AT&T (AT&T) name.

- 2006 - BellSouth shareholders approve the $67 billion sale of the company to AT&T, which would further expand AT&T's reach in the telecommunications sector and place Cingular under a single owner.

- 2007 - Avaya is acquired by TPG Capital and Silver Lake Partners for $8.2 billion.

- 2009 - Nortel Networks files for protection from their creditors, and is divesting the entire business. Avaya purchases Nortel Enterprise Solutions.

- 2011 - Qwest Communications acquired by CenturyLink.

- 2011 - AT&T acquires T-Mobile USA from Deutsche Telekom for $39 billion.

- 2011 - Avaya announces they will become a publicly traded company again.

- 2012 - AT&T sells Yellow Pages business to Cerberus for $950 million.

- 2013 - AT&T acquires Leap Wireless (Cricket) for $1.2 billion.

- 2014 - AT&T acquires IUSACELL (a Mexican wireless provider) for $2.5 billion.

- 2015 - AT&T acquires Nextel Mexico for $1.875 billion.

- 2015 - AT&T acquires DirecTV for $48.5 billion.

- 2015 - Verizon acquires AOL for $4.4 billion.

- 2018 - AT&T acquires Time Warner, Inc. for $85 billion.

31 - The Story of AT&T's Breakup

In the 1980s, AT&T concentrated on keeping the telephone monopoly unbroken. Federal officials who sought to dissolve corporations through forceful application of antitrust regulations - called trustbusters - had long accused AT&T of using its size and influence to obstruct rivals from entering the marketplace. Going back as far as 1913, the U.S. Department of Justice had filed legal action after legal action in attempts to restrain AT&T's power in the market. In the 1970s, AT&T was the world's largest corporation - with over a million employees - and was determined to maintain that dominant position. AT&T spent millions of dollars over the decades defending itself in court.

Number of Active Antitrust Cases Pending Against AT&T at Year End, 1960 - 1982

Year	Number of Cases	Year	Number of Cases	Year	Number of Cases
1960	1	1970	21	1980	51
1961	2	1971	26	1981	60
1962	3	1972	31	1982	59
1963	3	1973	29		
1964	5	1974	38		
1965	8	1975	47		
1966	9	1976	47		
1967	14	1977	50		
1968	15	1978	54		
1969	13	1979	50		

In January 1982, after over 70 years of legal battles and in the middle of another antitrust lawsuit, AT&T chairman Charles L. Brown announced that AT&T would work with the government to breakup American Telephone and Telegraph. Employees were outraged. Brown loved AT&T and what it stood for, but he had to face reality. The federal judge hearing the case, Judge Harold H. Greene, had already made it clear that he didn't think AT&T stood a chance of winning. Neither did Brown.

Brown's decision, which he called "wrenchingly difficult," would hopefully lead to a new era of competition and innovation that allowed consumers to choose their telephone equipment and services.

> *"It was time to act, time to put uncertainties behind us and to begin reshaping the Bell System to match the requirements of a new era."*

But the breakup led to widespread confusion among consumers and to an eruption of investment and resulting system overcapacity that overwhelmed much of the industry in the late 1990's.

Only a year after the break-up, Brown said in an interview that the breakup of AT&T had been ill-advised,

> *"I think the nation in the long run will be sorry it happened; it wasn't broken, and it didn't need fixing."*

Brown's decision was based on AT&T repeatedly defending itself against antitrust charges in dozens of States. AT&T had hundreds of lawyers working to keep up with all the motions (requests to a judge to make a decision about a case). The paperwork was overwhelming, and so was AT&T legal bills of around 360 million dollars. A new company in telecom, Microwave Communications Incorporated (later MCI) was pushing for Washington to rein in AT&T, and agencies who cooperated with AT&T for decades were suddenly looking for opportunities to take away some of AT&Ts position of power in the industry. There was no alternative but to work with Judge Greene.

Charles Brown spent all of 1982 and 1983 negotiating with the U.S. Department of Justice on behalf of the entire Bell Telephone system. During the negotiations, the Bell System's 22 operating companies was collapsed into 7 Regional Bell Operating Companies, or RBOCs, also known as "Baby Bells," and AT&T became a separate company. This eventually was folded into a final break-up decree which was overseen by Judge Greene in Washington. The AT&T Divestiture took effect on January 1, 1984, and all state actions against AT&T went away concurrent with the settlement.

Brown worked hard to divide the company fairly and evenly. Even so, many thought that AT&T was the victor by retaining long-distance, the world-famous AT&T brand name, Bell Telephone Laboratories, Western Electric manufacturing, and authorization to enter the computer business. Brown was certain that the computer business was the future of AT&T.

The RBOCs initially learned that they acquired 80% of AT&T's 100-year-old copper phone network - that was incredibly expensive to maintain - and the local phone customers. At the time, their disappointment was understandable as local phone service was just $10 a month, or less in most places, and it was heavily controlled and supervised. AT&T's long-distance customers by comparison, were paying $0.40 or more per minute for long-distance, and since long-distance was unregulated, AT&T could boost its prices at any time.

The RBOCs were also disappointed by losing out on the "long-distance subsidy" (money granted by the government to assist AT&T so that the price long-distance may remain low or competitive) which had been used to boost profits prior to divestiture. Long-distance service was priced high to offset the very low price of local phone service. After the break-up however, local phone service prices increased slightly to make up some of the difference. Under the new rules, the RBOCs were banned from manufacturing and providing any form of long-distance services. They were also assigned corporate names that nobody ever heard of: Nynex, Bell Atlanta, BellSouth, Ameritech, U.S. West, Pacific Telesis and Southwestern Bell.

The RBOCs did receive some benefits to placate them such as the Yellow Pages and Bellcore (Bell Communications Research, Inc.), a research group that had been drawn from Bell Telephone Laboratories. They also received operational licenses from AT&T for a brand-new service that on the surface appeared to have no future. On the day the break-up terms were announced, major news organizations declared that AT&T was the winner.

Everyone was wrong.

Those AT&T operational licenses that Charles L. Brown just signed over to the RBOCs were wireless licenses for the entire United States.

When wireless came out, AT&T's own internal studies determined that it wouldn't be successful. The wireless market might attract a million users at most. When a young attorney named John Zeglis - AT&T's longtime general counsel - urged Brown to sign over the licenses to the RBOCs, and he didn't hesitate.

AT&T had its family broken apart. AT&T's networks were long-haul carriers with a sole purpose to transmit calls from one area to another. The long-distance system was never engineered to be separated from the local telephone service. The RBOCs now controlled the last mile of the network that runs between a switching office and the customer. As simple as the concept of the last mile is, AT&T now couldn't get in or out of a home or business without that access.

Wireless-to-wireless and Internet calls are a completely different story which is one reason VoIP (Voice over Internet Protocol) services were so intimidating to the RBOCs.

Before the break-up, the revenues from long-distance and local service were essentially going into the same pocket. After the break-up, access fees became a major issue for both sides - AT&T would lose 40% of its annual revenues to access fees, and the Bells would get to keep all of the revenue they collected. Over the next 20 years, both sides tried to expand their industry while retaining control of their existing businesses.

The long-distance market was changing rapidly, but AT&T wasn't changing along with it. AT&T was carrying an average of 40 million calls a day in 1984, 100 million by 1989, and by 1999 the number escalated to 270 million. The reason for the soaring call volume was that long-distance prices were plummeting from a high of $0.50 for a long-distance minute, to $0.10 by the mid-1990s, and they were still dropping.

The RBOCs were aggressively working to get into long-distance, which meant that AT&T would lose even more business. AT&T had already lost about 40% of its market share, and was losing more each fiscal quarter. The RBOCs still controlled over 95% of the local phone lines, and while they did, the only available battle was for long-distance service. As long as the RBOCs had a lock on those "last mile" connections, no one else had a way to get calls into and out of the home. Until that changed, competition was never going to develop in Americas local phone markets.

In February 1996, Congress passed the Telecommunications Act of 1996, aimed at deregulating the U.S. market. The law encouraged local and long-distance companies to enter each other's markets. It also offered incentives for cable TV companies to get into phone service. The same wide competition was opened up for gas and electric companies.

The RBOCs were now able to enter the long-distance market, but not before they met the requirements of a checklist, developed primarily by AT&T, that clearly indicated that their local phone markets were open to competition. They also had to receive approval from regulators at the state and federal levels, but after 10 years of perseverance, the RBOCs finally had a pathway to enter the $100 billion long-distance market.

AT&T (and other rivals) was also now able to lease the "last miles" from the RBOCs in an arrangement known as "resale." Within hours of the law's passing, AT&T announced its intention to enter the local phone business in all 50 states, and started entering into resale negotiations with all 7 RBOCs. AT&T predicted that customers would switch immediately. The one obstacle was that the RBOCs still had 100% control over the last mile connections to the customer.

Within 3 months after the 1996 Telecommunications Act was signed into law, Bell Atlantic announced plans to buy Nynex, and Southwestern Bell (later named SBC - the Southwestern Bell Corporation) announced plans to buy Pacific Telesis. When the deals closed, Bell Atlantic and Southwestern Bell would have complete "last mile" control of the eastern and western halves of the United States.

Critics were quick to point out that the RBOCs were abusing the spirit of the Telecommunications Act. It was intended to stimulate competition, not help the RBOCs create their own monopolies. Regardless of what the merged RBOCs said, they were clearly after the $100 billion long-distance market.

In November 1996, Joe Nacchio, the head of AT&T's Consumer Services division, predicted at an executive session including 30 senior executives and support staff, that the long-distance business would fail - at a precipitous rate - and the situation will only get worse. Now that the RBOCs entered the market, they'd shortly own the long-distance business. The announcement foretold that AT&T's core long-distance business was essentially unsalvageable. Nacchio, his career now over with this prophecy of doom, resigned the very next month, December 1996, to become CEO of Quest Communications.

In the summer of 1997, AT&T's new CEO from IBM, Charles Michael Armstrong, needed a rescue plan. He assembled his senior executives, and for 12 punishing hours a day, for three exhausting months, they scrutinized every concern facing AT&T. When the dust settled, there was one option they were willing to study - buy a company that would bridge the gap between AT&T long-distance and the customer premises.

Teleport Communications Group (TCG), catered exclusively to business customers, and had its own local networks in 90 markets including top cities like New York and Boston.

Armstrong believed that with some engineering, TCG could compete with the RBOCs, and started discussions of a merger.

On January 8, 1998, the $11.3 billion AT&T-Teleport Deal was announced in headlines across the country. In Armstrong's prepared statement:

"Joining forces with Teleport will speed AT&T's entry into the local business market, reduce our costs, and enable us to provide businesses the 'any-distance' services they want."

Armstrong was certain that cable TV would provide exactly what it needed to compete with the RBOCs. They proceeded to court major cable providers, but all balked at AT&T's offers, and insisted that AT&T provide all financing, and give up some of the control that came with the AT&T name. All but Telecommunications Incorporated (TCI).

On June 24, 1998, AT&T announced that it would pay $48.3 billion to buy TCI. The press kit for the deal stated: "One cable, one company, countless possibilities." By purchasing TCI, AT&T was gaining access to 33 million homes across America, and securing its financial freedom. Armstrong declared:

"We have an exciting future. We can, and will, become an any-distance communication company, providing entertainment, telephony, and high-speed Internet to our customers."

In the spring of 1999, it was announced that Comcast would buy MediaOne for $60 billion. The MediaOne Group, Inc. was a cable company created in 1983 by US WEST Inc. - one of the original RBOCs. The merger would give Comcast access to more customers than AT&T, and AT&T was not about to become second place to anything.

On May 6, 1999, AT&T announced that it would buy MediaOne for $62 billion. As part of the agreement, AT&T agreed to sell Comcast 2 million of MediaOne's customers. Comcast correspondingly agreed to sign a large phone contract with AT&T, if AT&T could get two other big cable operators to do the same.

On November 4, 1997, WorldCom and MCI Communications announced their $37 billion merger to form MCI WorldCom, making it the largest corporate merger in U.S. history. WorldCom began as Long-distance Discount Service, Inc. (LDDS) during 1983, became LDDS WorldCom in 1995, and was ultimately acquired by Verizon Communications as MCI in 2006 for $7.6 billion.

In 1999, the new MCI was outperforming every other provider. AT&T was challenged to grow revenues, but many of its executives were puzzled how competitors were having such unparalleled growth.

Also, in 1999, AT&T was working on acquiring cable company Time Warner (the second biggest cable operator in America), and increasing AT&T's access to homes to over 80%.

On February 1, 1999, AT&T and Time Warner announced a $85 billion merger, and a 20-year agreement on phone service. Jerry Levin, Time Warner's chairman and CEO pointed out that the partnership was proof that fiber-optic cable networks are the surest, quickest route to the digital future. AT&T stock rose to $93.50 per share.

In March 1999, AT&T convinced Comcast and Cox Communications to sell part of @Home Networks - a high-speed cable Internet service provider - for $2.9 billion. It was a seriously bad idea. @Home had abysmal and skyrocketing technical problems (often crashing for hours at a time, locking up networks, and losing e-mails recklessly), and thousands of angry customers.

In late November 1999, AT&T was working on a deal called Concert, an AT&T global partnership with British Telecommunications PLC for $10 billion. The Concert deal closed in early January 2000.

By the end of March 2000, AT&T told Comcast and Cox Communications that they would agree to sell all of their holdings of @Home to AT&T, or AT&T would end their commitments to their portion of the @Home Network contract. After a few days of negotiating, the @Home deal was announced on March 28, 2000.

May 2, 2000, AT&T put out a press release that it would miss all of its targets. Investors sent the stock price down by 14% to close at $42, cutting AT&T's market value by $22 billion - one of the biggest single-day decline in U.S. history. The notion of AT&T filing for bankruptcy wasn't entirely far-fetched.

In the summer of 2000, AT&T Wireless was the number two wireless operator in the country behind Verizon Wireless, which was nearly double its size, followed closely by Cingular Wireless.

AT&T Wireless had to address a technology problem that had impeded its expansion. AT&T Wireless' networks were based on TDMA (time division multiple access) technology, Verizon used CDMA (code division multiple access), and a third standard was GSM (global system for mobile communications) - an international standard. The three standards weren't compatible, so customers would have to replace their cell phones if they decided to switch wireless carriers. To become more of a competitor in wireless, AT&T would have to aggressively convert to a different standard - GSM was selected - and that would be hugely expensive at an estimated cost of $7 billion.

Coincidentally, DoCoMo (**Do Co**mmunications over the **Mo**bile network, and later NTT DoCoMo), one of the biggest communications companies in Japan, was looking for a partner in the United States. They were willing to invest as much as $10 billion for a 16% portion of Wireless - if AT&T would spin off Wireless as a separate company, and if AT&T would commit to the GSM standard.

On November 30, 2000, the DoCoMo deal was announced, and AT&T Wireless was born.

Back in March 2000, AT&T was still struggling with the breakdown of Consumer Services (long-distance) whose revenue flow was declining by 10 percent a year. During that summer, the executive board of AT&T was fully considering the idea of spinning off Consumer Services.

This was the beginning of the end of American Telephone and Telegraph. AT&T was running out of money, out of options, and out of time.

AT&T's decision to break up the company was announced on Wednesday, October 25, 2000.

In the press release that followed, AT&T revealed plans to create four new companies: AT&T Broadband, AT&T Business Services, AT&T Consumer Services, and AT&T Wireless. Each company would support each other in the marketplace through inter-company agreements.

Enraged investors crashed the AT&T stock price by 54%, reducing it to $23.38 per share, (from a peak of $95 in February 1999) and eradicating an astonishing $105 billion in investor assets. AT&T was now collectively worth only $45 billion with $65 billion in debt (thanks to the MediaOne deal). The Wall Street Journal printed,

> *"It's a corporate funeral that took place today; the end of an icon, and no matter how they put a positive spin on it, it's the death of a corporate giant."*

Since 1881, AT&T's dividend had been stable or increased through 470-plus fiscal quarters, through two world wars, and the great depression. It had never been touched. Ever. But right before Christmas of 2000, AT&T announced that it was cutting its dividend by 83%. AT&T also warned that its fourth-quarter revenue would be lower than expected - its third revision in a year.

In the Summer of 2000, AT&T's stock was down 60% to $35 per share because of the endless collapse of long-distance. Everyone agreed that AT&T Broadband was stumbling badly, and its financial deterioration was painful to witness.

Comcast starting pursuing AT&T in January of 2001. At Salomon Smith Barney's (an American investment bank) annual media conference, Comcast made it clear to AT&T that it had serious intentions about buying AT&T Broadband. AT&T, in response, requested provisions that suggested to Comcast that AT&T didn't take them seriously.

It was Sunday, July 8, 2001, at 4 P.M. sharp, when Comcast's hostile takeover bid was faxed to AT&T Chairman and CEO, C. Michael Armstrong. The proposal was simultaneously released to news outlets, offering $58 billion for Broadband assets - half of what AT&T paid for them.

In a packed Monday meeting with investors and analysts, Comcast revealed bluntly that they believed overall strategic direction of AT&T Broadband was wrong, and that AT&T was bleeding up to $500 million annually on the AT&T CEO's failed phone-over-cable plan.

In September 2001, Business Week magazine published a story saying that AT&T was talking to BellSouth about a possible merger. Someone in AT&T was leaking confidential information, and AT&T still hadn't responded to Comcast's offer.

AT&T's executive board - essentially a who's who of CEOs of top corporations - went on a fact-finding mission to gain a true understanding of AT&T Broadband's challenges. What they received was two days of presentations by managers, and a self-important defense of his management decisions by the CEO of AT&T Broadband, Dan Somers.

The night after the final presentation, AT&T announced that it would be turning down Comcast's offer so it could consider "strategic alternatives."

AT&T attempted to create a bidding war between the three biggest cable operators in America: AOL Time Warner, Cox Communications, and Comcast. But AOL and Cox were never true contenders.

On December 19, 2001, Comcast agreed to buy AT&T Broadband for $72 billion. The new company, to be called AT&T Comcast Corporation, would be one of the leading and most powerful communications, media, and entertainment companies in the world. However, before the deal closed, the "AT&T" name was removed, and the resulting company became simply, a much larger Comcast Corporation.

On January 31, 2005, AT&T announced that it was selling itself to SBC Corporation (Southwestern Bell Corporation) for $16 billion. Within a year after the announcement, American Telephone and Telegraph, the world-famous phone company, and its iconic brand name, became the sole property of SBC.

AT&T Investor Notes During the Armstrong Era:

- 1994, June 25 - AT&T's stock price closed at $53.01 per share
- 1996, September 30 - Because of the spin-off, each AT&T shareholder received .324084 shares of Lucent for every AT&T share, and .0625 shares of NCR for each AT&T share.
- 1997, October 17 - AT&T's stock price closed at $45.19 per share.
- 1999, February 3 - AT&T's stock price peaked at $95 per share.
- 1999, April 15 - AT&T delivered a 3-for-2 stock split where every shareowner received an additional share for every 2 shares owned.
- 2001, July 9 - AT&T shareowners received .3218 shares of AT&T Wireless Services Inc. for every AT&T share owned.
- 2002, November 18 - Under the terms of the deal, a shareholder with 100 shares of AT&T on Monday will have about 32 Comcast shares, and 20 AT&T shares, because of the reverse split. The reason was that once the AT&T-Comcast deal was completed, the remaining value of AT&T shares was expected to be around $4.50 per share.

- 2004, June 30 - AT&T's stock price ended the second quarter at $14.21 per share.
- 2005, January 31 - The merger terms by SBC and AT&T implied $19.71 per share. Each AT&T share held would receive .77942 shares of SBC.

Michael J Balhoff, CFA, Balhoff and Rowe, LLC, wrote in an analysis of AT&T Stock on February 12, 2005,

"...longtime holders of AT&T stock have participated in a titanic collapse over the last decade."

32 - The 1982-1984 AT&T Divestiture

AT&T was the largest company in the world for most of the twentieth century, with $75 billion in assets and over a million employees. Unlike other corporations, AT&T was a regulated monopoly; the government allowed it to operate without competitors in return for high-quality, universal service.

Despite the Bell System providing the world's best telephone service, competitors, state regulators, legislators, and the federal government endlessly conspired to break it up. AT&T faced constant regulatory scrutiny. Many of the relationships rested on personal assurances, even after the Federal Communications Commission (FCC) was created to regulate telecommunications. The FCC gradually permitted competition, while technology accelerated the process. By the end of the 1970s, most sectors of telecom were on the way to becoming fully competitive.

Computer switching equipment, satellite communications, and fiber optics made it easier and less expensive for new companies to enter the market. The regulated monopoly of AT&T seemed like a relic and an enemy of the free-market economy.

In 1974, the government filed an antitrust suit. AT&T believed that any antitrust actions were unfair since the Bell System operated under rules that were incompatible with antitrust law. Essentially, AT&T resented being punished for observing its agreement. The FCC clearly did not understand the forces it had set in motion. The commission attempted to make incremental changes without adequately considering the long-term impact these decisions would have.

In March 1981, United States vs. AT&T came to trial under Assistant Attorney General William Baxter. AT&T chairman Charles L. Brown thought the company would be devastated. He realized that AT&T would lose and, in December 1981, agreed to negotiate with the Justice Department. Reaching an agreement less than a month later, Brown agreed to the divestiture - the best and only realistic alternative. AT&T's decision allowed it to retain its research and manufacturing arms. The decree (ruling), titled the Modification of Final Judgment, was an adjustment of the Consent Decree of 14 January 1956. Judge Harold H. Greene was given the authority over the modified decree.

The government's antitrust suit, allegedly protected from political scheming, turned out to be absolutely political, and it was for political reasons that kept President Reagan from ending the suit. Dismissing the antitrust case would have generated bad publicity and start a partisan fight between Congress and the President. Since there was simply no easy way for the Reagan administration to end the case, it did not act. The lack of Congressional control over telecom helped competitors enter the market. No single agency had authority over the entire process, so the breakup occurred, despite widespread political opposition.

In 1982, the U.S. government announced that AT&T would cease to exist as a monopolistic entity. On January 1, 1984, it was split into seven smaller regional companies, Bell South,

Bell Atlantic, NYNEX, American Information Technologies, Southwestern Bell, US West, and Pacific Telesis, to handle regional phone services in the U.S. AT&T retained control of its long-distance services, but was no longer protected from competition.

Our Foundation

The Modified Final Judgment, while ordering the divestiture of the Bell Operating Companies, leaves Western Electric, along with American Telephone & Telegraph International, American Bell International and Bell Telephone Laboratories, with AT&T.

A major difference to us as a supplier of telecommunications equipment is that, whereas under the 1956 consent decree we had limited opportunities, and were restricted to a specific market, we are now free to enter the general market. For the first time, we will be able, as our president, Donald Procknow, put it, to *"make anything we want and sell to anyone we want."*

You can't find a company executive who isn't excited about our prospects for the future. Senior executive vice president Paul Zweier put it as well as anyone when he said, *"why should we be afraid of the future? We're the guys who led the innovations in the first place. I mean, that's our thing and we're going to do all right."*

Our Strength

There's good reason for optimism; we've got a lot going for us. Again, quoting Paul Zweier: *"We're not novices at the game. And we're still part of a very solid team."* President Procknow says, *"We're a proud organization and we've adapted well to many changes through-out our history. We can draw upon our proven strengths - our engineering, manufacturing and service skills. We haven't been around for 113 years for nothing."*

As we said earlier, Bell Telephone Laboratories, the recognized top design group in the world, will still be working with us, providing its research and development expertise for projects undertaken by AT&T and Western Electric.

We've also been sharpening our skills at salesmanship, in preparation for entering the open market. Here again, we haven't been caught short. We've been working to set up a sales force ever since the early 1970's, when we created our account management and product planning groups.

Our Direction

As earlier stated, Western Electric is now free to compete in the open market, and we're ready to go. We're putting in place a sales and marketing operation in Morristown, New Jersey, under the direction of executive vice president Phil Hogin, in preparation for a thrust into the market with a line of components, including semiconductors, that we've been selling internally. And we're wooing a number of outside telecommunications firms with our newest and best state-of-the-art product lines.

While we have begun an expansion of those product lines, we're equally committed to the manufacture of telecommunications equipment, and we'll sell that equipment in the international and the national market. However, there should be no question that our first and primary commitment will continue to be to meet the needs of the Bell Operating Companies.

Our Competitors

Our competitors are not vague shadows, lurking almost unseen in the background. They're very real, and much larger in numbers than ever before. Prior to divestiture, an annual Buyers' Guide issue of Telephony magazine listed 344 firms as suppliers in the telecommunications business. A year later, the listing ran to 1,234 names, and their impact is being felt on all parts of our product line. For nearly every product we make and every service we perform, other companies have products, capabilities, and large appetites for sales growth.

The Sequence of Events of the Divestiture:

1910 - The Interstate Commerce Commission, formed in 1887, was given authority by the Mann-El-kins Act to regulate interstate telephone business, having jurisdiction over telephone companies in the following matters: just and reasonable charges; passes and franks (*permissions and authentications*); preferences and prejudices; filing contracts; reports to the commission; investigations; furnishing information; joint rates; uniform system of accounts; and preservation of records.

1913 - A letter from Nathan C. Kingsbury, AT&T vice president, to the U.S. Attorney General, committed AT&T to dispose of its telegraph stock. It also promised to provide long-distance connection of Bell System lines to independent telephone systems (where there was no local competition), and further agreed not to purchase any more independent telephone companies except as approved by the Interstate Commerce Commission. This letter is often referred to as "the Kingsbury Commitment."

1934 - The Communications Act, signed by President Franklin D. Roosevelt, brought interstate telephone business under regulation by the Federal Communications Commission instead of the Interstate Commerce Commission.

1949 - The U.S. Attorney General filed suit in the Federal District Court in New Jersey against AT&T and Western Electric, alleging violation of the Sherman Antitrust Act and asking that Western Electric be separated from the Bell System.

1956 - A consent decree (final judgment by consent) was entered in the U.S. District Court in Newark, N.J. It limited the Bell System to common carrier communications and government projects, but preserved the long-standing relationship between the manufacturing, research and operating arms of the system. It also mandated major concessions regarding patent protection.

1974 - March 7 - Microwave Communications Inc. (MCI) filed an antitrust suit against AT&T and the Bell associated companies in the U.S. District Court in Chicago. The four-count complaint, seeking triple damages, alleged that the Bell companies violated the Sherman Act by monopolizing or attempting to monopolize the business and data communications market.

1974 - November 20 - the Justice Department filed a civil antitrust suit against AT&T, charging monopolization and conspiracy to monopolize the supply of telecommunications service and equipment, and asked the separation of Western Electric from the Bell System. The suit also asked separation of some or all of the Long Lines Department and perhaps other parts of the Bell System. Besides AT&T, Western Electric and Bell Telephone Laboratories were named as defendants.

1976 - August - the FCC decided to re-examine the rules it set in its 1971 Computer Inquiry. The object of this second inquiry - called Computer Inquiry II - was, among other things, to find ways to allow common carriers to benefit from new data processing technology.

1976 - October 20 - Federal District Court Judge Joseph E. Waddy ruled that the Justice Department's antitrust suit was proper and that he had jurisdiction. AT&T appealed the decision.

1978 - The antitrust case was assigned to Judge Harold H. Greene because of the poor health of Judge Waddy. Judge Greene issued a pre-trial order that put both sides on a strict schedule designed to get the trial under way by fall, 1980.

1980 - April 7 - four years after it began Computer Inquiry II, the FCC announced one of the most momentous decisions in its history - the de-tariffing of all new customer premises equipment and of all enhanced communications services. AT&T and GTE were required to set up separate subsidiaries. The de-tariffing date was set as March 1, 1982. (Later, the subsidiary requirement was modified to apply only to the Bell System, and the de-tariffing date was extended to January 1, 1983.)

1982 - January 8 - AT&T and the Justice Department announced a resolution of the antitrust suit. AT&T agreed to divest the 22 Bell operating companies. This agreement is referred to as the Modification of Final Judgment (MFJ).

1983 - January 1 - the provisions of Computer Inquiry II were implemented, and AT&T's new subsidiary, American Bell, began operations.

33 - Lucent Technologies Bullet History

Lucent Technologies was composed of four operating units. Each unit was supported by Bell Laboratories Research and Development. All worked together to provide innovative and cost-effective solutions for customers.

Business Communications Systems:

- Business Communications Systems develops, manufactures, markets and services advanced voice and multimedia communications solutions for businesses worldwide.

Consumer Products:

- The Consumer Products unit of Lucent Technologies designs, manufactures, sells, services and leases communications products for consumer, small-office and home-office use. The majority of households in the United States have telephones made by this unit.

Microelectronics Group:

- This unit of Lucent Technologies is a world leader in communications-based microelectronics. It designs, manufactures and sells integrated circuits, power systems and optoelectronic components for various communications and computing applications.

Network Systems:

- The largest unit of Lucent Technologies, Network Systems designs, develops, manufactures and supports networking systems and software for telecommunications providers, wireless operators and cable television companies around the world. Network Systems products include switching and transmission systems, fiber-optic cables, wireless systems and the networking software needed to operate communications networks.

Significant Events

- 1995 - AT&T announced that it would split into three companies: a manufacturing and research and development company, a computer company, and a services company. NCR, AT&T Bell Laboratories and AT&T Technologies were to be spun off by 1997. In preparation for its spin-off, AT&T Technologies was renamed Lucent Technologies.

- 1996 - Lucent was completely spun off from AT&T in 1996. The word lucent dates back to the fifteenth century and means "glowing light." Lander Associates, a San Francisco design firm, came up with the name to describe the company's clarity of thought, purpose, and vision. Lucent's logo, a red, sketched circle, is called "the innovation ring."

- 1996 - One of the primary reasons AT&T chose to spin off its equipment manufacturing business was to permit it to sell to competing telecommunications providers who were reluctant to purchase from a direct competitor in the past. Bell Labs Innovations brought prestige to the new company, and revenue produced from thousands of patents.

- 1996 - September 30 - Lucent stock goes public at $7.97 per share. A 500-share purchase is worth $4,000.

- 1996 - Henry Schacht was brought in to oversee the transition from an arm of AT&T into an independent corporation.

Henry Schacht   **Rich McGinn**

- 1997 - Richard McGinn, who was serving as President and COO, succeeded Schacht as CEO, while Schacht remained chairman of the board.

- 1997 - Lucent acquired Octel Communications Corporation for $2.1 billion.

- 1998 - In April, with shares of Lucent stock selling for $132 per share, the company executes its first two-for-one stock split. That initial of 500 shares, are now equal to 1,000, and the investment is worth $33,000.

- 1999 - On April 5, Lucent executes its second two-for-one stock split. The initial investment, now 2,000 shares, is worth $111,750 on paper. On Dec. 2, Lucent stock closes at $81.75. The 2,000-share investment is worth $163,500. But now, the stock begins its descent.

- 1999 - Lucent acquired Ascend Communications $24 billion.

- 1997 - Lucent acquired Livingston Enterprises Inc. for $650 million in stock.

- 1995 - Carly Fiorina leads corporate operations.

- 1996 – Carly Fiorina was appointed president of Lucent's consumer products sector, reporting to president and chief operating officer Rich McGinn.

Carly Fiorina

- 1997 – Carly Fiorina was named group president for Lucent's $19 billion global service-provider business, overseeing marketing and sales for the company's largest customer segment.

- 1997 - Philips Consumer Communications - Carly Fiorina chaired a $2.5 billion joint venture between Lucent's consumer communications and Royal Philips Electronics.

- 1998 - January 26 - Lucent Technologies unveils WaveStar™ OLS 400G - a global optical networking system that delivers five times the bandwidth of current fiber-optic systems. 400 gigabit-per-second capacity over a single strand of optical fiber.

- 1998 - March 8 - Lucent announces the WaveStar™ BandWidth Manager that single-handedly routes all traffic - voice, ATM, Internet, and video - being handled by the largest telephone central offices. Saves carriers over 60% in equipment costs alone; has the processing power of 1,000 Pentium processors; eliminates up to 10,000 coaxial cables needed for equipment interconnections; advertised at "99.99999 percent reliability."

- 1998 - June - Lucent buys Yurie Systems, a maker of ATM (Asynchronous Transfer Mode) access Equipment for $1.1 billion - all cash. Lucent offers CEO of Yurie Systems, Jeong Kim, the position of President of Carrier Networks. Prior to the sale, Kim says, "This is Bell Labs Innovations with 130,000 people and 3 patents a day, and we have 250 employees and only 3 patents. For that they're going to pay $1.1 billion in cash."

- 1998 - Phillips's losses were at $500 million on sales of $2.5 billion.

- 1998 - Philips announced the closure of one-quarter of the company's 230 factories.

- 1999 - Lucent acquires Ascend Communications for $24 billion. Ascend was the number one vendor of ATM switches to phone companies, the second largest data networking company (after Cisco), and a 10-year-old company with over 4,000 employees. Lucent employees resented the merger as their new co-workers held larger amounts of Lucent stock than most lifetime Lucent employees. Culturally, Lucent and Ascend clashed. Lucent produced quality and 99.999% reliability, whereas Ascend concentrated on producing cutting-edge technology that may not be finalized. The Ascend deal was a short-term success and an abysmal long-term failure.

- 1999 - Lucent's initial public offering earns a record $3 billion.

- 1999 - Under Carly Fiorina, Lucent added 22,000 jobs and revenues seemed to grow from $19 billion to $38 billion. However, the real reason for Lucent encouraging sales was by lending money to their own customers.

- 1999 - According to Fortune magazine, *"In a neat bit of accounting magic, money from the loans began to appear on Lucent's income statement as new revenue while the dicey debt got stashed on its balance sheet as an allegedly solid asset"*. Lucent's stock price grew tenfold.

- 2000 - April - Lucent begins laying off workers as the telecommunications sector slumps. Over 5,000 workers are still employed in the Merrimack Valley facility at the end of the year.

- 2000 - It was finally recognized that the predicted demand for telecommunication switching and transmission equipment was an illusion. It was also discovered that Lucent's profits had been inflated by a practice of "helping its customers finance their equipment purchases." The ensuing effect was devastating. Lucent's revenue plunged. Its stock price which peaked at $84/share, fell below $2. The company cut tens of thousands of jobs, including thousands within Bell Labs Innovations. Workers were embarrassed to wear Lucent shirts or hats on the street. The company ultimately reduced its workforce from a high of 150,000 to about 40,000. In attempts to cut costs and energy consumption, every other light inside buildings were turned off. Lawns weren't mowed as often, and employees were requested to limit their telephone calls.

- 2000 - January 2nd - Lucent's Chief Executive Officer, Rich McGinn, makes an announce to the board - in a conference call - that the quarter would be a disappointment. Failure to make the numbers would come from "everywhere." Large customers fell short on forecasted purchases. AT&T was $250 million short, Saudi Arabia, $200 million, British Telecom, $100 million, and many other "deals fell off the table" at the end of December.

- 2000 - February - Lucent has its fiscal 2000 accounting practices investigated by the Securities and Exchange Commission's Enforcement Division. The investigation was triggered by Lucent's restatement of its last quarter revenues, inventory sent to distributors that was never sold to final customers, software licensing agreements, and onetime discounts called "non-recurring credits." The Securities and Exchange

Commission found that overstated earnings were because of improprieties by a number of individuals, but also that Lucent's internal controls were deficient. Lucent in fact failed to cooperate with the SEC, and actually hampered the investigation. Lucent was fined $25 million dollars.

- 2000 - Mid-March - Lucent on the NASDAQ reached an all-time high, then started a slow and steady descent. (NASDAQ is the electronic exchange where stocks are traded through an automated network of computers instead of a trading floor. It is the world's second-largest stock exchange. It stands for the "National Association of Securities Dealers Automated Quotations System").

- 2000 - April - Lucent sold its Consumer Products unit to VTech and Consumer Phone Services.

- 2000 - June - Lucent had grown too fast, tried to incorporate too many new product entities, and the strain on its system was evident. Lucent could not accurately forecast product demand, revenue, or earnings, because it had never fully integrated its own systems with those of its 38 acquisitions. Inventories grew by 34% in fiscal 2000 on products that no one wanted.

- 2000 - August - Bosco elected to retire, and was replaced with Jeong Kim and Bob Barron. Kim was just 39 years old. After analysis, Kim reported that Optical Development was poorly managed, the department was in disarray, and handoff between research and development and manufacturing was the weakest point. The sales force in Optical was underperforming, business was plummeting, and morale was sinking even faster. The product side of the business was unable to deliver, and salespeople had been given an impossible task. The Bell Telephone Laboratories development of OC-192 was woefully underfunded. *"We need to stop being our own worst enemy."*

Jeong Kim

- 2000 - During the year, the Lucent stock price plummeted, and thousands of union members lost their entire life savings. Retirements couldn't be considered because workers lost everything to their faith in Lucent stock.

- 2000 - Lucent's bubble burst while competitors like Nortel Networks and Alcatel were still going strong. It would be many months before the rest of the telecom industry collapsed.

- 2000 - Richard McGinn, chairman and CEO, was replaced by former CEO Henry Schacht.

- 2000 - Lucent had 14 straight quarters where it exceeded analysts' expectations, but on January 6, 2000, CEO Rich McGinn announced that Lucent, *"had run into problems during that quarter."*

- 2000 - Lucent stock to plunged by 28%, cutting $64 billion off of the company's stock value.

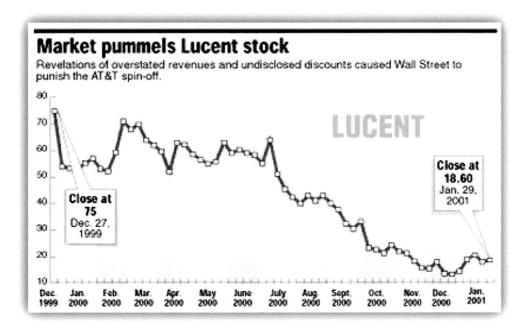

- 2000 - It was revealed that Lucent had used questionable accounting and sales practices to generate some of its earlier quarterly numbers, and Lucent fell from grace.

- 2000 - October - Lucent spun off its Business Systems division into Avaya, Inc.

- 2000 - November - Lucent revealed to the Securities and Exchange Commission that it had a $125 million accounting error for the third quarter of 2000.

- 2000 - December - Lucent reported it had overstated its revenues for its latest quarter by nearly $700 million.

- 2000 - Lucent was reduced to 30,500 employees, down from about 165,000 employees. The layoffs of so many experienced employees meant that the company was in a disastrous position to recover when the telecom market did improve in late 2003.

- 2001 - January - Employees and shareholders of Lucent Technologies heard about the company's outlay of over $40 million over the last two years to create one of the world's most exclusive golf courses. Although the project was never announced or spelled out in Lucent's financial documents, Lucent had backed the construction of the Hamilton Farm Golf Club, a rambling, 5,000 acre, 36-hole complex in New Jersey. The complex included a helicopter-landing pad, a guest home of 20,000 square feet with 10 suites, a wine cellar and tasting room, and a full-time concierge. Lucent had planned to sell memberships in the club to large corporations for $1 million each, in addition to charging annual fees of several hundred thousand dollars a year.

- 2001 - January - With 125,000 employees worldwide, Lucent announces a major restructuring plan to eliminate 10 percent of its work force in 60 days. Merrimack Valley plant was to be spared from the initial cuts.

- 2001 - Employees loyal to Lucent were deeply demoralized in anticipation of job cuts. Parking lots filled at 9:00, emptied at 4:30. There was no sense of urgency, no sense of accountability, essentially everyone was ignoring their work and looking for new jobs.

- 2001 - July - Lucent announces it will reduce its Merrimack Valley Works head count to between 700 and 800 by year's end, and puts the facility up for sale. The company tells stockholders it lost $3.25 billion and must lay off between 15,000 and 20,000 more workers.

- 2001 - The OC-192 miscalculation was a problem that Lucent was still living with.

- 2001 - McGinn was forced to resign as CEO and he was replaced by Schacht on an interim basis.

- 2001 - May - Lucent's CFO, Deborah Hopkins, left the company with Lucent's stock value at $9.06

- 2001 - Merger discussions between Lucent and Alcatel failed, causing Lucent's stock price to collapse.

- 2001 - November - Lucent sells its optical fiber business for $2.3 billion including the Atlanta Works, to Japanese-based Furukawa Electric Co. who creates OFS (Optical Fiber Cable and Connectivity Solutions), headquartered at the former Atlanta Works.

- 2002 - March - Lucent sells its manufacturing line to contractor Solectron, which sets up an A-Plus Manufacturing subsidiary in the Merrimack Valley Works building. Solectron hires 400 Lucent manufacturing workers for its manufacturing operation. The deal is dissolved a year later.

- 2002 - October - Shares of Lucent stock close at 0.58 cents per share on Oct. 11. The 2,000-share investment is worth $1,160, a net loss of over $2,800 from the initial investment six years earlier. On paper, stockholders take a nearly $162,000 hit.

- 2002 - Patricia Russo becomes Lucent's CEO. Henry Schacht remains on the Board of Directors.

- 2002 - June - Lucent spun off its microelectronics division into Agere Systems.

- 2002 - The spinoffs of the enterprise networking and wireless divisions removed Lucent from those markets.

- 2002 - October - the price of Lucent stock had bottomed at 0.55 cents per share.

- 2003 - September - Osgood St. LLC buys the Merrimack Valley Works for $16.86 million.

- 2003 - Patricia Russo becomes Lucent's Chairman of the Board.

- 2003 - Early - Lucent shares are worth $2.13.

- 2003 - Early - Lucent's market value was now $15.6 billion down from a peak of $258 billion.

- 2003 - Lucent continues to be active in the areas of telephone switching, optical, data and wireless networking.

- 2004 - December - By the end of the year, Lucent employs 31,500 workers worldwide, a 75 percent reduction over the course of three years. At the Merrimack Valley Works, the job losses are even more severe, with a 90 percent reduction in staff. Only 600 people out of 5,000 employed in 2000 remain.

- 2004 - Lucent reports its first profitable year and revenue increase since 2000.

- 2005 - Jeong Kim becomes Bell Labs Innovations' 11th President.

- 2005 - Lucent CEO Russo gets a $3.55 million bonus for 2005 versus $2.95 million for 2004.

- 2006 - January 24 - Lucent officials report that the company posted a net loss of $104 million, and sales slipped by 12 percent from the previous year to $2.05 billion.

- 2006 - January 31 - The stock closes at $2.67 for the month, that initial investment is now worth $5,340.

- 2006 - April 2 - Lucent announced a merger with Alcatel SA (Société Anonyme) forming Alcatel-Lucent. Alcatel SA agreed to acquire Lucent Technologies Inc. for $13.45 billion in stock. Lucent was priced at $3.01 a share. The merger failed to produce the expected results, and Lucent's assets that Alcatel purchased were significantly devalued.

- 2007 - Lucent settled Foreign Corrupt Practices Act charges with the DOJ and SEC. Its violations occurred before the merger with Alcatel. The settlement included a $1 million criminal fine, and $1.5 million in civil penalties. Lucent's offenses involved payment of travel expenses for Chinese government officials from 2000 to 2003.

- 2008 - July 29 - Alcatel-Lucent's Russo, Tchuruk to Quit; Loss Widens - Chief Executive Officer Patricia Russo and Chairman Serge Tchuruk quit after the sixth straight quarterly loss. Henry Schacht, Russo's predecessor as Lucent CEO, will step down from the board. The net loss widened to $1.7 billion.

- 2010 - Alcatel-Lucent S.A. and three subsidiaries agree to pay $92 million to resolve the Foreign Corrupt Practices Act investigation. Coordinated enforcement actions by Department of Justice and SEC resulted in penalties of over $137 million.

- 2010 - Alcatel-Lucent also paid $10 million to settle corruption charges brought by the government of Costa Rica.

- 2015 - Nokia Corporation announces its intentions to acquire Alcatel-Lucent for $16.6 billion.

- 2016 - Nokia gains control of Alcatel-Lucent. As of March 16, Nokia held a 91.8 percent stake in Alcatel-Lucent's total shares, and planned to complete the purchase of 100% by April 26.

- 2016 - The Alcatel-Lucent brand is abolished.

34 - Lucent's Terastrike Initiative

✓ 3-I-00 - Terastrike - The "Terastrike Initiative" is announced, and is tracked in a bi-weekly newsletter. Demand for 10G modules for September is 20 times the current rate. Over the next year, Merrimack Valley plans to shift 1,000 jobs into OLS, MUX, and Cross-connect focused factories through retraining and redeployment. Resources currently in circuit pack operations will be freed up through outsourcing.

✓ 3-II-00 - Terastrike - March plan for 10G output is 850 modules. January and February delivered 972 modules. Mobilization continues through hiring engineers, bringing in new test sets, moving production associates into 10G, making additional capital investments, and evaluating critical materials and space readiness. A parallel effort has been started at Lucent Ireland.

✓ 3-III-00 - Terastrike - March output is 127 of 850 modules scheduled. OC48 Data Team is created to address StarBase issues. WaveStar TDM production output increased 100% from 1Q00 to 2Q00. Terastrike investment will grow WaveStar TDM 4Q00 to a level 5 times current. Supplier quality and components engineering teams are working to improve incoming vendor quality.

✓ 3-IV-00 - Terastrike - March output is 135 of 850 modules scheduled. Order fill continues to rise with a 17% increase over last week. Output increased last week by 13%. Merrimack Valley is applying to Bell Atlantic for their prestigious Balaguer Environmental Excellence Award.

✓ 4-I-00 - Terastrike - March output closed with 624 of 850 modules promised. Merrimack Valley now has 355 job openings for 323 production associates, and 32 engineers. Manufacturing projections are for 6,789 modules over three months.

✓ 4-II-00 - Terastrike - April output is 18 modules of 1,518 promised. A two-month major non-conformance affecting TDM circuit packs was found to be an intermittent faceplate latch and micro-switch assembly. Merrimack Valley is re-certified by the Canadian Standards Association (CSA) for meeting safety standards for fire and personal injury. Nippon Telephone and Telegraph (NTT) performs successful New Quality Assurance System (NQAS) re-certification audit on Merrimack Valley's quality systems. "SWAT" teams are working to re-engineer processes to shorten intervals, improve process layouts, reduce analysis mills, and increase capacity at bottleneck operations.

✓ 4-III-00 - Terastrike - April output is 161 modules of 1,518 promised - only 6% of the 3rd quarter target. Det Norske Veritas (DNV) conducts successful periodic audit of WaveStar DACS product line, maintaining their ISO-9001 certification.

✓ 5-I-00 - Terastrike - April closed with output of 465 modules shipped of 1,518 promised

✓ 5-IV-00 - Terastrike - May output closes is 1004 modules shipped over a schedule of 810 promised

✓ 6-III-00 - Terastrike - June output is 237 of 1,734 promised. SDH department has vacated 14,500 square feet of floor space to be upgraded and prepared to receive new OLS production facilities. The remaining 21,000 feet in the area will be released to OLS by July 1st. Order fill is currently below expectation.

✓ 6-V-00 - Terastrike - ONG modules delivered are up 204% from the 2nd quarter. Ongoing materials shortages in the telecommunications marketplace have impacted on performance - which is still an all-time record for Merrimack Valley. Whole-order delivery was 93% for ONG and 88% for all of Merrimack Valley. The factory is on-schedule against budget to layout expected test capacity and step-up test set deployments. Optical components market is projected to grow from $6.7Billion in 1999 to over $23Billion in 2003. Majority of non-ONG product lines are being relocated to other Lucent locations and outside contract manufacturing houses to support the need for additional OLS factory floor space

✓ 6-00 - Terastrike - June output was 1,784 of 1,734 modules promised.

✓ 7-00 - Terastrike - July output is 2,297 of 2,000 modules promised.

✓ 8-III-00 - Terastrike - August output is currently 771 of 4,000 modules promised. Lucent is responsible for 33% of overall North American Market, and 84% of AT&T's demand for optical equipment. AT&T orders $2.9Billion of WDM and Optical Cross-connect through 2003. Jeong Kim is appointed the new president of Lucent's Optical Networking Group.

✓ 8-00 - Terastrike - August output is 2,987 of 4,000 modules promised.

✓ 9-II-00 - Terastrike - September output is currently 453 of 5,674 modules promised. The biggest defect category for TDM (at 71%) and OLS (at 28%) products is "Critical Operation Omitted".

✓ 10-I-00 - Terastrike - Product transfers because of Terastrike drive to gain floor space are DACS II to Solectron, XTSI to Kansas City, ECU to Celestica, PVG to Oklahoma City, and USEC / ASSET moved to Lucent at Charlotte, North Carolina.

✓ 10-I-00 - Terastrike - Ends - Backlog of customer Owings for Merrimack Valley is up a whopping 485% from 4Q99 to 4Q00. Over $74 Million was spent in fiscal 2000 on test set deployment. Personnel retention is a major challenge for Merrimack Valleys competitors and start-ups are tapping the experienced talent base.

10I-Wk

Terastrike Post

Lucent Technologies

Final Edition!

WE DID IT AGAIN! A RECORD 4TH QUARTER!

ONG Growth	
4Q99 vs. 4Q00	Up 247%
3Q00 vs. 4Q00	Up 7%
10G Module 3Q00 vs. 4Q00	Up 323%
Performance to Commitment	
4Q00 Output vs. 4Q00 Commitment	Below by 16%
10G 4Q00 Module Output vs. Plan	Up 1%
Quality	
OC-192 Functional Test Yield 4Q00 vs. 3Q00	Up 3%
Delivery Performance	
4Q99 vs. 4Q00	Past due up 485%
3Q00 vs. 4Q00	Up 10%

Mike's Corner

"The tremendous effort on everyone's part resulted in another record output quarter for Merrimack Valley. Congratulations and Thank you! There were many encouraging signs that indicate we're heading in the right direction. Our output of 10G Modules doubled over last quarter. OC-192 Functional Test Yields continue to improve, as do yields in OLS and T3M.

Unfortunately, supply chain issues continue to plague our ability to meet our commitments. This has driven our past due customer order log and inventory to unacceptable levels. Although many actions are in place to improve the supply chain, current market conditions will continue to make this a challenge for all of us. Every organization will have goals and objectives established for 2001 focused on improving customer service and improving inventory turns.

We continue to invest in our future. Test capacity continued to increase during the quarter. We spent $74M in fiscal 2000 on test set deployment and we will continue to grow our capabilities in 2001. We also plan to grow our talent base in the area of New Product Introduction.

Retention is a major challenge for us. Competitors and start-ups recognize the talent base that exists within Merrimack Valley Works. We've captured extensive feedback in the past six months pertaining to the individual needs you have.

We are prioritizing how these needs should be fulfilled to create an environment that encourages you to stay with Lucent. The environment will change. We have initiated a training program for managers that focuses on retention issues.

The growth of this business has created exceptional opportunity. Progress has also been made in obtaining talented resources. Seven critical management openings and 174 key occupational positions have been filled through transfers, promotions and new hires.

Looking forward, Merrimack Valley must be a safe, exciting and rewarding place to be. We'll be re-inventing ourselves in 2001 into an agile, aggressive business. We will be scheduling strategy forums in early November to discuss our role as an ONG Integration Center. You will have an opportunity to hear and discuss our new strategy with the Directors of the business."

Note: The Terastrike Post was created to track our progress with the 10G Program. Due to our success in meeting our goal, this will be the final issue of this publication.

Lucent Technologies Proprietary

34 - Bell Telephone Laboratories

Bell Telephone Laboratories was the best funded and most successful corporate research laboratory the world has ever known. At the Holmdel site, Bell researchers discovered background radiation which was a critical step in the development of the Big Bang hypothesis. In its decades—long prime, beginning in the 1930s and extending until the end of AT&T, the labs produced nine Nobel Prize—winning discoveries and helped the United States win World War II.

Bell Telephone Laboratories was home to ingenious minds that contributed to some of the greatest technological advancements of the twentieth century. Selected examples are highlighted below:

- 1924 — Telephotography Machine — Sends political convention photos long-distance

- 1925 - Bell Telephone Laboratories born in New York City; AT&T International Business sold.

- 1927 — Long-distance Television Machine — Sends images of Herbert Hoover via phone lines from Washington to New York

- 1939 — Binary Digital Computer — George Stibitz designs the Complex Number Calculator, which performs mathematical operations in binary form using one—off relays and finds the quotient of two 8—digit numbers in 30 seconds.

- 1941 - Bell Telephone Laboratories opens facility in Murray Hill, New Jersey.

- 1947 - Transistor (a combination of the words of "transconductance" and "resistor") — Invented by John Bardeen, Walter Brattain, and William Shockley. This first "solid vacuum tube" resulted in the transistor: a fundamental building block of modern electronic devices winning the Nobel Prize in 1956.

- 1954 — Microwave Tower Stations — 400 stations are scattered across the country, by 1958 the microwave carrier made up 13,000,000 miles of American telephone circuits.

- 1956 - First TransAtlantic Telephone Cable — Connects the US with Europe by carrying up to 36 simultaneous calls.

- 1958 - LASER - 'Light Amplification by Stimulated Emission Radiation' — Harnessed excited molecules and atoms to make light in an extremely pure form which led to all digital LASER technologies.

- 1959 - Horn Antenna & Transmission Dish — Picks up a static noise providing the strongest evidence to date that the universe was created in a 'Big Bang' explosion.

- 1960s - Cellular technology developed.

- 1961 - Continuously Operated LASER Beam — Led to fiber optic communications

- 1962 - Telstar I — First orbiting satellite to receive, amplify, and transmit voice and data

- 1963/1964 - Touch-Tone Service and Telephones introduced — Enables voicemail and call centers.

- 1964 - There could be arrogance at Bell Telephone Laboratories when it came to developing new products, and the Picturephone was a prime example. Developed by Bell Telephone Laboratories during the mid—1960s, and introduced into service in Chicago in 1971, consumers simply did not want it. Bell Telephone Laboratories executive vice president Julius P. Molnar championed the Picturephone at Bell Telephone Laboratories, and it cost over $500 million to develop. The only consumer research was a demonstration at the New York World's Fair of 1964. The result was what came to be called "the Bell System's Edsel."

- 1969—1972 - "C" Programming Language and Unix Operating System — The Gold standard of operating systems and the Internet's foundation, developed by Ken Thompson, Dennis Ritchie.

- 1973 - Bell Telephone Laboratories develops new way to manufacture ultra-transparent glass fibers

- 1976 - The First 4ESS telephone office goes into service

- 1978—1980 - Commercial Cellular Network and Digital Cellular Phones

- 1980 - Digital signal processor chip is introduced

- 1982 - The First 5ESS Switch goes into service

- 1988 - Fiber Optic Cable Laid Across Atlantic — Leads to global connectivity and would not have been possible if AT&T Bell Laboratories had not developed the technology to make optical fiber practical

Bell Telephone Laboratories was a unique place, in many ways. The list of innovations and discoveries that came from Bell Telephone Laboratories is extraordinary. Today's information age and digital era came from, or was initiated by, Bell Telephone Laboratories. The number of people affiliated with Bell Telephone Laboratories who obtained Nobel Prizes is remarkable, particularly for an industrial research facility. Bell Telephone Laboratories scientists have received myriad honors over the years including being elected to the National Academy of Sciences, the National Academy of Engineering, earning the National Medal of Technology, the National Medal of Science, and receiving innumerable technical society awards.

Bell Telephone Laboratories Official Names:

1925 - 1984	Bell Telephone Laboratories
1984 - 1996	AT&T Bell Laboratories
1996 - 2007	Bell Labs Innovations
2007 - Current	Nokia Bell Labs

Bell Laboratories Patents:

Between October and December 1999, the United States Patent and Trademark Office issued Bell Laboratories 389 patents — as stated in the Bell Telephone Laboratories Technical Journal V5, N1. This was just an example of the limitless design, development, and engineering work that went on at Bell Telephone Laboratories daily.

At the time of this writing, Bell Laboratories innovations are responsible for the creation of over 33,000 U.S. patents.

Transistor Electronics - Major Milestones in from Bell Telephone Laboratories:

- 1948 - Point Contact Transistor
- 1950 - Single-Crystal Germanium
- 1951 - Grown Junction Transistor
- 1952 - Alloy Junction Transistor
- 1952 - Zone Melting and Refining
- 1952 - Single-Crystal Silicon
- 1955 - Diffused -Base Transistors
- 1957 - Oxide Masking
- 1960 - Planar Transistor
- 1960 - MOS Transistor
- 1960 - Epitaxial Transistor
- 1961 - Integrated Circuits

The Nobel Prize:

The Nobel Prize is a set of annual international awards in several categories in recognition of academic, cultural, or scientific advances. The categories are peace, physics, chemistry, physiology or medicine, and literature. Swedish chemist, engineer and industrialist Alfred Nobel established the five Nobel prizes in 1895.

Bell Telephone Laboratories scientists and engineers are the recipients of 9 Nobel prizes.

- 1937 - The Wave Nature of Matter
  [Physics — Clinton Davisson and George Thomson]

- 1956 - The Transistor
  [Physics — John Bardeen, Walter Brattain, and William Shockley]

- 1977 - Condensed Matter Theory
  [Physics — Philip Anderson, John van Vleck and Nevill Mott]

- 1978 - The Cosmic Microwave Background
  [Physics — Arno Penzias and Robert Wilson]

- 1997 - LASER Trapping of Atoms
  [Physics - Steven Chu, William Phillips and Claude Cohen—Tannoudji]

- 1998 - Fractional Quantum Hall Effect
  [Physics - Horst Störmer, Daniel Tsui and Robert Laughlin]

- 2009 - Charge—coupled Device,
  [Physics - Willard S. Boyle and George E. Smith]

- 2014 - Super—resolved fluorescence microscopy
  [Chemistry - Eric Betzig, Stefan W. Hell and William E. Moerner]

- 2018 - Optical tweezers and their application to biological systems
  [Physics - Arthur Ashkin, Gérard Mourou and Donna Strickland]

The Turing Award:

The Turing Award is an annual prize given by the Association for Computing Machinery to an individual selected for contributions "of lasting and major technical importance to the computer field". The Turing Award is generally recognized as the highest distinction in computer science and the "Nobel Prize of computing".

The award is named after Alan Turing, a British mathematician and reader in mathematics at the University of Manchester. Turing is often credited as being the key founder of theoretical computer science and artificial intelligence.

The Turing Award has been received four times by Bell Telephone Laboratories researchers.

- 1968 - Richard Hamming for his work on numerical methods, automatic coding systems, and error—detecting and error—correcting codes.

- 1983 - Ken Thompson and Dennis Ritchie for their work on operating system theory, and for developing Unix.

- 1986 - Robert Tarjan with John Hopcroft, for fundamental achievements in the design and analysis of algorithms and data structures.

- 2018 - Yann LeCun and Yoshua Bengio shared the Turing Award with Geoffrey Hinton for their work in Deep Learning.

U.S. National Medal of Science:

Established by the United States Congress in 1959 and first awarded in 1963, the National Medal of Science is presented by the U.S. President to individuals "deserving of special recognition by reason of their outstanding contributions to knowledge in the physical, biological, mathematical, or engineering sciences."

The U.S. National Medal of Science has been won twelve times by Bell Telephone Laboratories researchers.

- 1996 — C. Kumar, N. Patel — For fundamental contributions to quantum electronics and invention of the carbon dioxide LASER, which have had significant impact on industrial, scientific, medical, and defense applications.

- 1996 — James L. Flanagan — Applying engineering techniques and speech science to solve underlying problems in speech communication.

- 1993 — Alfred Y. Cho — Pioneering research leading to the development of molecular beam epitaxy, a technique that revolutionized thin film growth making atomically accurate structures for electronic and optoelectronic devices, and for the study of new quantum phenomena.

- 1991 — Arthur L. Schawlow — The conception of the LASER and in advancing its applications, especially in LASER spectroscopy.

- 1988 — William O. Baker — Pioneering studies of the complex relationships between the molecular structures and physical properties of polymers; a distinguished record of leadership in the combined disciplines of science and engineering; distinguished service to government and education.

- 1986 — Solomon J. Buchsbaum — For his wise contributions to national science and technology policy, and for his studies of solid-state plasmas.

- 1982 — Philip W. Anderson — Fundamental contributions to the theoretical understanding of condensed matter.

- 1982 — Charles H. Townes — Contributions to the understanding of matter through its interaction with electromagnetic radiations and the application of this knowledge towards the invention of the maser and LASER.

- 1974 — Rudolf Kompfner — Invention of the traveling—wave tube and highly significant scientific insights underlying communication satellites and optical communications.

- 1973 — John Wilder Tukey — Mathematical and theoretical statistical contributions including the analytical tool known as fast Fourier transform for understanding waveforms in fields from astrophysics to electrical engineering.

- 1966 — Claude E. Shannon — Brilliant contributions to the mathematical theories of communications and information processing.

- 1963 — John R. Pierce — Contributions to communications theory, electron optics and traveling wave tubes, and for the analysis leading to world—wide radio communications using artificial earth satellites.

U.S. National Medal of Technology & Innovation:

Established by the United States Congress in 1980, and first awarded in 1985, the National Medal of Technology is presented by the United States President to individuals, teams, or companies, for accomplishments in the innovation, development, commercialization, and management of technology.

The U.S. National Medal of Technology & Innovation has been won eleven times by Bell Telephone Laboratories.

- 2010 — Michael F. Tompsett — For pioneering work in materials and electronic technologies including the design and development of the first charge—coupled device (CCD) imagers.

- 2006 — Herwig Kogelnik — Pioneering research and leadership associated with LASERs, optoelectronics, integrated optics, and Lightwave communication systems.

- 2006 — James E. West — Co—invention of the electret microphone in 1962. Ninety percent of the two billion microphones produced annually and used in everyday items such as telephones, hearing aids, camcorders, and multimedia computers employ electret technology.

- 2005 — Alfred Y. Cho — Invention of the molecular beam epitaxy (MBE) technology and the development of the MBE technology into an advanced electronic and photonic devices production tool.

- 2001 — Arun N. Netravali — Leadership in the field of communication systems and for pioneering contributions that transformed TV from analog-to-digital.

- 1998 — Dennis M. Ritchie and Kenneth L. Thompson — Development of UNIX® operating system and the C programming language.

- 1994 — Richard F. Frenkiel and Joel S. Engel — Contributions to the theory, design, and development of cellular mobile communications systems.

- 1993 — Amos E. Joel, Jr. — Vision and leadership in introducing electronic switching and other related communications technology.

- 1992 — W. Lincoln Hawkins — Research leading to long—lived plastic coatings for communications cable that has saved billions of dollars for telephone companies around the world.

- 1990 — John S. Mayo — Role in managing the conversion of the national switched telephone network from analog-to-digital—based technology.

- 1985 — Bell Laboratories — Contributions over decades to modern communications systems. It was the first institution ever to be recognized with this honor.

Bell Laboratories Location - Murray Hill, New Jersey:

By the early 1940s, Bell Telephone Laboratories engineers and scientists had begun to move away from the congestion and distractions of New York City, and in 1967 Bell Telephone Laboratories headquarters was officially relocated from New York City to Murray Hill, New Jersey.

The headquarters of Bell Telephone Laboratories was at the Murray Hill, NJ facility. The president of Bell Telephone Laboratories had his office there. The personnel, legal, and public relations areas were also there. During much of its early years, the entire Bell Telephone Laboratories was housed there after moving from West Street in New York City, although the West Street address remained the official corporate address until 1966.

The property had to be used for research purposes only, with no manufacturing allowed.

The mission of Bell Telephone Laboratories was to assure the future of communication - and that included educating the public about the science and technology of communication. The result of such education was the next generation of scientists and engineers. And this was being done in the 1950s and 1960s - without any Federal support. STEM (Science Technology Engineering and Mathematics) programs are today's attempt to attract students to careers in science and technology. However, these programs lack the support of an organization with the broad practical mission of a Bell Telephone Laboratories.

Bell Laboratories Location – Murray Hill, New Jersey

Bell Laboratories Location — Holmdel, New Jersey:

Much of the Lightwave research and engineering designs for Merrimack Valley's products were performed by the brilliant engineers of the Bell Laboratories location in Holmdel, New Jersey. This is a small outline of that incredible facility.

In 1961, AT&T opened a Holmdel, New Jersey, building to house its growing R&D division, Bell Telephone Laboratories — some of the best minds in science who performed fundamental work on communications systems.

Designed by architect Eero Saarinen, who died a year after it opened, Holmdel was both stylish and immense, costing $20 million to build in 1959 dollars ($167 million in today's dollars). AT&T expanded it in the mid—1960s and the mid—1980s to its current size.

The glass—walled structure contained 6,000 scientists, engineers, and other workers. Decades before the first smartphone, researchers at Bell Telephone Laboratories in central New Jersey developed the technology that ushered in the digital age. The scientists who worked here were pioneers in developing the transistor, cellphones, touch—tone dialing, and fiber optic communications.

When Alcatel—Lucent took over Bell Telephone Laboratories and the Holmdel building in 2006. The company shut down and closed the 473 acre, 1.9 million square foot site in 2007.

Bell Laboratories Location — Holmdel, New Jersey

35 - 9/11 Restoration Stories

[The following is a compilation of stories of Lucent's response to the devastation of customer systems after the 9/11 terrorist attacks. Lucent's successful restoration of service comes from decades of expertise collected from Western Electric, AT&T, and Bell Laboratories. The disaster recovery that happened in an unimaginably short time, will likely never happen again.]

AT&T Equipment Survived Trade Center Collapse

September 12, 2001

AT&T Corporation, the number one United States long-distance telephone and cable television company, said its communications network carried a flood of heavy calling volume on Wednesday, but remained unharmed after its equipment survived the collapse of the World Trade Center.

Calling volume on "the network is running about 20 percent above a typical Wednesday morning," AT&T spokesman Dave Johnson said. "There's heavy inbound surge to the New York and Washington areas and some network congestion, but nothing like yesterday."

AT&T handles about 300 million voice telephone calls a day. It carried 431 million calls on Tuesday as customers flooded the telephone lines in the wake of the attacks on the World Trade Center and Pentagon, making it the heaviest business day in the company's network history, Johnson said.

AT&T's local network switching equipment, which routes telephone calls, was in the basement of the World Trade Center towers and survived the implosion of the buildings, Johnson said.

"It appears the equipment has survived. It was up and alive and still providing dial tone by 4 o'clock yesterday afternoon. Once the back-up batteries ran out, we took them offline, but the equipment is still working," Johnson said.

"We were amazed," he said. "It's several stories underground and all I can say is that they must have built up that basement very sturdy."

The switching equipment handled calls for AT&T business customers in Lower Manhattan. The company rerouted calls and suffered no network outages.

AT&T will retrieve the equipment once it gets approval from New York City and disaster teams to approach the rubble of the World

Trade Center. None of AT&Ts' employees were injured or killed in the attacks.

Lucent Rebuilds the World Trade Center Communications after the 9/11 Attacks

Verizon's Darrin Zirpoli is a native Long Islander and was a Lucent installer for three years, in charge of a team of nine others working at the company's 140 West Street building on the morning of Sept. 11, 2001. At the edge of the World Trade Center complex, his building was a neighbor to 7 World Trade Center and stood in the shadows of the soaring towers.

At 8:46, a loud roar and huge explosion made Zirpoli think something was coming through the ceiling. He ran to the windows and saw a huge gaping hole in the North tower.

The Verizon building was evacuated, sending everyone into the streets. When the second plane hit, the team scattered. Zirpoli stayed on to make sure everyone was accounted for, and found himself running for his life ahead of the dense gray cloud that rushed into the streets as Tower 2 fell.

Eventually, all the Lucent team members made their way back to the downtown office at 304 Hudson St., to check on the others and make sure everyone had made it out safely.

A mile and a half away in mid-town Manhattan, Jim Modlin, Lucent Worldwide Services (LWS) Installation's director of Northeast Region Operations, was preparing a conference call. Screams and shouts brought him to the office windows on the tenth floor at 5 Penn Plaza, to stand with other Lucent employees and stare in disbelief, wondering what had caused the fire and billowing black smoke in the north tower.

They were facing the side of the building where the first plane hit, and could see fire and smoke, but didn't know that it had been a plane until they tuned in to CNN. Then the second plane struck, and with the rest of the country, they understood what had happened as more information became available.

Discussing the crisis, they agreed their first concern was to ensure any Lucent people assigned to the area had gotten out safely.

It was clear that restoring communications in the area was going to be a vital concern, and Modlin and his team began to brainstorm what would be required to best position the New York City services team for rapid response and ensure communications were maintained with the rest of the LWS teams. The team in Warren - Landmann, Nick De Tura, North America Program Management vice president, and Denise Palombo, Lucent's Program Management vice president for AT&T, called in Supply Chain Network's (SCN's) Project Manager Caren Crew and connected with Joe Frazetti, Program Management vice president for Verizon in Hunt Valley, Md.

Together they tried to predict how customers might ask them to respond. They wouldn't have any specific answers for a few days, but the first step in New York City would be getting people in teams and setting up a 24/7 operation center. Phone lines and computers were quickly pulled into the conference room next to his office, and a staff was scheduled to be there at all times. Later, they would connect to similar centers in Warren and Hunt Valley.

John Pitre, Operations director for the New York City area, knew the minute he saw the fire in the first tower that there would be communications concerns for downtown Manhattan.

But when the towers fell, he realized just how serious the problems would be. Facilities in the Verizon building at 140 West St. that stood adjacent to the World Trade Center complex had to be severely damaged. The Verizon building is a communications hub for Verizon, AT&T, Verizon Wireless and AT&T Wireless, along with many other, smaller providers. Much of their equipment and facilities had turned to dust as the buildings collapsed.

The disaster damaged three of AT&T's local switches and destroyed a local transport and access hub residing in the basement of one of the World Trade Center towers, wiping out the heart of a network which had been built over 15 years, and was AT&T's largest, and densest local network in the country.

Then 7 World Trade Center collapsed on Verizon's huge 140 West St. nerve center, tearing out the side of the building and sending dirt, dust and rubble through gaping holes to blanket its 24 floors.

At the time, no one could know the extent of the damage, but Pitre, who is in charge of all of the area's Installers, Supervisors, and Operations Area managers, hurried to get teams together.

Frazetti remembers getting his Maryland team up and running within an hour in an established operations center.

Frazetti had called Modlin within minutes of the attacks to verify the impact on the World Trade Center complex. The Hunt Valley operations center had handled other disasters, and was prepared with maps of downtown Manhattan, showing where every piece of Lucent equipment was located. Connected to the Lucent operations centers in Warren and mid-town Manhattan, and to Verizon, the team went to work.

That night Frazetti's team began to order the equipment and materials we knew we had to have, even though Verizon had not yet asked us to.

Lucent has always been good in fire and flood, but this was the worst and the most complex anyone had ever seen. We were dealing with multiple buildings, many different technologies, and lots of pressure. President Bush was expected on the 14th, so wireless had to be ready. Trading on Wall Street would begin on the 17th.

These networks had to be restored.

Meanwhile, the Hunt Valley office was also responding to the attack on the Pentagon, where Lucent had recently completed a new network, and the Maryland team was establishing cellular service in Pennsylvania at the site where the fourth plane had crashed.

The first Lucent employees to enter lower Manhattan were Mobility installers, who worked near Ground Zero most of the night of Sept. 11, relocating equipment and moving in COWS (Cells on Wheels) to reestablish wireless service for AT&T Wireless, Verizon Wireless and other wireless customers.

They worked nonstop from Tuesday through Friday and got wireless service restored very quickly. Several small wireline service providers called to ask if there were any Lucent technicians who could cover for their techs for a few hours so they could get some sleep. It was a time of national crisis.

On the afternoon of Sept. 12, the first Lucent employees made their way into Verizon's 140 West St. building to restore service to the two 5ESS Switches on the seventh floor, changing out circuit packs and cleaning debris.

Modlin and Pitre were there within days of the collapse, making the mile-and-a-half journey in an hour-and-half, passing through ten security checkpoints on the way. What the world saw on a television screen could not convey the enormity of the destruction.

In the days and weeks that followed, there would be hundreds of Lucent installers and managers working in the area, up to 600 during the peak of the restoration efforts. They came from all over the east coast and also from the west, leaving their families and working 12 to 15 hour shifts six days a week, sleeping in hotels for however long it would take.

Frazetti said that the emotion everyone felt after the attacks became energy for the people working in the area. They could actually do something, and turn their feelings into something positive.

One task was to build the biggest Lucent 5ESS switch ever, with 88,000 trunks and 100,000 lines, in a ridiculously short amount of time. The massive switch would replace the two already in the building.

Because 7 World Trade Center had collapsed and tore of portions of the Verizon building, the building had to be gutted and cleaned from top to bottom before the team could begin installing the switch.

Ordinarily it would take up to a year and a half to prepare the building space, engineer, build, and install a switch of this magnitude. The switch was built in Oklahoma City, transported to New York, and installed in 28 days. Most of Manhattan's Lower East Side was served by the switches at 140 West St. The work was key to helping restore New York's communications system.

Time was also important to the teams restoring AT&T's networks in lower Manhattan. They were under pressure to get the network restored over that first weekend, so the New York Stock Exchange could open on Monday.

Working 24/7 were the Lucent employees staffing the operations centers, ready to pick up a customer's call on the first ring

The NYSE opened as scheduled on Nov. 17, and though the panic selling that followed was distressing, the systems worked. On Nov. 23, a small ceremony at 140 West St. marked the handing over of the new switch to Verizon, to many thanks from the customer.

Lucent had finished 95 percent of the restoration by Thanksgiving, and now, only a few loose ends of the massive restoration remained. Customers touched by the event couldn't say enough. And neither could Lucent executives, who worked side-by- side with their teams and proudly watched as they accomplished the impossible.

It was an unbelievable feat, a heroic act - it showed the power of Lucent Worldwide Services. Nobody could have done what was done to create an end-to-end plan and execute it flawlessly.

AT&T Recognizes Lucent for World Trade Center Disaster Recovery Efforts

January 30, 2002

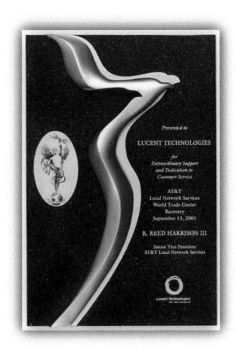

"This was personal... and we won't forget." With those words, AT&T's Vice President for Local Network Services Engineering and Operations Ron Shurter, and Senior Vice President - Local Network Services, Reed Harrison, thanked Lucent, its AT&T Customer Team and the thousands of Lucent employees who helped get AT&T's lower Manhattan network back up and running after the Sept. 11 attacks.

The disaster damaged three local switches and destroyed a local transport and access hub residing in the basement of one of the World Trade Center towers, wiping out the heart of a network which had been built over the past 15 years and was AT&T's largest, densest local network in the country. Lucent people went to work, even before AT&T called, and in one-week major portions of the network were operational, supporting the re-opening of the New York Stock Exchange on Sept. 17.

This past December, Harrison set his company's gratitude for that service in stone, presenting a green granite plaque for "Extraordinary Support and Dedication to Customer Service" to Lucent's Tony Otero, AT&T Customer Team vice president. On Monday, Jan. 21, Otero shared the honor with the rest of the Lucent family in an unveiling ceremony at Murray Hill that recalled the sacrifice and success of the days and weeks after the crisis.

"It was an incredible effort to support one of our most important customers," Otero said. "We leveraged Lucent's knowledge of AT&T's network, the quality and reliability of our technologies, the expertise of our Engineering, Installation and Technical Support teams, and, most importantly, our people's collective dedication to serving our customer. The Lucent team asked over and over 'What can I do to help?'"

There was more to do than anyone could have predicted, according to Nick De Tura, LWS Global Program Management vice president, who attended the ceremony with John Heindel, LWS president. Guided by Denise Palombo, Program Management vice president for the AT&T team, Lucent's Program Management team managed over 80 projects that required heroic efforts and personal sacrifices from many Lucent employees.

"We opened factories at night to get what the customer needed," Palombo said. "We moved material and people into the region when there were no airplanes flying. Things that typically take weeks and months, we did in minutes and hours."

Otero noted particularly the role that Lucent's Supply Chain Networks (SCN), interfacing with manufacturing, played in the effort.

"They did a phenomenal job," he said, citing the efforts of Caren Crew, SCN Process Management director in Warren, N.J., Tony Damelio, SCN Strategic Planning and Management director and Carolyn Collins, AT&T Manufacturing general manager at Merrimack Valley. "SCN interfaced with the factories and managed the outflow. They put a stop to all outgoing orders and let affected customers have first choice."

Jimmy Curtin, Lucent sales manager for New York, who slept on a cot in AT&T's "war room" for three weeks following Sept. 11, knows that the customer is very aware of the total effort of Lucent employees. "They are extremely happy with what we did," he said. "They know we care."

Some members of the cross-functional team gathered at the ceremony in Murray Hill: (from left to right) Denise Palombo, Claudia Grandjean, Mike Bonadies, Val Koricki, Michele Petrek, John Heindel, Doug Carter,

Tony Otero, Barbara Landmann, Patty Begane, Sandy Horan, Jimmy Curtin, Keith Lerch, John Wheelen, Tony Damelio, John Brereton, Caren Crew, Jim Modlin, Nick DeTura. They were joined by colleagues from many locations on a phone bridge.

Participants in the ceremony relived the event as they watched a videotape provided to them by AT&T, which interwove scenes of the disaster and their planning and rebuilding efforts with the personal memories of AT&T managers.

Acknowledging that it would be impossible to thank everyone involved in the effort personally, Otero recognized the locations where employees had been invited to dial in to the ceremony - Atlanta; Lisle/Naperville, Ill.; Merrimack Valley, Mass.; Columbus, Ohio; Greensboro, N.C.; Oklahoma City; and Dublin, Ireland.

"It's appropriate to gather together on Martin Luther King Day," Otero said. "It's a day that represents the triumph of the American values of freedom, hard work and resolve, and that's what this team represents."

36 - The Telephone Pioneers of America

The original Bell System lives on in the Telephone Pioneers of America. A group that has probably provided more service to the less fortunate than any comparable organization in the world.

The Pioneers are over 800,000 strong, spreading community service and fellowship throughout the continental United States and Canada.

The Pioneers is an active international volunteer organization made up of employees from the telecommunications industry. In the last days of Lucent at Merrimack Valley Works in 2000 alone, the Pioneers clocked in 169,000 hours volunteering in New England.

The "essence of pioneering" is the secret of success as to why this organization continued to survive and flourish through the Great Depression, two world wars, and the breakup of the Bell System. It evolved from its original social-oriented focus to becoming the largest and foremost industry-affiliated community service organization in the world.

The idea for the organization was envisioned in 1910 when three veteran telephone employees - Henry Pope, Charles Truex, and Thomas Doolittle - wrote down the names of all the telephone old-timers they could think of. All three were prominent telephone people who had been part of the industry since its inception.

Pope organized the National Telephone Exchange Association, and presided at its first convention at Niagara Falls in 1880. Truex had been active in the business since 1879, hired by Theodore Vail to establish exchanges throughout the United States. Doolittle was an innovator who had made many contributions to the improvement of telephone service, the most notable being the invention of hard-drawn copper wire. Its conduction abilities over that of the previously-used iron wire was a huge step towards making long-distance transmission practical.

As the idea for an organization began to take shape, the three founders enlisted the support of Theodore Vail, who enthusiastically embrace the idea of (what was then) a social organization for veteran telephone employees.

"We've all worked together to the same ended and to the same purpose," Vail wrote, *"and it is only fitting that we should sometimes play together."*

With Pope as the driving force, the three drafted a formal membership paper, dated October 1, 1910, which they distributed to all the veteran telephone people they could reach. Word spread, and within a year, they were 493 members. Alexander Graham Bell was granted the honor of being named the first honorary pioneer.

The first meeting was held in Boston, on November 2 and 3, 1911, with 244 Pioneers in attendance, which was nearly half the total membership. Theodore Vail was elected president, and would be re-elected president every year until his death in 1920. Alexander Graham Bell received membership card No. 1.

While service has become synonymous with the Pioneers, this was not always the case. Volunteerism evolved as an offshoot of the Pioneers' Hobbies programs, which were designed to help members make the transition from full-time jobs to retirement. Volunteerism was also fostered by the dedication to service that is deeply rooted in telephone people by their obligation to fulfilled the public trust.

At the 1958 Pioneer general assembly at The Statler-Hilton Inn Hotel in Chicago, community service - long a focus of the Pioneer activities - was officially declared a part of their mission. The theme of that meeting - Community Service - was illustrated by a new banner showing the Pioneer triangle flanked by six crests symbolizing areas of participation - civic, health, education, youth, welfare, and church. Pioneer President William Kahler (also President of Illinois Bell) called service of the community:

> *"The New Tradition. In the Telephone Pioneers of America, we have literally an army of men and women who are organized into Chapters, Councils, and Clubs, in thousands of communities throughout the United States and Canada. We have a great history and a great heritage. We only need to remember that to do something worthwhile requires us to do more than pass a resolution. It requires work, and the Telephone Pioneers of America are uniquely capable of that."*

Thirty years later, at the 1988 Dallas General Assembly, a Pioneer symbol was modified with the addition of the now famous words under the triangle: "Answering the call of those in need." The Pioneers continue to answer that call and are making the world a better place.

The Pioneers Pin Defined:

- The 3 sides stand for Fellowship, Loyalty, and Service.
- 1875 is the 06/02/1875 invention of the telephone.
- 1911 refers to the original organization of the Telephone Pioneers on 11/02/1911
- The number 174465 on the bell is the patent number of the telephone

In interviews with dozens of Pioneers from around the U.S. and Canada, two consistent patterns emerge regarding the organization. First is enthusiasm and pride in the fellowship and service Pioneering provides; the second is a desire for Pioneering to remain strong.

The Merrimack Valley Works, Chapter 78, Pioneers of America, was chartered in 1970 as a result of an explosive growth in membership. The Chapter was an outgrowth of the North Andover Council, formed in 1967. Membership at the time of the Chapter's formation was almost 1,000.

Prior to the North Andover Council, members were part of the Merrimack Valley Council which included all Bell System employees in New England.

Bell Laboratories Pioneers, formerly associated with the Frank Jewett Chapter of Murray Hill, NJ, joined the North Andover Council in 1969. At the same time the retired Pioneers from Western Electric and the Laboratories officially formed their own Life Member Pioneers Club who are retired pioneers. The conversion to Chapter status was accelerated by the addition of these two groups.

Paul E. Hughes was the Chapter's first president, and the inventor of the Audio ball.

At the Merrimack Valley Works, Chapter 78, some of the most popular projects handled by retirees included building and repairing Audio Balls or "Beepballs," a ball invented by Pioneers for blind players, talking books for the blind, and one local retiree crafted wooden checkerboards for the blind.

In 1981, 25 to 30 Life Members of Chapter 78 assembled Audio Balls one morning each week, a project that started in 1970. The Audio Ball is a regulation-size softball for the blind, containing an electronic device that makes a beeping sound.

In 1972, Merrimack Valley and Bell Telephone Laboratories engineers, redesigned the ball, improving its durability. The first redesign was improved in 1975, and again in 1980 featuring a poly-injected Polyurethane ball. Balls are distributed throughout the United States and the world by Pioneer Chapters and Councils. Thousands had been assembled at the Merrimack Valley Works since the project started.

MV Pioneers were known for visiting veteran's hospitals, organizing events at nursing homes and holding an annual Special Olympics for disabled Merrimack Valley residents.

The Pioneers clown troupe, made up of 45 volunteers, visited cancer wards and nursing homes and marched in local parades. It was one of the costliest projects, and most popular.

Dudley H. Farquhar, a long-time president of the Pioneers, and a Merrimack Valley Works employee for many years, said employees often looked at the Pioneers as a way to repay their good fortune. With 8,000 active and retired members at its peak, the Merrimack Valley chapter had considerable muscle to commit to a cause:

> *"We would try to involve the whole factory, and when you are talking about a place that at its height employed over 11,000 people, you have the possibility for a tremendous upswing in what can be accomplished."*

On March 30, 2000, Lucent Technologies discontinued their support of the Telephone Pioneers of America, the organization that was the passion of about 5,000 retirees and 3,000 employees in the local Merrimack Valley chapter. The company no longer provided money, backed their affiliation with the national group, or automatically withdrew dues from employees who wanted to support the group.

Lucent's New Jersey headquarters claimed that the decision was not financial, but was made because fewer than 25 percent of Lucent employees are members of the Pioneers, and fewer than 5 percent take part in the group's events.

Lucent, once referred to as a corporate giant with a heart, saved about $1.5 million a year by withdrawing support from the Pioneers.

At the time, and as part of its cost-cutting measures, Lucent did not only withdraw its support from the Pioneers, but it eliminated a thrift store at Merrimack Valley Works that the club maintained in the plant to help fund causes.

Despite the abandonment by Lucent, it has continued to grow to an organization of about 830,000 members, consisting primarily of actively employed and retired employees in the telecommunications industry, making it one of the world's largest corporate volunteer organizations.

Pioneers volunteer over 10 million hours annually responding to the individual needs of their communities throughout the United States and Canada.

The Pioneers receive generous financial and moral support from their sponsor companies, beginning with Theodore Vail and continuing to the modern-day telecommunications giants and charitable public donations. Voluntary in every sense of the word, Pioneering is a tremendous asset for those sponsors, paying huge dividends in employee morale, community service, and positive public relations.

It is the sort of Goodwill that cannot be purchased by writing a check, because it requires both the donation of the Pioneers' time, and the opening up of their hearts.

Pioneer Headquarters

5680 Greenwood Plaza Blvd, Suite 500
Greenwood Village, CO 80111
Telephone: 800-872-5995, Fax: 888-477-3351

Telephone Pioneers: Merrimack Valley Works Events:

- 1945 - 14 Haverhill employees become associated with Telephone Pioneers of America. 21 years of service necessary for eligibility. John J. Shaughnessy (father of MV guard force head, Lt. Richard Shaughnessy) elected president of the Haverhill Club.

- 1951 - The Telephone Pioneers of America form a subdivision of the Thomas Sherwin Chapter of the Merrimack Valley Council with 25 members in the Haverhill Shops.

- 1979 - Merrimack Valley Works Pioneers begin sponsorship of annual special field games.

- 1979 - Merrimack Valley Works Pioneers win TPA President's award in Washington, D.C. First Lady Rosalyn Carter is the luncheon speaker. Award recognizes ten years of audio ball production.

- 1982 - Beep Balls - Originally called the "audio ball," was invented in 1951 by Charlie Fairbanks, a telephone engineer with Mountain Bell in Colorado. In 1976, the National Beep Baseball Association (NBBA) was formed and developed official rules. The balls themselves are assembled by life members of the Merrimack Valley Chapter of the Pioneers, and they can't turn them out fast enough. Last year they made some 1,700, which sounds like a lot until you consider the pounding that the transmitter has to withstand and the number of teams clamoring for them.

- 1986 - Merrimack Valley Works Pioneers raise $50,000 to help restore the Statue of Liberty.

- 2001 - April 3 - The Telephone Pioneers of America - a national volunteer network of 830,000 members (5,000 retirees and 3,000 current employees in the Merrimack Valley chapter), and the oldest industrial, fraternal organization in the world - will no longer be supported by Lucent Technologies.

Pioneers Update - The New Outlook Pioneers

The New Outlook Pioneers are an independent Pioneer group - with no company sponsorship - comprised of the employees and retirees of Western Electric, Lucent Technologies, Avaya Communication, and Agere. As plants closed and the corporation spun off parts of the business, the community service group known as the Telephone Pioneers of America, continued in the communities where the plants had been located. Lucent

Technologies stopped supporting the groups, and the Pioneers became a volunteer and self-supporting group. A recent count for the New Outlook Pioneers is over 82,700 of the entire Pioneer Membership. The Pioneers volunteer network is comprised of over 530,000 strong, and have members throughout the United States.

New Outlook Pioneers are organized into seven Chapters, and Chapters are subdivided into Councils and Clubs. New Outlook Pioneers are proud to be a part of TelecomPioneers, a 501(c)(3) organization. To learn more about TelecomPioneers, please go to their web site [http://newoutlookpioneers.net/].

Membership will be granted to any individual who is willing to support the mission of TelecomPioneers and who will commit to supporting their community, the TelecomPioneers and our projects. Members will pay annual dues and will have full membership privileges, including the right to vote and to hold elective office.

Northeast Chapter 131

The Northeast Chapter 131 is part of the *New Outlook Pioneers* group, within the pioneer volunteer network of TelecomPioneers. We are comprised of employees and retirees of Western Electric, AT&T Network Systems, Lucent Technologies, Alcatel-Lucent, and Agere Systems, and represent the industry's commitment to responsible citizenship by volunteering to address community needs "answering the call of those in need."

- Northeast Chapter 131 President: Teresa Gagnon
- Club President: Kathy Henze

Operation Platoon Mom

Operation Platoon Mom raises funds to provide snacks and coffee to troops currently deployed in Afghanistan and Iraq. Cookies are made by boys at NFI — Northeast Family Institute — and Dianne's Pastries. Coffee is discounted by Dean's Beans and Seattle's Best.

Operation Platoon Mom is led by Dudley Farquhar.

Hug-A-Bear

The Hug-A-Bear Project makes felt teddy bears with embroidered faces, poly-filled and stuffed by board members and children at the YMCA, and distributed to nursing homes by the dozens.

Project Hug-A-Bear is led by Lucia Amenta.

Project HOT Trikes

The Pioneers' HOT (Hand-Operated Tricycle) Trikes are designed to be used by children who are unable to walk. By using their arms to power the tricycle from the handlebars, disabled children can enjoy the special thrill of riding a bike. When a child has outgrown the trike, the Pioneers ask that it is returned to be refurbished, and stored until we receive another request. Project HOT Trikes is led by Kathy Henze.

Special Field Games (Special Olympics)

The annual Special Field Games is a sporting event for people of all ages with special needs. Hundreds of guests have fun taking part in many athletic events. The Games started in 1979, bringing together as co-sponsors the Pioneers from Western Electric and Bell Telephone Laboratories, and the Employees' Association of Bon Secours Hospital in Methuen, MA.

A tradition of service to the community has continued by Pioneers over the years. No project better depicts this service than the Special Field Games for special needs children and adults.

The Special Field Games were held at Northern Essex Community College in Haverhill. Local special needs persons took part in relay races, Frisbee and softball toss, soccer ball kick and other events tailored to fit their capabilities. The Games are held to create a greater awareness and understanding by the general public to the needs of special people, and at the same time offer these people the opportunity to experience the pride and satisfaction that can come through competition.

In the years since Lucent's 2007 closure of its North Andover location, the Special Field Games have been carried on by Paul & Kellie Martin.

TELEPHONE PIONEERS: Employees giving back to the community

Cheryl Senter/*Staff photos*
The Pioneers, volunteers based at the Valley Works, devised many items for the blind and disabled. This chess board's white squares are covered with felt.

Western Electric retiree Richard Hamel of North Andover holds an audio baseball for the blind, developed by the Pioneers.

Lucent Pioneers working on items for the blind and disabled include Paul Boucher (front) of Haverhill, Norman Parron (back left) of Portsmouth, N.H., and Renato Salvador of Windham N.H.

The following headlines are proof of the nationwide contributions of the Telephone Pioneers of America.

Albany Sunday Herald	*Telephone Pioneers donate Time and Materials When Installing Lifelines*
Arizona Sun-News	*Telephone Pioneers Donate Therapeutic Devices to Rehab Center*
Atlanta Record Eagle	*Telephone Pioneers Wage War on Alcohol and Drug Abusers*
Chicago Tribune	*Telephone Pioneers Focused Efforts on a Home for Children Separated from their Families*
Columbus Enterprise	*Telephone Pioneers Donate Time and Materials to Build Bridge in Historical Park*
Cumberland Times	*Telephone Pioneers Stage Variety Show, Proceeds to Convalescent Home*
Florida Forum	*Telephone Pioneers Make and Donate Audio (Beeper) Balls to Blind*
Houston Post	*Telephone Pioneers Adopt Angels through Salvation Army*
Kansas Independent Reporter	*Telephone Pioneers Build and Donate Safe Playground Equipment to Accommodate Handicapped Children*
Lawrence Eagle Tribune	*Merrimack Valley Works Pioneers raise $50,000 to help restore the Statue of Liberty.*
Michigan Gross Pointe News	*Telephone Pioneers Sponsor Screening Program to Catch Infant Hearing Loss Early*
Minnesota Gazette	*Telephone Pioneer Fundraising Buys Two Wheelchairs*
Morristown Daily Record	*Telephone Pioneers Donate Telecommunications Devices (TDD) to the Deaf*
Muncie Evening Post	*Telephone Pioneers Donate Crocheted Slippers and Lap Robes to North End Nursing Home*
Nashville Banner	*Telephone Pioneers Make Beeping Eggs and Sponsor Easter Egg Hunt for Blind Children*
New York Herald	*Telephone Pioneers have Major Involvement in Olympic Torch Run*
Oregon Bulletin	*Telephone Pioneers Donate Hearing Aid Dog*
Reading Times	*Telephone Pioneers Donate Braille Writers to the Blind*
Spokane Republic-Extra	*Telephone Pioneers Plant Flowers and Trees along Highway*
Toronto News	*Telephone Pioneers Raise $3,000,000 for Restoration of the Statue of Liberty*

Vancouver Echo	*Telephone Pioneers Sponsor Aid to Immigrant Youth*
Waterloo Courier	*Telephone Pioneers Donate Handmade, Specially Designed Tricycles to Handicapped Children*
Winston-Salem Journal	*Telephone Pioneers Give Party for Patients at Hospital*
Wisconsin Reporter	*Telephone Pioneers Build Ramp at Fishing Access to Accommodate Wheelchairs*

Special Field Games - The 15th Special Field Games were held on May 16, 1993 at Northern Essex Community College in Haverhill. This year, 230 local special needs persons participated in relay races, Frisbee and softball toss, soccer ball kick and other events tailored to fit their capabilities. A look at the collage will show just how much fun it was for contestants and volunteers!

37 - Tubes to Transistors

The World's First Electronic Telephone Exchange Planned Using Transistors Instead of Vacuum Tubes

[First published in the Merrimack Valley Works Communicator in February 1956]

February 1956 - The revolutionary recent advances of modern electronics will be put to work within the next few years to streamline the Bell System's gigantic task of interconnecting millions of telephone users, whether across the street or across the nation.

The world's first electronic telephone exchange - forerunner of a radically improved and faster means of routing telephone calls - will go into experimental operation in Morris, Illinois, in two or three years, according to a recent Bell Telephone Laboratories announcement. It will provide telephone service to about 2,500 customers. Installation of the new exchange will mark the start of a gradual change to all electronic switching systems throughout the country over a period of years.

Western Electric engineers have begun development work on processes for manufacturing the electronic switching equipment. Production of equipment for the electronic telephone exchange at Morris is expected to begin at Hawthorne Works before the end of 1956.

Dial switching systems in use throughout the country today use electro-mechanical switches called relays, which at the command of the customer's dial automatically connect the customer with the telephone being called. These relays operate in about a thousandth of a second, but the elements in the new electronic switching system are expected to operate a thousand times as fast - in a millionth of a second. This tremendously fast operation will not only provide speedier service, without sacrificing reliability, but, because of its speed, fewer units of equipment will be required to serve a standardized exchange.

A key part of the all-electronic system will be the transistor, also invented at Bell Telephone Laboratories, which does most of the things a vacuum tube can do, and has many advantages for the telephone business.

The transistors and other modern electronic devices to be used in the new system - resistors, varistors, capacitors, and other components which affect the flow of electricity in various ways - are very small in size, so small as to make considerable space saving possible. Not only will there be fewer units of equipment but because of fast operation, but the units themselves will be much smaller in size. Eventually, the result will be a saving in the building space needed.

Creation of electronic switching systems is not simply the substitution of new devices for present switching mechanisms. Whole new systems involving complex circuitry must be devised. Planning and development are required to ensure that Bell System objectives of service reliability and economy will be met.

"Packaged units" comprising groups of components and their circuitry are foreseen as system building blocks. Transistors are expected to have relatively long life but to make maintenance easier, it is probable that these packaged units will be built so that they may be plugged in place or removed from the equipment easily. Automatic indicators will signal an attendant in the event of trouble and indicate the cause so that faults can be corrected quickly.

The average telephone user will probably never realize that the call is going over the new electronic system except for the increased speed with which the connection is made and one other thing. As part of the changeover to electronic switching, the familiar telephone ring will probably be replaced by a distinctive musical tone to signal the called party. The musical tone will be heard through a small loudspeaker built in to the base of the telephone. It has been found pleasing, and as effective as a bell. The musical tone is better suited to electronic switching because it uses considerably less power than is needed to ring a bell.

The Merrimack Valley Shops will have a part in the manufacturing of this epoch-making world's first electronic telephone exchange. Many of the transformers, inductors, and capacitors required for this first installation will come from this area.

38 - AT&T and the Picturephone

The idea of adding a visual component to audio for person-to-person communications is almost as old as the telephone itself, but little could be done to bring it about before the electronics era.

The Bell System's television transmission experiments went back to as far as the late twenties and early thirties, but the push to research visual displays as an addition to the telephone was delayed for about 20 years by the importance of developing network television.

Starting in the 1950s, the availability of less expensive video cameras, cathode-ray-tube displays, and solid-state devices rekindled interest in the prospect of face-to-face communications. Serious work was resumed in Bell Laboratories.

In August 1956, a system employing a tiny picture with transmission over ordinary telephone wire pairs was demonstrated to The Institute of Radio Engineers. The picture was semi-animated with still images that were updated every 2 seconds. By October 1959, enough progress had been made in devices and understanding that the decision was made to develop a station set which was called Mod I.

By early 1964, all the components for a full system test were available. A number of terminal sets were constructed and provided to the Bell Laboratories employees at Murray Hill and Holmdel, New Jersey for the first operation in an office environment.

Later that same year, a major demonstration was conducted at the 1964 New York World's Fair. The exhibit consisted of six booths for calls within the exhibit, and one booth that was linked by a microwave radio channel to a booth at Disneyland in California. Subjects to try the system were selected at random from visitors to the Bell exhibit at the fair.

NEW LOOK **PICTUREPHONE**
Now you can *see* as well as talk. The Picturephone has Touch-Tone controls to make calls and control the television screen so you can see the person you're talking to, be seen yourself, or have a darkened screen. Attended service between New York, Washington and Chicago began in 1964.

Picturephone visual telephone service was popular with the participants in these tests, and participants were reluctant to part with their sets when the tests were complete. The Bell Laboratories users were more critical than the public at the World's Fair, and only 65% judged the picture to be good or better in quality. In addition, all parties agreed that graphics were essential to supplement the face-to-face picture, and graphics required a higher resolution. This feedback-initiated development which was directed towards a 1-megahertz design with improved controls called Mod II.

Development of the Mod II system was probably the largest developmental undertaking directed towards a new service offering in Bell Labs history. Almost every area was involved - devices, station terminals, transmission, switching - and all of which required new capabilities.

A six-month service trial began in February 1969, with 40 Mod II terminals installed in the Pittsburgh and New York offices of Westinghouse. The trial was judged to be successful, and commercial service was launched on a local basis in both Pittsburgh and Chicago. In 1970 service in New York was postponed because of severe service problems at the time.

1969 **PICTUREPHONE® SET**
See the person you're talking to? It's the newest step in telephone equipment. This is the Mod II Picturephone set now in pilot production at Western Electric. The picture unit has a "zoom" feature which permits individual or group viewing. Mod II includes a new 12 button Touch-Tone® telephone.

About 500 stations were installed - mostly in Chicago - but subscribers were slow to appear. The reasons caused much debate. The limited number of sets was obviously a factor. It was difficult to interest customers in the new service when they were so few others to call. The equipment was also expensive and charges were high - basic rates were in the vicinity of $100 per month, which included a fee for the terminal set - and a connection charge.

For whatever reason, the service did not become popular. When Illinois Bell significantly reduced rates, subscriptions still did not pick up. Active marketing was terminated.

The technology was ready, but the public was not.

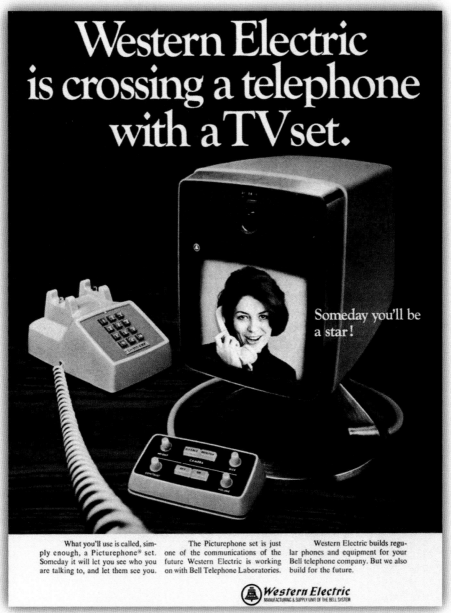

Western Electric is crossing a telephone with a TV set.

Someday you'll be a star!

What you'll use is called, simply enough, a Picturephone® set. Someday it will let you see who you are talking to, and let them see you.

The Picturephone set is just one of the communications of the future Western Electric is working on with Bell Telephone Laboratories.

Western Electric builds regular phones and equipment for your Bell telephone company. But we also build for the future.

Western Electric
MANUFACTURING & SUPPLY UNIT OF THE BELL SYSTEM

39 - Merrimack Valley in the Movies

In the Merrimack Valley (1959)

This promotional film emphasizes the relationship between the local community, employees, and the Bell System. The film follows a day in the life of fictional Western Electric supervisor, "Ed Jones," and his job at the modern electronic manufacturing works known as the Merrimack Valley Works where telephone carrier equipment was produced. The film is set in Haverhill, Lawrence, and North Andover, Massachusetts.

Owners of the massive Osgood Landing found out that 600,000 square feet of vacant property is a find for Hollywood producers.

The 600,000 square feet — the equivalent of 10 & 1/2 football fields — is a film producer's dream, according to Massachusetts Film Office Executive Director Nick Paleologos.

> *"I didn't quite have a sense of it until I walked through and realized how vast it is,"* Paleologos said of his recent tour. *"It's huge, and it's in great shape. A lot of these warehouses filmmakers are using haven't been occupied for 10 years."*

The former Lucent plant on Route 125 has landed on a short list of prime filming spots across the state.

The building's executives didn't seek out the status, but weren't about to pass up a chance to make some money on space that has otherwise been unprofitable. They've now made it their mission to court state film officials.

> *"We met and told the Massachusetts Film Office we were definitely interested in more films,"* said Ellen Keller, vice president of commercial real estate for Osgood Landing. *"We certainly hope more come."*

The Massachusetts Film Office toured the site in a meeting that was brokered by the state Office of Business Development with an eye toward future filmmaking. Prior to that, Osgood Landing had been transformed into a set for two films in just seven months: "The Box" and "The Invention of Lying."

The films brought big stars, such as Cameron Diaz, Tina Fey, Rob Lowe, James Marsden, and Ricky Gervais. They also have drummed up business at local restaurants, thrift shops — even the airport.

You never know who is in the planes, but there are more jets since filming started in Haverhill, Andover, Lawrence and Lowell. The airport receives a $10 landing fee for the small, single-engine planes and as much as $100 for small jets.

Star sightings are causing a stir with people camping out by Osgood Landing for autographs. Rob Lowe, who starred in "The Invention of Lying," dined at several local eateries, including Palmers in Andover, and Orzo Trattoria in North Andover.

The following pages highlight two popular movies where the Merrimack Valley location is prominent.

The Box (2009)

PG-13 - 1h 55min - Drama, Fantasy, Mystery

Stars: Cameron Diaz, James Marsden, Frank Langella

Synopsis: A small wooden box arrives on the doorstep of a married couple, who know that opening it will grant them a million dollars and kill someone they don't know.

The Invention of Lying (2009)

PG-13 - 1h 40min - Comedy, Fantasy, Romance

Stars: Ricky Gervais, Jennifer Garner, Jonah Hill

Synopsis: A comedy set in a world where no one has ever lied, until a writer seizes the opportunity for personal gain.

Surrogates (2009)

PG-13 - 1h 29min - Action, Sci-Fi, Thriller

Stars: Bruce Willis, Radha Mitchell, Rosamund Pike, James Cromwell, Ving Rhames

Synopsis: Set in a futuristic world where humans live in isolation and interact through surrogate robots, a cop is forced to leave his home for the first time in years in order to investigate the murders of others' surrogates.

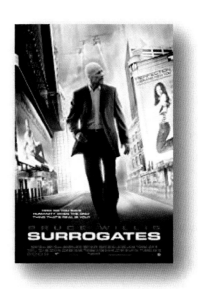

40 - Telephone Trivia

Alexander Graham Bell

Born: March 3, 1847 in Edinburgh, Scotland

Credited with inventing the first practical telephone. He considered his most famous invention an intrusion on his real work as a scientist, however, and refused to have a telephone in his study.

Died: August 2, 1922 (aged 75) from complications from diabetes

First Telephone

The Liquid Telephone - March 10, 1876 - Experiment conducted in the attic of a boardinghouse at 5 Exeter Place in Boston, MA - A diaphragm touching an acid-water mixture in a metal cup. During the experiment, some of the mixture was spilled onto Alexander Graham Bell's pants causing him to exclaim, "Mr. Watson, come here, I want you."

"Leave the beaten track occasionally and dive into the woods. You will be certain to find something you have never seen before." - Alexander Graham Bell 1876

First Telephone Patent

The patent for the first working telephone was filed at the United States Patent Office in Washington D.C. on February 14, 1876, by friend and later father-in-law, Gardiner Greene Hubbard, a prominent Boston lawyer, and President of the Clarke School for the Deaf in North Hampton, MA, on Bell's behalf. Patent number 174,465 exists as Alexander Graham Bell's legal claim to the telephone patent, and the foundation of the Bell System. In January of 1877, Bell's second telephone patent was the combined receiver and transmitter instrument.

Telephone

Etymology from Ancient Greek (têle, "afar") + (phōnḗ, "voice, sound").

Bell System Logos

The Bell System logo was placed on telephone booths and symbolized quality service. Variations of it, becoming more modern over time, were used from 1889 to the final dissolution of the Bell System in 1984.

1889   1900   1921   1939   1964   1969

First Long-distance Telephone Call

On February 12, 1877, Alexander Graham Bell made the first long-distance telephone call between Boston and Salem, Massachusetts. Bell was quoted: *"The day will come when the man at the telephone will be able to see the distant person to whom he is speaking."*

Bell's Photophone

History was made on Feb. 19, 1880 in Washington, D.C., when Sumner Tainter sent his voice 700 feet over a flickering beam of sunlight to Alexander Graham Bell. The invention that made this possible was Bell's new photophone.

Bell was so excited by the success of this photophone demonstration that he suggested to his wife, Mabel, that they name their newly born daughter "Photophone." (Fortunately, they named her Marian.) The June 21, 1880, experiment was the culmination of an idea that began developing in Bell's mind in 1878. On Feb. 19, 1880, Bell and Tainter first sent their voices along a short ray of sunlight at his laboratory. In a letter to his father, Bell excitedly wrote, *"I have heard articulate speech produced by sunlight! I have heard a ray of the sun laugh and cough and sing!"* The transmitter of the version they used that day was simplicity itself.

It consisted of a thin mirror that reflected a ray of sunlight toward Bell's lab.

When Tainter spoke into a mouthpiece attached to the back of the mirror, the mirror vibrated in step with his voice.

A reflector that resembled a small satellite dish antenna captured the beam of sunlight from the photophone. The fluctuations in the light caused by Tainter's voice were converted back to sound by means of a light-sensitive detector installed at the focus of the reflector, a battery and a telephone receiver. On Feb. 19, 1980, exactly 100 years after Bell and Tainter sent their voices over a short beam of light in their lab, representatives from the Smithsonian Institution, the National Geographic Society and Bell Laboratories assembled at the site of Bell's former laboratory at 1325 L St. in Washington.

Their purpose was to commemorate the Photophone Centennial, an event proposed to Melville Bell Grosvenor, Bell's grandson, during a visit to his National Geographic office in 1977.

Much has happened to advance the field of optical fiber communications in the years since the Photophone Centennial, including the development of the high-speed Internet connection that sent these words to the newspaper.

In 1921, shortly before his death, Bell told an interviewer that, "*In the importance of the principles involved, I regard the Photophone as the greatest invention I have ever made, greater than the telephone.*"

Origin of the Phone Number:

Technically, a telephone number is simply a sequence of digits assigned to a fixed-line telephone subscriber station, connected to a telephone line, or to a wireless electronic telephone device - such as a radio telephone, a mobile telephone, or to other devices - for data transmission via the public switched telephone network or another public or private network.

The telephone number serves as an address for calls using a system of destination routing. Telephone numbers are dialed by a calling party on the originating telephone set, which transmits the sequence of digits in the process of signaling a telephone exchange. The exchange completes the call to another locally connected subscriber. Telephone numbers are assigned within the framework of a national or regional telephone numbering plan.

Lowell, Massachusetts was the first town in America to issue phone numbers to individual subscribers because of a measles outbreak in 1879. A local physician feared that if one or more of the town's four telephone operators would fall ill, the city's phone system would collapse, so he recommended giving users "numbers" so that the operators could connect calls more efficiently.

Dr. Theodore Edson Parker was the head of the Department of Public Health in Lowell, and was an early investor in Alexander Graham Bell's telephone. Bell gave him ownership for the invention of phone numbers. Dr. Parker is buried in Lowell Cemetery.

Over the course of telephone history, telephone numbers had various lengths and formats, and even included most letters of the alphabet in leading positions when telephone exchange names were in common use until the 1960s.

Telephone Operators

In the earliest days of the telephone, people couldn't dial directly. They needed a go-between to connect their calls through a central switchboard to another telephone. It became a critical service that helped telephone technology flourish.

In April 1877, George W. Coy attended a lecture by Alexander Graham Bell in which Bell demonstrated how he could speak with two colleagues using a device called the telephone. Coy, who worked in the telegraph business, soon originated a business with Bell implementing a central switchboard that could connect any two telephones.

In 1878, the first telephone exchange launched in New Haven, Connecticut, with 21 clients, including a pharmacy, the police, and the post office.

Coy originally selected teenaged boys to perform the operator duties, but soon found that they were often distracted, ignored call requests, and tussled around the sensitive equipment. Phone companies soon began to recruit young women who would be more attentive to their duties.

As the number of telephones expanded, so did the demand for operators. In 1910, there were 88,000 telephone operators in the United States. By 1930, 235,000.

In the telephone's earliest days, one phone could simply be connected to another by cables. A caller would give the operator the name of the person he or she wanted to speak with, and the operator would use a patch cord to connect the two parties. Long-distance calls would require the local exchange to route the call to more distant exchanges through a series of cables. Later, as the exchanges added more and more customers, phones were assigned numbers, and callers could request to be connected that way.

By the 1930s, technology allowed telephone users to simply dial another phone without the aid of an operator. Phone companies then cut their workforces, and thousands of operators lost their jobs. The Bureau of Labor Statistics reports in 2021 that only 5,000 workers are classified as "telephone operators," and 69,900 as "switchboard operators (including answering services)."

A Book Published in 2007 Claimed that Bell Stole Key Telephone Ideas

In "The Telephone Gambit: Chasing Alexander Graham Bell's Secret," journalist Seth Shulman argued that Bell - aided by aggressive lawyers and a corrupt patent examiner - got an improper peek at patent documents Elisha Gray had filed, and that Bell was erroneously credited with filing first - further claiming that Alexander Graham Bell stole ideas for the telephone from rival, Elisha Gray.

Shulman believes Bell's lab notebook, which was restricted by Bell's family until 1976, then digitized and made widely available in 1999, details false starts Bell encountered as he and assistant Thomas Watson tried transmitting sound electromagnetically over a wire. Then, after a 12-day gap in 1876 - when Bell went to Washington to sort out patent questions about his work - he suddenly began trying another kind of voice transmitter. That method was the one that proved successful.

As Bell described that new approach, he sketched a diagram of a person speaking into a device. Gray's patent documents, which describe a similar technique, also feature a very similar diagram.

THOMAS SANDERS of Haverhill, personal friend of Mr. Bell, encouraged the inventor and advanced the larger part of the money it cost to make the telephone a commercial success.

Western Electric Company Trivia

How was Bell's Telephone Invention Funded?

Thomas Sanders, a Haverhill businessman, provided early financial backing for Alexander Graham Bell, who spent considerable time in Haverhill initially as a tutor to Sanders' deaf son. Sanders, whose shop cut soles for shoe manufacturers, advanced much of the money spent on the early development of the telephone, between the years 1874 to 1878. He stretched his credit to the limit in his friend's behalf before "the scientific toy" began to show signs of being a financial success. The 4th AT&T stock certificate for 1,497 shares was issued to Thomas Sanders in repayment.

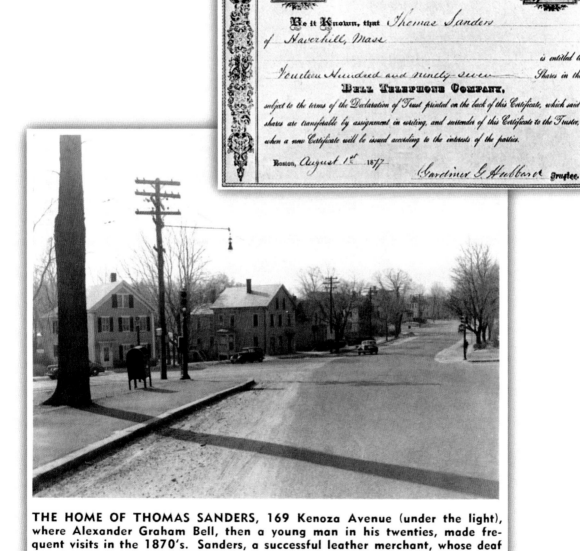

THE HOME OF THOMAS SANDERS, 169 Kenoza Avenue (under the light), where Alexander Graham Bell, then a young man in his twenties, made frequent visits in the 1870's. Sanders, a successful leather merchant, whose deaf son George was one of Bell's private pupils, showed his faith in young Bell by running $100,000 in debt to help launch the telephone.

When did Western electric become part of the Bell System?

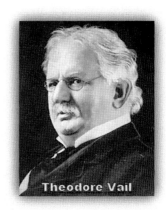

In 1881, Theodore Newton Vail paid $150,000 dollars in cash to Western Union for 1,000 shares of Western Electric Manufacturing Company stock. Incorporated on November 26, 1881, the new company merged Western Electric with Gilliland Telephone Manufacturing Company (Ezra Gilliland was an inventor who designed the telephone switchboard), and Charles Williams, Jr. (an important manufacturer of telegraph instruments during the 19th century).

Where were the factories at the time?

In 1882, Western Electric was global almost from the start, with factories in Chicago, New York, Boston, Indianapolis, and Antwerp, Belgium.

What were some products other than telephone equipment?

Western Electric manufactured washing machines, cameras, curling irons, fans, irons, light bulbs, vacuum cleaners, electric stoves, electric drills, radios, and wrought-iron tile-top tables in three sizes.

Did you know?

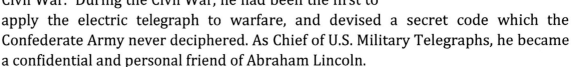

General Anson Stager, (April 20, 1825 - March 26, 1885) the co-founder of Western Union, the first president of Western Electric Manufacturing Company, and a Union Army officer, was head of the Military Telegraph Department during the American Civil War. During the Civil War, he had been the first to apply the electric telegraph to warfare, and devised a secret code which the Confederate Army never deciphered. As Chief of U.S. Military Telegraphs, he became a confidential and personal friend of Abraham Lincoln.

Did you know?

On May 15, 1845, the world's first telecommunications company was officially established. The **Magnetic Telegraph Company**'s articles of incorporation established that for every fifty dollars subscribed in the capital of the company, one share of common stock valued at $100 would be issued. The articles further stated that for every share issued, another would be issued to the patentees, who included founders Samuel F. B. Morse, F.O.J. Smith, Leonard Gale, and Alfred Vali.

Did you know?

The youngest son of President Abraham Lincoln, Robert Todd Lincoln, served as a director and president of the Chicago Telephone Company - the forerunner of Illinois Bell. He was named director of the Chicago Telephone Company in 1891. Robert Lincoln died on July 26, 1926.

Did you know?

Alexander Graham Bell Referred Helen Keller's Parents to Anne Sullivan's School. Not a lot of people know that Alexander Graham Bell devoted a lot of time and energy to helping deaf people speak and hear. This urge most likely went back to his own mother's hearing loss. Today, Bell's work is considered somewhat controversial (he fought to ban sign language in the education of deaf people). In 1886, at the height of his fame, he agreed to meet with Arthur and Kate Keller and discuss the hardships facing their daughter. On their first meeting, Helen said she, *"loved him at once,"* after he made his pocket watch chime so she could feel the vibration. It was Bell who referred the Keller's to the Perkins Institution in Boston. And, though Bell referred Keller to another doctor, he maintained an active interest in her education. The two maintained a lifelong friendship.

Did you know?

Bell picked out his middle name himself around the time of his 11th birthday. Prior to this time, he didn't have a middle name. For whatever reason, Bell drew inspiration from one of his father's former students, Alexander Graham, to add "Graham" to his name, but he was still known to his family as simply "Alec" or "Aleck."

Did you know?

Bell started out as an instructor at a boys' boarding school when he was only 16. His father had developed "Visible Speech," a system of phonetic symbols. These symbols showed how to physically make the sounds needed to say any word. Bell was able to use this system with deaf students to help them learn to talk and improve their diction. Bell also had some of his own methods. His mother had suffered severe hearing loss after an illness as a child, and Bell had used different ways to communicate with her.

Did you know?

Bell filed his patent for his version of the telephone on February 14, 1876. Later that same day, a lawyer working for Elisha Gray submitted a caveat, a type of announcement of an invention, for the telephone on his behalf. As he wrote to his parents in 1874, Bell had been aware of his competitor's efforts and felt enormous pressure to finish his own design.

Did you know?

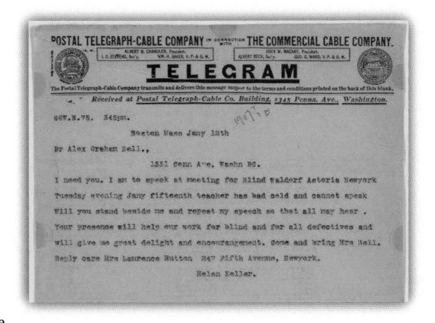

In the early 1900s people frequently communicated via telegram. In a 1907 telegram, Helen Keller, who was deaf and blind, yet still became a noted speaker and activist, contacted Alexander Graham Bell, who invented the telephone and was also an advocate for deaf people. In the telegram, sent before Keller delivered a talk in New York, she asks Bell if he will *"stand beside me and repeat my speech so that all may hear?"*

Did you know?

President James Garfield was shot in an assassination attempt on July 2, 1881. Doctors tried to keep the president alive and remove the bullet from his body, but they misjudged its trajectory and could not locate it. Each attempt to dig it out only worsened the president's condition.

Alexander Graham Bell was convinced science would prevail and came to the rescue with an electromagnetic machine he had previously tested to locate bullets in Civil War veterans. Unfortunately, the bullet was not found and President Garfield passed away on Sept. 19.

Bell believed the steel springs in the mattress interfered with his device, and doctors only allowed him to examine the president's right side, where they believed the bullet was lodged. After his passing, the bullet was found in his left side.

Did you know?

An AP syndicated article in 1953 predicted cellphones?

Mark R. Sullivan, San Francisco, president and director of the Pacific Telephone & Telegraph Co., said in an address Thursday night: *"Just what form the future telephone will take is, of course, pure speculation. Here is my prophecy: In its final development, the telephone will be carried about by the individual, perhaps as we carry a watch today. It probably will require no dial or equivalent, and I think the users will be able to see each other, if they want, as they talk. Who knows but what it may actually translate from one language to another?"*

Did you know?

Alexander Graham Bell discovered that the tetrahedral truss, created from three-dimensional triangles, could support considerable weight even when constructed out of light-weight materials. Bell made extensive aerodynamic studies with these kites before attempting to build airplanes. His Aerial Experiment Association achieved the first manned flight in Canada.

Did you know?

The American inventor Lee De Forest (1873-1961) is one of several pioneers of radio development. De Forest experimented with receiving long-distance radio signals, and in 1907 patented an electronic device named the audion. Until this time, the radion was considered little more than "wireless <u>telagraphy</u>," since it sent Morse code (dots and dashes) instead of conveying actual sound. De Forest's new three-electrode (triode) vacuum tube boosted radio waves as they were received and made possible what was then called "wireless <u>telephony</u>," which allowed the human voice, music, or any broadcast signal to be heard loud and clear.

Did you know?

In 1912, Western Electric sold Indian Motorcycles?

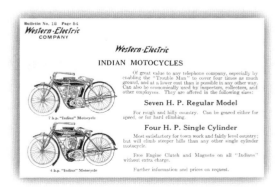

Did you know?

On May 10, 1877, the 19th President, Rutherford B. Hayes, had the White House's first telephone installed in the mansion's telegraph room. President Hayes embraced the new technology, though he rarely received phone calls. In fact, the Treasury Department possessed the only other direct phone line to the White House at that time. The White House phone number was "1." Phone service throughout the country was in its infancy in 1877. It was not until a year later that the first telephone exchange was set up in Connecticut.

It would be 50 more years until President Herbert Hoover had the first telephone line installed at the president's desk in the Oval Office.

The Morris Internet Worm Source Code

This disk contains the complete source code of the Morris Internet Worm program. This tiny, 99-line program brought large pieces of the Internet to a standstill on November 2, 1988. This worm was the first of many intrusive programs that use the Internet to spread.

This pleasantly landscaped building is the repeater station just over the Haverhill line in North Andover. Here, and in similar stations along the telephone lines, carrier and voice frequency waves are amplified to compensate for loss in signal strength caused by distance.

ICE SHAKER — Unique method of getting rid of unwanted ice on wires is illustrated in this photo of a chartered Pacific Telephone helicopter blasting frozen fog from long distance lines in Central Oregon. The ice, at some points as thick around as a silver dollar, was blown off the wires by down draft from the helicopter's rotors. The ice formation interferes with carrier system channels on open wire lines, and, if permitted to build up, could break the wires.

Lucent Trivia - circa 1999 - the data would be quite different prior to Lucent.

What is the total factory count including joint ventures?

- ✓ 58 factories around the world

How many factories in each region?

- 26 in the United States
- 11 in EMEA (Europe, the Middle East and Africa)
- 11 in Asia-Pacific
- 7 in China
- 3 in CALA (Caribbean and Latin America)

What is the biggest factory in square footage?

- ✓ Omaha Works with 2,200,000 sq. ft.

What is the biggest factory in employee count?

- ✓ Merrimack Valley with 4,280 employees (at one time, over 12,000)

What is the smallest location in square feet?

- ✓ Brisbane, Australia with 5,000 sq. ft.

What is the smallest location in employee count?

- ✓ Milpitas, California with 10 employees

Which factory is farthest north?

- ✓ St. Petersburg, Russia

Which factory is the farthest south?

- ✓ Brisbane, Australia

Which 18 manufacturing sites were also Global Provisioning Centers (GPCs)?

1. Merrimack Valley Works
2. Columbus, Ohio
3. Atlanta, Georgia
4. Dallas, Texas
5. Kansas City, Kansas
6. Oklahoma City, Oklahoma
7. Omaha, Nebraska
8. Bydgoszcz, Poland
9. Campinas, Brazil
10. Chernigov, Ukraine
11. Nuremberg, Germany
12. Qingdao, China
13. Rouen, France

41 - Periodicals

Over the years, Western Electric, AT&T, and Lucent Technologies, and many related organizations, published weekly and monthly journals, bulletins, and magazines to keep employees informed of what was going on in our Merrimack Valley communities. Images representative of the many publications are reproduced below. I'm positive that there are many that are missing to the passing of time.

1944

1945

1957

1966

1969

1972

1973

1975

1976

1976

1977

1977

1977/1978

1978

1981

1983

1986

1988

1989

1998

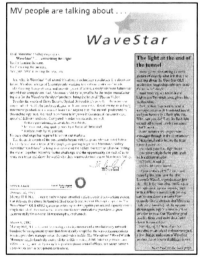

2001

42 - Communicator / Valley Voice Staff

"It takes a lot of good people"

- Andrew Gaunt - Artist
- Andy Clancy - Correspondent
- Anna Klashka - Photography
- Anne Venetta Richard - Contributor
- Arthur (A.J.) Belleville - Associate Editor / Editor
- Barbara Arnold - Photography
- Bernie Mooers - Special Consultant / Editor
- Bill Collins, Jr. - Editor
- Bob David - Correspondent
- Bob Gablosky - Editor / Artist / Photo Collage Master / Contributor
- Bob Grieco - Correspondent
- Bob Landes - Correspondent
- Bob Richardson - Writer
- Bob Zingali - Correspondent
- Bonnie Haley - Correspondent
- Bonnie Magoon - Correspondent
- Bruce Simon - Correspondent
- Carolyn Hodge - Editorial Staff
- Charlie Cote - Correspondent
- Claire Faucher - Correspondent
- Colleen Burke Collins - Correspondent
- Cynthia C. Karston - Photographer
- Daniel R. Balsley - Photographer / Editor / Reporter
- Denise Stewart - Artist
- Diane Solomon - Correspondent
- Dianne Coppola - Editor / Photographer
- Ed Crespo - Correspondent
- Ed Eich - Photography
- Elaine Webb - Contributor
- Ellen Lahlum - Reporter
- George Ares - Artist

- Guy Williams - Photography
- Herb Surrette - Artist
- Irene Dumas - Editor
- James Hajjar - Correspondent
- James P. Chasse - Photographer
- Joe Ponti - Correspondent
- John Perrone - Correspondent
- Kathy Peterson - Correspondent
- Larry Fisher - Contributor
- Lena Bistany - Correspondent
- Linda Lemerise - Production Assistant
- Lisa Descoteau - Assistant Editor / Intern
- Lois Kelly - Editor
- Margaret Smutek - Correspondent
- Marie Hodgdon - Associate Editor / Intern from Merrimack College
- Mary Owen - Correspondent
- Merrill Whiting - Editor / Correspondent / Pioneer Page
- Mike Deloge - Correspondent
- Mirga Girnius - Contributor
- Nanci Ross - Correspondent
- Nancy (Rigazio) Csaplar - Editor
- Nick Carnett - Special Consultant
- Pauline Sullivan - Pioneer correspondent
- Peter Bajor - Contributor
- Peter Nizza - Artist
- Regina Londergan - Editor
- Roger Culliford - Photography
- Ron Quinn - Graphic Artist
- Ruth Despirito - Special Services
- Ruth Sapienze - Correspondent
- Stephanie Kearns - Photographer
- Steve Jaskelevicus - Correspondent
- Tim Donovan - Correspondent / Editor

43 - Bibliography

Adams, Stephen B., and Orville R. Butler. *Manufacturing the Future: A History of Western Electric.* Cambridge Univ. Press, 2008.

Balzer, Richard. *Clockwork: Life in and Outside an American Factory.* Doubleday, 1976.

Bernstein, Jeremy. *Three Degrees above Zero: Bell Labs in the Information Age.* Affiliated East-West Press, 1988.

Brooks, John. *Telephone: The First Hundred Years.* Harper & Row, 1976.

Cauley, Leslie. *End of the Line - The Rise and Fall of AT&T.* Free Press, 2005.

Coll, Steve. *The Deal of the Century: The Breakup of AT&T.* Simon and Schuster, 1988.

Endlich, Lisa. *Optical Illusions: Lucent and the Crash of Telecom.* Simon & Schuster, 2004.

Frailey, J. D., and James M. Velayas. *In the Spirit of Service: Telecommunications from the Founders to the Future.* Columbus Creek Pub., 1993.

Gertner, Jon. *The Idea Factory: Bell Labs and the Great Age of American Innovation.* Penguin Books, 2013.

Gutteridge, Thomas G., et al. *Organizational Career Development: Benchmarks for Building a World-Class Workforce.* Jossey-Bass, 1993.

Iardella, Albert B. *Western Electric and the Bell System: A Survey of Service.* Western Electric Co., 1964.

Kraus, Constantine Raymond, and Alfred W. Duerig. *The Rape of Ma Bell: The Criminal Wrecking of the Best Telephone System in the World.* Lyle Stuart, 1988.

Rey, R. F. *Engineering and Operations in the Bell System.* AT&T Bell Telephone Laboratories, 1983.

Stone, Alan. *Wrong Number: The Breakup of AT&T.* Basic Books, 1988.

Temin, Peter, and Louis Galambos. *The Fall of the Bell System: A Study in Prices and Politics.* Cambridge University Press, 1989.

Tunstall, W. B. *Disconnecting Parties: Managing the Bell System Break-Up an Inside View.* McGraw-Hill Book Company, 1985.

Walton, Mary, and William Edwards Deming. *The Deming Management Method.* Mercury Books, 1989.

Books of Interest on our Companies

Western Electric

Clockwork: Life in and outside an American Factory - 1976
Richard Balzer

This is the story of a writer, Richard Balzer, who with the cooperation of management, was hired to work as a 32-grade bench hand, and observe and write a story of his experiences in the Merrimack Valley Works in the early 1970s.

AT&T Network Systems

The Rape of Ma Bell: The Criminal Wrecking of the Best Telephone System in the World - 1988
Constantine Raymond Kraus and Alfred W. Duerig

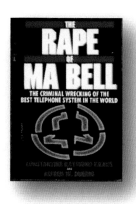

Two former Bell system engineers argue a strong case that the 1983 antitrust breakup of the AT&T-Bell-Western Electric "natural" regulated monopoly was a public-interest "crime" and communications "disaster." Among the consequences: a now-crippled Bell Labs, a much costlier and less efficient U.S. Defense communications network, and a $45 billion annual cost increase to private and business phone customers who receive equipment and service of greatly reduced quality. The authors make many additional charges, including a "conspiracy" theory of media "silence" regarding the Justice Department's assault on Ma Bell.

Lucent Technologies

Optical Illusions -Lucent and the Crash of Telecom - 2004
Lisa Endlich

In 1996, because of deregulation in the telecommunications industry, AT&T split and spun off Lucent Technologies, a portion of Bell Laboratories that was its equipment-manufacturing division. The investment community embraced Lucent because it was a high-tech company that actually had tangible products and had its roots in one of the biggest companies of all time. But this darling of the industry rode the high-tech boom and bust with the rest of them. Endlich's story reveals that conditions inside the company were never too rosy, and as it struggled to compete as a high-tech giant with old-tech values, (at the time) it lost 70 percent of its employees and 99 percent of its stock value.

Some Books of Interest (in order by publication date):

*Western Electric
and the Bell System
1964*

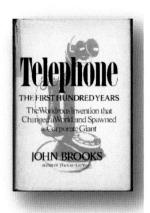

*Telephone: The First
Hundred Years
1976*

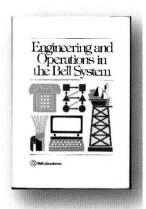

*Engineering and
Operations in the
Bell System
1977*

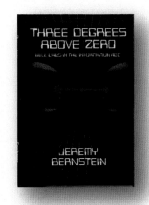

*Three Degrees Above
Zero - Bell Labs in
the Information Age
1984*

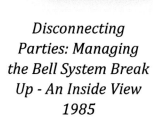

*Disconnecting
Parties: Managing
the Bell System Break
Up - An Inside View
1985*

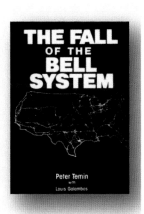

*The Fall of the Bell
System

1987*

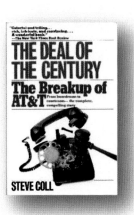

*The Deal of the
Century: The
Breakup of AT&T
1988*

*Wrong Number: The
Breakup of AT&T
1989*

In the Spirit of Service: Telecommunications from the Founders to the Future 1998

Manufacturing the Future: A History of Western Electric 1999

End of the Line - The Rise and Fall of AT&T 2005

The Idea Factory: Bell Labs and the Great Age of American Innovation 2012

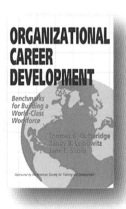

The Deming Management Method 1989

Organizational Career Development: Benchmarks for Building a World-Class Workforce 1993

44 - Merrimack Valley Works Glossary

Author's Note: Convention dictates that there should be a List of Acronyms separate from a Glossary. In this instance, I saw no good reason to overly complicate the lookup process.

ABI	American Bell Incorporated
ABM	Anti-Ballistic Missile
AGV	Automatic Guided Vehicle
AIM	Automated In-line Manufacturing
AIS	Advanced Information System
ALDS	Apollo Launch Data System - is a radio and cable complex of data, television, and teletypewriter circuits that check the Apollo spacecraft, controls the launch, and directs the booster engine as it achieves orbit.
AMAPS	Advanced Manufacturing Accounting Production System
AMPS	Advanced Mobile Phone Service
APICS	American Production and Inventory Control Society
AR6A	Introduced in 1981 - provided 6,000 voice circuits - AM Radio technology (**AM R**adio, **6** Ghz, "**A**" version)
ASQC	American Society of Quality Control
AT&T-NOG	American Telephone & Telegraph - Network Operating Group
ATM	Asynchronous Transfer Mode
ATTIS	AT&T Information Systems
ATTIX	American Telephone and Telegraph Interexchange Entity
BOC	Bell Operating Company
BOM	Bill of Materials: Consists of all the lists of raw materials, parts, components, assemblies, sub-assemblies, and all other items required to manufacture, repair, or reconstruct an item.
BRPS	Bit Rate Per Second - bitrate refers to the number of bits that are processed in a given unit of time.
CAD	Computer Aided Design

CAD/CAM	Computer Aided Design / Computer Aided Manufacturing
CAM	Computer Aided Manufacturing
CAPP	Computer Aided Process Planning
CARP	Computer Aided Reliability Program
CASTL	Customer Acceptance Systems Test Laboratory
CC&PS	Common Components & Power Systems - a division of AT&T Technology Systems
CCRA	Consumer Communications Reform Act
CCSA	Common Controlled Switching Arrangement
CEC	Corporate Education Center
CET	Certified Electronic Technician / Cutting Edge Technology
CGI	Computer Generated Image
CI-2	Computer Inquiry II
CIM	Computer Integrated Manufacturing
CLEC	Competitive Local Exchange Carrier - a telephone company that competes with the already established local telephone business by providing its own network and switching.
CMOS	Complementary Metal Oxide Semiconductor
Comptometry	The skilled use of arithmetic operations
COPAC	Computer Oriented Procurement Analysis and Control
CORNET	CORporation NETwork
CPE	Consumer Premises Equipment
CPIM	Certified in Production and Inventory Management - Preferred by employers worldwide, the APICS CPIM is recognized globally as the standard of professional competence.
CPRP	Corporate Product Realization Process
CRSD	Customer Requested Ship Date - when the customer wants his/her purchase delivered.

CSQP	Customer / Supplier Quality Process - Bellcore and the RBOCs chose Merrimack Valley Works as one of four suppliers to take part in the program to develop a closer customer/supplier relationship.
DACS	Digital Access and Cross-connect System
Dataphone®	Data Communications Services
DDI	Direct Dial In: Europe and Oceania's version of "DID"
DDS	Dataphone Digital Service / Digital Data Service
DID	Direct Inward Dialing: a telecommunication service offered to subscribers who operate a private branch exchange (PBX) system.
DIF	Digital Interface Frame
DQA	Dual Quadrant Assemblies - reduces crosstalk in FTSG DS3 channels
DR-6	Introduced in 1983 - 1,344 voice circuits - Digital Radio technology
DSP	A digital signal processor is a specialized microprocessor chip, with its architecture optimized for the operational needs of digital signal processing. Digital Signal Processing is the process of analyzing and modifying a signal to optimize or improve its efficiency or performance. It involves applying various mathematical algorithms to analog and digital signals to produce a signal that's of higher quality than the original signal.
EBO	Embedded Base Organization
EC	Echo Canceller
EIEP	Employee Information Exchange Panel
ENFIA	Exchange Network Facilities for Interstate Access
EOS/ESD	Electrical OverStress / ElectroStatic Discharge
EPIC	Engineering for Purchased Integrated Circuits
ERP	Enterprise Resource Planning
ERP II	Enterprise Resource Planning with Web / Internet Functionality

ESD	ElectroStatic Discharge: a sudden transfer of the electrical charge usually built up between two objects.
ESS	Electronic Switching System
ETOP	Employee Training Opportunity Program / Enhanced Training Opportunities Program
FAA	Federal Aviation Administration
FASE	Fundamentally Analyzable Simplified English
FCC	Federal Communications Commission
FDM	Frequency Division Multiplex
FIC	Film Integrated Circuit
FM	Frequency Modulation
FOA	First Office Application - the first deployment (pilot) of the equipment or technology in an actual customer environment after internal test and acceptance phases are completed.
FR-8	Introduced in 1981- providing 2,400 voice circuits, FM Radio
FSS	Fully Separated Subsidiary
GaAsFET	Gallium Arsenide Field-Effect Transmitter
GDX	Gated Diode Crosspoint
Ghz	Gigahertz
GTE	General Telephone and Electronics
HASL	Hot Air Solder Leveler
HIC	Hybrid Integrated Circuit - a combination of a Silicon Integrated Circuit (SIC) and a Film Integrated Circuit (FIC)
ICA	Initial Customer Application - provides extra operational support with first installations
ICBM	Inter-Continental Ballistic Missile
IEEE	Institute of Electrical and Electronics Engineers
IMPAC	Integrated Manufacture Planning And Control

IMS	Information Management Systems
INFORMIX®	A vendor database that provides solid data on vendor quality, ensuring that materials of the highest quality are delivered to the shop floor.
IP Switch	Internet Protocol Switch
IPCS	Information Planning and Control of Storeroom
IPCS	Integrated Production Control System
IPH	Installation Procedures Handbook
ISDN	Integrated Services Digital Network
JIT	Just In Time
Khz	Kilohertz
LATA	Local Access and Transport Area
LIEF	Launch Information Exchange Facility - a system designed for NASA by the Bell System. Four times each second, a checklist of 1,000 Apollo items is scanned and fed into computers for interpretation.
LOB	Line of Business
LTE	Long Term Evolution
MACCS	Maintenance and Calibration Control System - MACCS keeps track of all breakdown reports and keeps a history of maintenance and calibration for each piece of equipment.
MC-CDMA	Multicarrier Code Division Multiple Access
MCM	Multi Chip Module
MFJ	Modification of Final Judgement
MIMO	Multiple-Input Multiple-Output
MIS	Management Information Systems
MOS	Metal Oxide Semiconductor - The "MOS" refers to the transistors in a component, called MOSFETs (metal oxide semiconductor field effect transistors). It is a technology used to produce integrated circuits.

MOVES	Material Operations Velocity System - a receiving software system that allows materials to be received and sent to its next destination quickly and accurately.
MOVES-SC	Materials Operations Velocity Systems - Stores Control system. MOVES-SC communicates with the IMPAC material management system to coordinate work and inventory quantities.
MPCS	Manufacturing Process Control System
MPS	Master Production Schedule
MRP	Manufacturing Resource Planning: MRP generates production schedules for operations and raw material purchases.
MRP II	Manufacturing Resource Planning II: Coordinating sales, manufacturing, purchasing and engineering, to produce the best results for the company.
MSDS	Material Safety Data Sheets
NASCOM	NASA (Ground) Communications System - manages terrestrial communications between ground stations, mission control centers, and other elements of spacecraft ground segments. Includes the Bell System designed LEIF and ALDS systems.
NEXT	Near-End Crosstalk
NMOS	N-type Metal-Oxide-Semiconductor
NPIC	New Product Introduction Center
OASIS	Online Access to Storeroom Inventory System
OATS	Open Area Test Site - This facility was constructed with an air-supported fabric dome over a precisely engineered concrete floor. The facility was used to measure radio frequency energy coming from equipment made at MV. It was the big white bubble behind the plant.
Oceania	A geographic region that includes Australia, Melanesia, Micronesia and Polynesia.
OFCC	Office of Federal Contract Compliance
OFDMA	Orthogonal Frequency-Division Multiple Access
OLS	Optical Line System - Products included: OLS-40G, WaveStar-OLS-400G
OSHA	Occupational Safety and Health Administration

PAE	Physical Address Extension - In computing, a memory management feature for the x86 architecture.
PAEs	Professional Administrative Employees
PBX	Private Branch Exchange - a private telephone network used within a company or organization.
PCA	Protective Connecting Arrangement
PCAP	Packet Capture - In the field of computer network administration, PCAP is an application programming interface (API) for capturing network traffic.
PCC	Policy And Charging Control
PCEF	Policy And Charging Enforcement Function
PCRF	Policy And Charging Rules Function
PECC	Product Engineering Control Center
PLM	Product Line Management
PLPM	Product Line Planning and Management
POTS	Plain Old Telephone System
PPI	Purchased Product Inspection
PPM	Parts Per Million
PQR	Product Quality Review
PRC	Product Realization Center
PUC	Public Utilities Commission
PWB	Printed Wiring Board
QA	Quality Assurance: An organization - independent of company manufacturing and service operations - that provides information used in reporting the shipped quality of products, and keeps management informed of the quality status of all products and services.
QAM	Quadrature Amplitude Modulation
QIT	Quality Improvement Team

QMP	Quality Measurement Plan: The evaluation of current quality, using a time interval of six rating periods in length
QPE	Quality Program Evaluation: The on-site review of a potential supplier's quality program, measuring the extent to which it conforms to engineering specifications and industry standards.
Quality Clusters	The subdivision of a process into a logical grouping of operations and employees such that meaningful statistical data can be obtained. The objectives are to provide faster problem identification and a mechanism to effect continuing improvements to the process.
QWL	Quality of Work Life: A concept with three basic elements. Worker participation, union
R&D	Research & Development
RAM	Random Access Memory
RBOC	Regional Bell Operating Company - known as the "Baby Bells"
RF	Radio Frequency
RFID	Radio-frequency identification (RFID) uses electromagnetic fields to automatically identify and track tags attached to objects.
SARTS	Switched Access Remote Test System - an operations support system designed to access and remotely test special service telephone circuits.
SAW	Surface Acoustical Wave devices
SBU	Strategic Business Unit
SCAMA	Switching, Conferencing, And Monitoring Arrangement - In 1968, this was the most elaborate switching system in the world. It could arrange 40 simultaneous conferences with any station on the network, including Comsat satellites and deep space probes.
SDH	Synchronous Digital Hierarchy Products included: WaveStar ADM, ISM, SLM, DACS-VI 2000
SDP	Synchronous Distributed Processor
Sentinel	Sentinel was a US Army anti-ballistic missile (ABM) system designed to provide protection over the entire United States, able to defend against small ICBM strikes. In November 1967, the first ten locations were announced, with Boston being the first on the list.
SIC	Silicon Integrated Circuit

SIPP	Sales, Inventory, and Production Planning
Six Sigma	6σ is a set of techniques for process improvement introduced by Motorola in 1986. A six-sigma process is one in which 99.99966% of all opportunities to produce a part are statistically expected to be free of defects.
SLC	Subscriber Loop Carrier
SLM	Subscriber Loop Multiplex
SMAS	Standard Metropolitan Statistical Area
SONET	Synchronous Optical NETwork - The ability to interconnect multiple products efficiently over a new type of network.
SQC	Statistical Quality Control: an aggregate of activities, such as design analysis and statistical sampling with inspection for defects, designed to ensure adequate quality in manufactured products.
SRDC	Sub-Rate Data Cross-Connect
TASI	Time Assignment Speech Interpolation
TED	Transmission Equipment Division
TELCOMP	TELCOMP was a programming language developed at Bolt, Beranek and Newman (BBN) in about 1964, and in use until at least 1974.
TOR	Turn Over Ratio
TRIM	Total Resource and Inventory Management
TWIN	Tribute to Women in Industry Award
UHF	Ultra-High Frequency
VF	Voice Frequency
VHF	Very High Frequency
VIF	Voice band Interface Frame
VPP	Voluntary Protection Program
WATS	Wide Area Telecommunications Service

45 - Index